Getting
Finance
in
South Asia
2009

Getting Finance in South Asia 2009

Indicators and Analysis of the Commercial Banking Sector

Kiatchai Sophastienphong

Anoma Kulathunga

© 2008 The International Bank for Reconstruction and Development / The World Bank
1818 H Street NW
Washington DC 20433
Telephone: 202-473-1000
Internet: www.worldbank.org
E-mail: feedback@worldbank.org

All rights reserved

1 2 3 4 5 11 10 09 08

This volume is a product of the staff of the International Bank for Reconstruction and Development / The World Bank. The findings, interpretations, and conclusions expressed in this volume do not necessarily reflect the views of the Executive Directors of The World Bank or the governments they represent.

The World Bank does not guarantee the accuracy of the data included in this work. The boundaries, colors, denominations, and other information shown on any map in this work do not imply any judgement on the part of The World Bank concerning the legal status of any territory or the endorsement or acceptance of such boundaries.

Rights and Permissions

The material in this publication is copyrighted. Copying and/or transmitting portions or all of this work without permission may be a violation of applicable law. The International Bank for Reconstruction and Development / The World Bank encourages dissemination of its work and will normally grant permission to reproduce portions of the work promptly.

For permission to photocopy or reprint any part of this work, please send a request with complete information to the Copyright Clearance Center Inc., 222 Rosewood Drive, Danvers, MA 01923, USA; telephone: 978-750-8400; fax: 978-750-4470; Internet: www.copyright.com.

All other queries on rights and licenses, including subsidiary rights, should be addressed to the Office of the Publisher, The World Bank, 1818 H Street NW, Washington, DC 20433, USA; fax: 202-522-2422; e-mail: pubrights@worldbank.org.

ISBN-13: 978-0-8213-7571-6
eISBN: 978-0-8213-7572-3
DOI: 10.1596/978-0-8213-7571-6

Library of Congress Cataloging-in-Publication Data

Sophastienphong, Kiatchai.
  Getting finance in South Asia 2009 : indicators and analysis of the commercial banking sector / Kiatchai Sophastienphong and Anoma Kulathunga.
    p. cm.
  Includes bibliographical references.
  ISBN 978-0-8213-7571-6 — ISBN 978-0-8213-7572-3 (electronic)
  1. Banks and banking—Asia, South—Case studies. 2. Microfinance—Asia, South—Case studies. 3. Finance—Asia, South—Case studies. I. Kulathunga, Anoma. II. Title.
  HG3270.3.A6S66 2008
  332.1'20954—dc22

Cover design by Drew Fasick.

Contents

Foreword ix
Acknowledgments xi
About the Authors xiii
Acronyms and Abbreviations xv

PART I: ANALYSIS

1. INTRODUCTION 3
Background 3
Development Dimensions and Micro Indicators 4
   Access to Finance 4
   Performance and Efficiency 5
   Financial Stability 5
   Capital Market Development 6
   Market Concentration and Competitiveness 6
   Corporate Governance 7
The Methodology 7
Development of Benchmarks 8
Interpretation of Ranks 9
The Role of Microfinance in South Asia 10

2. THE GETTING FINANCE INDICATORS: COUNTRY PERSPECTIVE 13
Bangladesh 13
   Access to Finance 15
   Performance and Efficiency 16
   Financial Stability 16
   Capital Market Development 17
   Market Concentration and Competitiveness 17
   Corporate Governance 18
India 19
   Access to Finance 21
   Performance and Efficiency 21
   Financial Stability 22

   Capital Market Development 22
   Market Concentration and Competitiveness 23
   Corporate Governance 23
  Nepal 25
   Access to Finance 26
   Performance and Efficiency 26
   Financial Stability 27
   Capital Market Development 28
   Market Concentration and Competitiveness 29
   Corporate Governance 29
  Pakistan 31
   Access to Finance 31
   Performance and Efficiency 33
   Financial Stability 33
   Capital Market Development 34
   Market Concentration and Competitiveness 34
   Corporate Governance 35
  Sri Lanka 37
   Access to Finance 38
   Performance and Efficiency 38
   Financial Stability 39
   Capital Market Development 40
   Market Concentration and Competitiveness 40
   Corporate Governance 40

3. COUNTRY RANKINGS ON THE GETTING FINANCE INDICATORS 43
  Overall Rankings on Development Dimensions 43
  Individual Rankings on Micro Indicators 46
   Access to Finance 46
   Performance and Efficiency 46
   Financial Stability 47
   Capital Market Development 47
   Market Concentration and Competitiveness 47
   Corporate Governance 47

4. AN INTERNATIONAL PERSPECTIVE 51
  Benchmark Comparison (2006) 51
   Access to Finance 51
   Performance and Efficiency 52
   Financial Stability 52
   Capital Market Development 54
   Market Concentration and Competitiveness 54

International Comparison of Financial Ratios—Benchmark Countries (2006) 55
International Comparison of Financial Ratios—Comparator Groups (2005) 58

5. FINDINGS AND OBSERVATIONS 63
Access to Finance 63
Performance and Efficiency 64
Financial Stability 64
Capital Market Development 64
Market Concentration and Competitiveness 64
Corporate Governance 65
Benchmarking and Comparability 65

PART II: INDICATORS

6. COMPILATION GUIDE FOR THE GETTING FINANCE INDICATORS FOR SOUTH ASIA 69
Access to Finance 69
Performance and Efficiency 71
Financial Stability 73
Capital Market Development 75
Market Concentration and Competitiveness 76
Corporate Governance 78

7. METHODOLOGY 79
Data Compilation 79
Choice of Indicators 79
Method for Country Rankings 80
Corporate Governance 80

8. MAJOR POLICY DEVELOPMENTS IN THE PRUDENTIAL REGULATIONS OF SOUTH ASIA, 2005–06 85
Bangladesh 85
Implementation of the New Capital Adequacy Framework (Basel II) in Bangladesh 85
Prudential Regulations 85
Other Policy Developments 87
India 88
Implementation of the New Capital Adequacy Framework (Basel II) in India 88
Prudential Regulations 88
Other Policy Developments 91

Nepal 92
   Implementation of the New Capital Adequacy Framework (Basel II) in Nepal 92
   Prudential Regulations 93
   Other Policy Developments 95
Pakistan 96
   Implementation of the New Capital Adequacy Framework (Basel II) in Pakistan 96
   Prudential Regulations 97
   Other Policy Developments 100
Sri Lanka 100
   Implementation of the New Capital Adequacy Framework (Basel II) in Sri Lanka 100
   Prudential Regulations 101
   Other Policy Developments 102

9. INTERNATIONAL BEST PRACTICES IN CORPORATE GOVERNANCE 105
Organisation for Economic Co-operation and Development 105
Basel Committee on Banking Supervision 105

APPENDIXES 109
Appendix 1.   Getting Finance Indicators for South Asia, by Country and Year 110
Appendix 2.a. Getting Finance Indicators for benchmark countries, 2001–06 132
Appendix 2.b. Benchmark Countries: Data Sources and Notes 138
Appendix 3.   Corporate Governance Matrix: Questionnaire Responses, 2006 139

REFERENCES 145

INDEX 149

Foreword

The Poverty Reduction, Economic Management, Finance and Private Sector Development Unit of the World Bank's South Asia Region has embarked on a regional initiative to develop standardized indicators to measure the soundness and performance of the financial sector in the Region. In the first three phases of this initiative, the Bank developed Getting Finance Indicators under the categories of access to finance, performance and efficiency, corporate governance, and financial stability. These categories represent different dimensions of financial sector development. Under these dimensions, micro indicators were compiled to assess the financial performance and soundness of the banking sector in five different countries in the region—Bangladesh, India, Nepal, Pakistan, and Sri Lanka—against its prudential regulations and against its South Asian peers. To provide a more holistic perspective of getting finance in South Asia, and to improve the understanding of the financial systems in the region, two more dimensions—capital market development, and market concentration and competitiveness—are added in this current volume. Another important enhancement is the compilation of benchmark indicators for selected high-income Organisation for Economic Co-operation and Development (OECD) member and nonmember countries, and a comparator group of Asian countries. This enhancement provides an opportunity to assess the performance and soundness of the South Asian group in a global perspective. Data on these indicators have been compiled and analyzed only for the commercial banking sector for the six years from 2001 to 2006.

This report, *Getting Finance in South Asia 2009*, published annually by our unit, reaffirms the World Bank's commitment to working with developing member countries to promote financial sector development and create financial systems that are sound, stable, supportive of growth, and responsive to people's needs. This program has enabled the Bank to initiate a dialogue with the supervisory authorities in South Asia to improve their data collection efforts, which will in turn strengthen their off-site supervision work. It also provides the impetus for the Bank to expand its monitoring and evaluation work. The Getting Finance Indicators, and the country rankings that are based on them, are expected to become an increasingly important reference tool for the Bank in monitoring and evaluating development objectives and outcomes in its financial sector operations. These indicators should also prove to be a valuable tool for financial sector supervisory agencies in South Asia. The updated indicators, country rankings, and benchmarks should better equip these agencies to monitor the health of their respective country's banking system and to assess its robustness and sustainability relative to others in South Asia and in more developed economies.

Ernesto May

Sector Director
Poverty Reduction, Economic Management, Finance and
Private Sector Development
South Asia Region

Acknowledgments

Kiatchai Sophastienphong (senior financial sector specialist) and Anoma Kulathunga (consultant) acknowledge the invaluable contributions of many individuals to this report.

We gratefully acknowledge the comments, guidance, and encouragements from Simon Bell (sector manager, SASFP) throughout the series. Several members of World Bank country teams facilitated the research and operational visits and commented on the study, including Shah Nur Quayyum (financial sector analyst), Shamsuddin Ahmad (senior financial sector specialist), A. K. M. Abdullah (financial analyst), and Sadruddin Muhammad Salman (extended term consultant) for Bangladesh; Niraj Verma (financial specialist) and K. R. Ramamoorthy (consultant) for India; Sabin Raj Shrestha (financial sector specialist) and Lalima Maskey (program assistant) for Nepal; Isfandyar Zaman Khan (research analyst) for Pakistan; and Sriyani Hulugalle (senior economist) and Lohitha Karunasekera (team assistant) for Sri Lanka. We offer them special thanks.

We thank the representatives of central banks and other authorities who participated in this study, including the following from Bangladesh Bank's Department of Offsite Supervision: Md. Golam Mostafa (deputy general manager), Debaprosad Debnath (deputy general manager), M. Zahir Hossain and Ashok K. Karmaker (assistant directors); from Nepal Rastra Bank's Bank Supervision Department and Bank and Financial Institution Regulation Department: Surendra Man Pradhan (executive director), Bhisma Raj Dhungana (director), and Pralhad Thapa (deputy director); from the State Bank of Pakistan's Banking Surveillance Department: Jameel Ahmad (executive director), Lubna Farooq Malik (director), Muhammad Javaid Ismail (senior joint director), Salman Ahmed (junior joint director), Naushad Kamil (junior, joint director), Rizwana Rifat (assistant director), Abdul Samad (assistant director), and Muhammad Rizwan (assistant director); and from the Central Bank of Sri Lanka's Bank Supervision Department: P. Samarasiri (director), A. A. M. Thassim (deputy director), and H. D. Ajith (senior examiner).

We are indebted to Ahmad Ahsan (lead economist); Pipat Luengnaruemitchai (economist); Anjali Kumar (financial sector operations and policy department); and Priya Basu, Mark Dutz, Varsha Marathe, Kyoo-Won Oh, Henry Bagazonzya, Gaby Afram, and Tatiana Menova (South Asia Region's finance and private sector development unit), all of whom provided invaluable inputs as peer reviewers of the concept note and the report. Finally, yet importantly, we express our thanks to Vivi Zhang (consultant) and Maria Marjorie Espiritu (program assistant), who provided invaluable research, technical support, and typesetting.

About the Authors

Kiatchai Sophastienphong is Senior Financial Sector Specialist, Poverty Reduction, Economic Management, Finance and Private Sector Development at the World Bank, South Asia Region. Recently Mr. Sophasienphong has led the Financial Sector Assessment Program (FSAP) update mission to Sri Lanka; helped to design and implement restructuring and bank privatization programs in Bangladesh, Nepal, and Pakistan; and guided the dialogue on financial sector issues in several client countries at both the policy and technical levels. He has designed the overall financial sector strategies for these countries and developed a program to implement these strategies. Prior to joining the Bank, he held senior executive positions at the Bank of Thailand (the central bank) and two private commercial banks in Thailand. He also worked as the Senior Financial Economist in the Regional and Sustainable Development Department at the Asian Development Bank. In addition to this publication, he recently co-authored the book *South Asian Bond Markets: Developing Long-Term Finance for Growth* (to be published by the World Bank). His research interests include bank restructuring and privatization, corporate debt restructuring, and bond market developments. He received a BA and an MA in Economics from the University of Cambridge, United Kingdom.

Anoma Kulathunga is a doctoral student at the George Washington University Business School in Washington, D.C., and a consultant at the World Bank. Prior to her doctoral studies, Ms. Kulathunga had worked for the Central Bank of Sri Lanka for 15 years. She received an MA in Finance from the George Washington University and an MBA from the University of Sri Jayewardenepura, Sri Lanka. She is an associate member of the Chartered Institute of Management Accountants, U.K. In addition to this publication, she recently co-authored a chapter in *Islamic Finance: The Regulatory Challenge* (published by John Wiley & Sons). Her research interests include financial sector development, Islamic banking, worker remittances, and international banking.

Acronyms and Abbreviations

AA	Articles of Association
ADB	Asian Development Bank
AGM	Annual General Meeting
AIG	Accord Implementation Group
AOF	Account Opening Form
AR	annual report
ATM	automated teller machine
BB	Bangladesh Bank
BCO	Banking Companies Ordinance of 1962
BOD	board of directors
BPSS	Board for Regulation and Supervision of Payment and Settlement System
BRPD	Banking Regulation and Policy Department
CAAP	Capital Adequacy Assessment Process
CAR	capital adequacy ratio
CAMEL	Capital adequacy, Asset quality, Management quality, Earnings, and Liquidity
CBSL	Central Bank of Sri Lanka
CEO	chief executive officer
CFO	chief financial officer
CIB	Credit Information Bureau
CR	Concentration Ratio
CRR	Cash Reserve Requirement
CSO	civil society organization
CTS	Cheque Truncation System
DFI	development finance institution
DMA	direct marketing agent
DSA	direct selling agent
ECAI	External Credit Assessment Institutions
EPZ	Export Processing Zone
FIs	financial institutions
FII	foreign institutional investor
FPSI	Financial Performance and Soundness Indicators

FPT	fit-and-proper test
FTRA	Financial Transactions Reporting Act
GAAP	Generally Accepted Accounting Principals
GDP	gross domestic product
GNI	gross national income
HFT	Held for Trading
HHI	Herfindahl-Hirschman Index
HMG	His Majesty's Government
IAS	International Accounting Standards
IASC	International Accounting Standards Committee
IFR	Investment Fluctuation Reserve
IFS	International Financial Statistics
IMF	International Monetary Fund
IPDI	Innovative Perpetual Debt Instruments
IPO	initial public offering
IRB	Internal Rating-Based Approach
IT	information technology
JCR-VIS	JCR-VIS Credit Rating Co. Ltd.
KIBOR	Karachi Inter-Bank Offered Rate
KYC	Know Your Customer
MB	Monetary Board (of the Central Bank of Sri Lanka)
MF	mutual funds
MFI	microfinance institution
MOF	Ministry of Finance
MRAA	Microcredit Regulatory Authority Act
MRRU	Microfinance Research and Reference Unit
NBFC	nonbank financial companies
NBFI	nonbank financial institution
NCBs	nationalized commercial banks
NEFT	National Electronic Fund Transfer
NGO	nongovernmental organization
NOC	no objection certificate
NPA	nonperforming assets
NPC	National Payments Council
NPL	nonperforming loans
NRB	Nepal Rastra Bank
NRs	Nepal rupees
OBU	Offshore Banking Unit
OECD	Organisation for Economic Co-operation and Development
PACRA	The Pakistan Credit Rating Agency
PAN	permanent account number
PLS	profit and loss sharing

PMLA	Prevention of Money Laundering Act
PREM	Poverty Reduction and Economic Management
PRs	Pakistan rupees
PSS	Payment Settlement Systems
QIS	Quantitative Impact Study
RBI	Reserve Bank of India
ROA	return on assets
ROE	return on equity
ROSC	Report on the Observance of Standards and Codes
RRB	Regional Rural Banks
Rs	Indian rupees
RTGS	real-time gross settlement system
SBL	Single Borrower Limit
SBP	State Bank of Pakistan
SEANZA	South East Asia, New Zealand, and Australia
SEBI	Securities and Exchange Board of India
SEC	Securities and Exchange Commission
SHG	Self-Help Group
SLR	Statutory Liquidity Requirement
SL Rs	Sri Lanka rupees
SMA	Special Mention Account
SME	small and medium enterprise
TOR	Terms of Reference
Tk	Bangladesh taka
US	United States of America
VAT	value added tax
WDI	World Development Indicators
WOS	Wholly Owned Subsidiary
WTO	World Trade Organization

Part I

Analysis

1

Introduction

Background

Banks play an important role in the economic development process by mobilizing and allocating funds toward productive investments, reducing informational costs, and providing better access to assets and markets through their intermediation process. While the ensuing productivity increases lead to economic development, it is equally important to achieve financial inclusion, because it contributes directly to the income-generating capacity of the underprivileged. Thus, supporting the development and strengthening of the financial sectors would reduce risk and vulnerability for the poorest and enable them to participate in and benefit from the growth process.

Four years ago, the World Bank launched a regional initiative in South Asia to develop standardized indicators to measure the performance and soundness of the financial sector—the Financial Performance and Soundness Indicators (FPSI), now commonly known as the Getting Finance Indicators. Phases I and II of this initiative developed and compiled micro indicators to analyze the banking sector development in five South Asian countries—Bangladesh, India, Nepal, Pakistan, and Sri Lanka—assessing the sector's performance against the country's prudential regulations and against its peers in South Asia. In addition, phase II provided a comprehensive set of micro indicators for nonbank financial institutions (NBFIs) comparable to those for commercial banks (see World Bank 2005b). In phase III, the Getting Finance Indicators covered two additional dimensions of banking sector robustness (access to finance and corporate governance) along with the more traditional measures of financial stability and performance and efficiency. The phase III study used fewer micro indicators in each category than the earlier studies; however, it also provided a time-series analysis, a cluster analysis, and country soundness rankings based on the indicators (see World Bank 2006d).

In the fourth edition, to provide a more holistic perspective of Getting Finance in South Asia, and to improve our understanding of the financial systems in the region, two additional dimensions—capital market development, and market concentration and competitiveness—are included. Another important addition is the compilation of benchmark indicators for selected high-income Organisation for Economic Co-operation and Development (OECD) member and nonmember countries and a comparator group of Asian countries. These benchmarks provide the needed measure to assess the performance and soundness of the South Asian group from a global perspective.

To ensure comparability of the indicators across the region as well as consistent interpretation and analysis, a compilation guide was prepared, setting out the definitions and underlying concepts for both the compilers and the users of the indicators (see chapter 6). The definitions and methodology for computing these indicators that appear in the previous editions remain the same (see World Bank 2004, 2005b, 2006d).

Development Dimensions and Micro Indicators

As noted, six dimensions of financial sector development are analyzed: access to finance, performance and efficiency, financial stability, capital market development, market concentration, and competitiveness and corporate governance. Each category in turn includes six micro indicators, except for corporate governance, for which a questionnaire was developed to assess governance from the four major perspectives of ownership structure and influence of external stakeholders; investor rights and relations; transparency and disclosure; and board structure and effectiveness. For the comparative analysis, data have been compiled for the six years from 2001 to 2006 only for the commercial banking sector.

Access to Finance

Access to financial services is important in raising the standard of living of the poor and the underserved segments of society. In almost every part of the world, limited access to finance is considered a key constraint to private sector growth (see Beck, Demirgüç-Kunt, and Martinez Peria 2005). This is especially true in developing countries, where people have little influence over policy reforms and where financial sector development often benefits the rich disproportionately.

In countries seeking to develop financial markets, it is important to monitor and measure the level of access to finance. This knowledge provides a more balanced picture of financial outreach. Hence, it helps policy makers and regulatory authorities better target their development efforts.

As an initial step, the study analyzes access to finance using data relating to providers of finance (supply-side data). Building a more complete set of data would require collecting demand-side data as well, but this was ruled out by time and resource constraints. Access to finance is measured in terms of the physical availability, access, and use of financial services using the following six micro indicators:

- Demographic branch penetration (branches per 100,000 people)
- Demographic ATM penetration (automated teller machines per 100,000 people)
- Deposit accounts per 1,000 people
- Loan accounts per 1,000 people
- Geographic branch penetration (branches per 1,000 km^2)
- Geographic ATM penetration (automated teller machines per 1,000 km^2)

Demographic penetration indicates the availability of financial services to a given number of people. Geographic penetration indicates physical access to financial services in a given geographic area, while deposit and loan ratios show the use of such services.

Performance and Efficiency

The efficiency of banks is important for the robustness and resilience of the financial sector. The study uses traditional measures of bank efficiency in terms of returns efficiency and cost efficiency.

Two of the most popular measures of efficiency are used to assess scope for banks' earnings to offset losses relative to capital or assets, sustainability of its capital position, and efficiency in using its capital or assets:

- Return on equity
- Return on assets

Two ratios measure banks' efficiency in terms of staff and operating expenses:

- Staff cost ratio (personnel expenses as a percentage of operating expenses)
- Operating cost ratio (operating expenses as a percentage of net interest earnings)

In addition, two ratios measure the earning strength and overall operating efficiency of the banking sector:

- Net interest margin ratio (net interest earnings as a percentage of the average value of total assets)
- Recurring earning power ratio (preprovision profits as a percentage of the average value of total assets)

Financial Stability

Maintaining stability in a financial system—that is, avoiding significant disruptions to the system and its functions—is key to achieving low inflation as well as sustainable economic growth. In a stable financial system, markets function without disruptions, financial institutions can operate efficiently, and asset prices are realistic.

To measure the stability of financial systems, the study uses ratios on capital adequacy, asset quality, and liquidity. The capital adequacy ratios (CARs) measure the capacity of a financial institution to absorb losses and, thus indicate the level of its financial strength. The asset quality and liquidity ratios reflect vulnerabilities relating to credit risk and liquidity risk, respectively. The study does not measure market risk, a third source of vulnerability, because of the lack of data across countries and over a reasonable period, a problem also experienced in compiling data for previous studies.

Two ratios measure banks' financial strength in terms of its capital adequacy:

- Capital adequacy ratio (regulatory capital funds as a percentage of risk-weighted assets)
- Leverage ratio (total equity as a percentage of total on balance sheet assets)

Two ratios measure banks' asset quality in terms of credit risk:

- Gross nonperforming loans ratio (gross NPLs as a percentage of total advances)
- Provisions to nonperforming loans ratio (loan loss provisions as a percentage of gross NPLs)

The last two ratios measure banks' vulnerability to loss of funds and liquidity mismatch in terms of liquidity risk:

- Liquid assets ratio (liquid assets as a percentage of total assets)
- Liquid assets to liabilities ratio (liquid assets as a percentage of liquid liabilities)

Capital Market Development

The development of capital markets is a powerful indicator of the depth of the financial sector. By allocating funds for viable investment projects, healthy capital markets diversify the channels of financial intermediation, thus providing a countervailing force to the banking business. This would allow perceived risks to be monitored on a continual basis and be minimized.

Bond markets provide borrowers an alternative to bank lending as a form of long-term finance and allow a lender to convert illiquid assets into tradable securities. An active bond market allows credit risk to be spread over a wide range of investors and provides up-to-date information about a market player's creditworthiness. An active stock market suggests strong economic and institutional fundamentals. Hence, any shortfall would identify the need for reform measures to achieve higher levels of economic and institutional development. To measure the level of capital market development in terms of depth, efficiency, and liquidity, the study uses the following ratios:

- Ratio of domestic bond market as a percentage of equity market capitalization
- Ratio of domestic public bonds outstanding as a percentage of gross domestic product (GDP)
- Ratio of trading value of top 10 stocks as a percentage of total trading value
- Ratio of stock market capitalization as a percentage of GDP
- Ratio of stock trading value as a percentage of GDP
- Stock market turnover ratio (total value of shares traded as a percentage of average stock market capitalization)

Market Concentration and Competitiveness

The study examines the market structure of the banking sector to evaluate the banking system's proneness to instability and crises. A high level of concentration in the banking industry, by reducing competition and increasing cost, has a negative impact on efficiency: the financing obstacle will be higher and the likelihood of receiving bank financing will be lower. At the same time, a highly competitive banking sector might be more prone to crisis, due to increased fragility resulting from intense competition, than a more concentrated one. Hence, striking the right balance between the two is important for the optimal functioning and stability of the financial sector.

To measure market concentration and competitiveness, the study uses three concentration ratios and the Herfindahl-Hirschman Index (HHI). The U.S. Department of Justice and the Federal Trade Commission has issued (under horizontal merger guidelines) HHI standards,[1] which are used by the European Union, the United States, and many other countries, as a measure of market concentration (see U.S. Department of Justice and the Federal Trade Commission 1997).

Also, both simplicity and limited data requirements make the K-bank concentration ratio one of the most frequently used measures of concentration in the empirical literature (see Al-Muharrami, Matthews, and Khabari 2006).

The six micro indicators used are as follows:

- HHI
- K-bank concentration ratio (K = 3) – based on assets
- K-bank concentration ratio (K = 3) – based on deposits
- K-bank concentration ratio (K = 3) – based on loans

- Ratio of private credit extended by banks as a percentage of GDP
- Ratio of commercial banking assets as a percentage of GDP

Corporate Governance

Sound corporate governance creates an environment that promotes banking efficiency, mitigates financial risks, and increases stability and therefore the credibility of financial institutions. Developing countries have much to gain by improving their corporate governance standards, still mostly in the development stage. The basic principles of sound corporate governance are the same everywhere: fairness, transparency, accountability, and responsibility are the minimum standards that provide legitimacy to banks, reduce vulnerability to financial crisis, and broaden and deepen access to capital.

Corporate governance scoring is challenging and must be approached with care. Unlike other forms of financial analysis, where quantitative measures can provide "hard" benchmarks to guide more qualitative aspects of analysis, assessment of corporate governance is largely a qualitative exercise (see Standard & Poor's 2004). A questionnaire was developed to assess sound corporate governance in terms of ownership structure and influence of external stakeholders, investor rights, transparency and disclosure, and board structure and effectiveness. The good governance practices outlined by the OECD serve as the basis for the questionnaire developed to assess the corporate governance of South Asian countries in this report (see chapter 9). In February 2006, the Basel Committee on Banking Supervision also issued a guidance paper on corporate governance articulating the eight principles to enhance corporate governance for banking organizations, and to guide the actions of the directors, managers, and supervisors of a diverse range of banks (see chapter 9). Corporate governance is assessed through a series of straightforward questions, and no definitions or guidelines are provided in the compilation guide for those questions or the resulting indicators. Because the collection of data for the corporate governance analysis was confined to this simple questionnaire, the observations on corporate governance in this report should be viewed as preliminary at best.

The Methodology

For this study, just as for the earlier studies, South Asia is represented by Bangladesh, India, Nepal, Pakistan, and Sri Lanka. Annual data on the commercial banking sector of each of the countries were compiled for the six years from 2001 to 2006. These six years of data are analyzed to evaluate the performance and soundness of the financial system in each country. A simple-average ranking method is used to aid this evaluation process. (For more on collection of data, choice of indicators, and ranking methodology, see chapter 7.)

The compilation of comparable data for a set of financial sector soundness indicators in South Asia was an important contribution of the phase I and II reports. These time-series financial data, coupled with a comparative study of the prudential banking regulations of South Asian countries as well as international best practices, provide a useful tool for supervisory authorities. This would enable them to assess their prudential norms relative to those of their regional peers and of more advanced countries so that they can bring those norms, and their country's financial indicators, in line with international best practices. The third edition of Getting Finance in South Asia added another useful tool to supplement those already available to supervisory agencies in the region—that is, a ranking of South Asian countries based on a selected set of financial and corporate governance indicators that reflect the soundness of the financial system.

In this fourth edition, two new development dimensions—capital market development and market concentration and competitiveness—should provide a more holistic perspective of Getting Finance in South Asia. Another important enhancement is the compilation of benchmark indicators for selected high-income OECD member and nonmember countries and a comparator group of Asian countries. These benchmarks help the supervisory authorities identify industry and international averages, trends, and any significant variations to these norms. Once such variances are detected, the supervisory authorities should be prompted to determine the cause and to identify corrective action.

The rankings and analysis presented in this report are based mainly on the data gathered from each country. Thus, the findings, interpretations, and conclusions in the report depend on the accuracy of these data as well as on the indicators selected. The results of the analysis should draw attention to the importance of sound corporate governance, broad access to finance, and stable, efficient, and well-performing banks for maintaining a sound and robust financial system.

An unstable financial system entails heightened risk of financial crisis. Thus, a stable financial system, which shows promise of diversification by developing capital markets and welcomes fair competition, has the capacity not only to prevent financial crises from occurring but also to contain the effects of those that do occur and prevent them from spilling over into the real economy. Rather than serving as a reference, this and similar studies should prompt the regulatory authorities in South Asia to reflect on their country's position within the dynamic international financial arena and make timely adjustments needed to stay ahead of the game. Constant surveillance and monitoring of the structural trends in financial markets are needed to identify early warnings of the onset and potential impact of financial instability. To assist such surveillance, through this exercise, the World Bank seeks to compile the financial data, analysis, and benchmarks needed for monitoring risks to domestic financial stability.

Development of Benchmarks

Benchmarking helps a country to view its performance relative to its peers in the region and internationally. They are particularly useful as diagnostic tools to assess a country's performance and capabilities relative to international standards to identify gaps to improve performance; however, they are not well suited to describe the unique characteristics of the financial systems under consideration. While benchmarking, by itself, does not improve performance, it can be used in formulating strategic decisions. In this study, comparable data for selected high-income OECD member and nonmember countries—including Australia; Canada; Hong Kong, China; New Zealand; Singapore; the United Kingdom; and the United States—are compiled to serve as the benchmark. The choice of countries was based on two considerations: (1) standard-setting countries in the case of OECD member countries; and (2) for nonmember countries, members of South East Asia, New Zealand, and Australia (SEANZA).[2] The choice of countries was also affected by the availability of data.

For this benchmark group, data have been compiled for the six-year period from 2001 to 2006 only for the commercial banking sector. This data compilation was confined only to financial data; corporate governance information was not gathered (for underlying data, see appendix 2.A; for data sources, see appendix 2.B). For each indicator, the high (low) values of these seven countries were selected as the benchmark range. However, data for Hong Kong, China and Singapore were removed as outliers from geographic branch penetration ratio and geographic ATM penetration ratio because of their unique positions as international financial centers and their small land areas. These benchmarks provide an opportunity to assess the performance and soundness of the South Asian group in a global perspective.

Interpretation of Ranks

South Asian authorities actively pursue financial reform measures to build stable financial systems that are resilient to economic shocks. In this process, they have pursued many things—including policy changes, technological changes, market infrastructure improvements, and prudential guideline revisions—that would ensure safety and soundness of the financial system through greater transparency and accountability. They have initiated action to implement Basel II capital framework in the near future so that banks are able to strengthen the link between regulatory capital and risk management. Furthermore, all South Asian countries have attempted to introduce corporate governance guidelines. The positive effects of these reforms are discernible.

Overall progress is commendable for most countries. Analysis of the Getting Finance Indicators confirms that commercial banking sectors in Bangladesh, India, Nepal, Pakistan, and Sri Lanka have made great strides in some dimensions (returns, capital adequacy, and market concentration), whereas other dimensions (credit quality, provisioning, and access measures) need further improvements to compare well with the benchmark groups. Rankings of these countries aid the evaluation process to pinpoint areas in which performance is strong and areas in which improvements are most needed. India leads the region in overall ranking—indicating they lead the financial sector development efforts among the South Asian countries—followed by Pakistan, Sri Lanka, Bangladesh, and Nepal. However, rankings differ in each of the six areas assessed.

On access to finance, Sri Lanka ranks at the top (0.93 of the composite score[3]), followed by Bangladesh, India, Pakistan, and Nepal. Over the six-year period, Sri Lanka improved its financial outreach by providing physical access to financial services and encouraging their use. Except for geographic branch penetration, Sri Lanka leads in all access indicators. Access is lowest in Nepal.

On performance and efficiency, the top ranking goes to Pakistan (0.80)—due to higher returns, better earnings power, and somewhat lower costs—followed by Sri Lanka and India. Bangladesh and Nepal share fourth place. All the countries have enjoyed good returns resulting from wider interest rate spreads and increased credit volumes. Nepal still faces effects of negative regulatory capital; however, it leads the group in operating cost efficiencies. In addition, Bangladesh continues to be straddled with high operating costs, although returns appear to be reasonable.

On financial stability, India leads the region (0.89)—denoting superior capital position, better liquidity management, and improved credit quality—followed by Pakistan, Sri Lanka, Bangladesh, and Nepal. All countries except Nepal recorded higher CARs. Pakistan has the best provisions ratio. Nepal still faces negative regulatory capital and its liquidity position should be monitored to avoid a collapse of market liquidity.

The area on which South Asian countries need to focus most seems to be capital market development. India ranks at the top (0.91), followed by Pakistan, Sri Lanka, Bangladesh, and Nepal. Except for India, all other capital markets are at developmental stages. When compared with other countries, South Asian markets have relied less heavily on bond financing than equity financing. This factor is not readily observable with the selected indicators, however, as the bulk of the securities represents government debt. One other reason is the continued reliance on bank financing.

Market concentration and competitiveness category is led by India (0.89)—signifying healthy competition in the banking sector—followed by Bangladesh, Nepal, Pakistan, and Sri Lanka. Except for Sri Lanka, all other countries have low market concentration ratios. On the HHI, Sri Lanka is classified as moderately concentrated with the top three banks accounting for more than 50 percent of all assets, deposits, and loans. Private credit is high in most countries and needs careful monitoring to reduce the possibility of increased credit risk. Rapid expansion of bank credit to the private sector, if not coupled with prudential credit risk management systems, would make banks vulnerable if economic activities slowed down. This vulnerability happens when banks try to meet the increasing demand for credit during economic boom times by changing the composition of their asset portfolios and by increasing external borrowings, thus reducing profit margins (see Hilbers, Otker-Robe, and Pazarbaşıoğlu 2006). This fact is especially significant to South Asia because bank credit is the main source of financing for the private sector ahead of either equity or bond financing. As expected, commercial banking assets as a percentage of GDP are significant in all countries.

Finally, on average, South Asian countries show the most efforts and improvements in corporate governance. Pakistan takes the lead (0.84)—indicating significant reform efforts in this area—followed by India, Sri Lanka, Nepal, and Bangladesh. India, Pakistan, and, more recently, Sri Lanka, have issued detailed guidelines. Still, all countries need to review their corporate governance guidelines and strengthen them in areas such as stakeholder rights, disclosure of beneficial ownership, transparency and disclosure, and adherence to international standards. Enforcement of the corporate governance guidelines by the supervisory authorities also needs attention.

Overall, when comparative data over the six-year period are examined, it is evident that South Asia is showing commendable progress in making its banking systems more efficient.

The Role of Microfinance in South Asia

Because of comparability and data issues, the analysis is limited in coverage to commercial banks and ignores a range of other deposit-taking financial institutions, such as post office savings schemes, cooperative banks, microfinance institutions, and so on. Therefore, the interpretations and the general applicability of the findings on access to finance dimension is limited only to the commercial banking sector. For example, the microfinance movement, as a medium of financial access, is a significant feature in the economic structure of South Asia. Box 1.1 illustrates the significance of this important aspect in South Asian financial inclusion.

Box 1.1 Microfinance in South Asia

Overall, microfinance has been established as a significant part of the economic landscape of South Asia. By 2005, microfinance in the region covered at least 35 million of some 270 million families in the region and met some 15 percent of the overall credit requirements of low-income families. In Bangladesh and Sri Lanka, coverage was particularly impressive, with more than 60 percent of the poor covered by microfinance services.

Estimated breadth of microfinance outreach in South Asia

Country	Population[a] (millions)	Poverty ratio[b] (%)	Poor families[c] (millions)	Microfinance clients (millions)	MF poverty outreach[d] (%)	MF coverage of poor families[c] (%)
Afghanistan	22	55	2.0	0.12	50	3
Bangladesh	143	50	13.0	16.00	50	62
India	1,100	30	60.0	15.00	35	9
Nepal	26	35	1.6	0.50	45	14
Pakistan	155	33	8.5	0.58	35	2
Sri Lanka	20	25	1.0	2.50	25	63
South Asia	1,466	33	86.2	34.70	41	17

Source: Authors' estimates based on data available from the Asian Development Bank and others.
Note: MF = microfinance.
a. Population figures from World Bank Web site (updated from 2004 to 2005).
b. Poverty information for India and Bangladesh match World Bank information; informed estimates for other countries.
c. Poor families are defined as families subsisting on less than government-defined poverty thresholds, using an estimated family size of 5 for Sri Lanka; 5.5 for India, Bangladesh, and Nepal; and 6 for Pakistan and Afghanistan.
d. Poverty outreach from EDA Rural Systems Private Limited, India, studies for Bangladesh and India; for other countries, informed estimates based on secondary sources.

All six of the larger countries in the region either have a microfinance regulation in place (Nepal and Pakistan), are considering a draft law (Bangladesh, India, and Sri Lanka), or are actively debating what kind of regulation should be adopted (Afghanistan).

The microfinance movement provides most of the access to financial services available to low-income people in South Asia, but it is still largely a separate part of the financial system, with few examples of direct service provision to the poor by "mainstream" commercial institutions. And, despite the growing discussion about and enthusiasm for developing a seamless, inclusive financial sector, there is little evidence that this will happen to any great extent in the near future. Only in India are there significant examples of bank involvement in microfinance. This includes the linkage models with microfinance institutions (MFIs), the large and growing bank-SHG (self-help group) links, and involvement in the market of large commercial banks such as ICICI Bank, including international banks like ABN Amro and CitiBank. Also, several local and international social investment funds offering debt and equity products are active in India, something that has not taken off elsewhere in the region. But even in India, aside from the bank-SHG model, which has its own special characteristics, evidence of mainstreaming remains limited to a relatively small part of total outreach.

In some countries, major impediments need to be removed before an inclusive financial sector can develop. In Sri Lanka, especially, the dominating presence of a large government subsidized microfinance programs impedes the growth of well-managed MFIs and even commercial banks that want to enter the sector. In Pakistan, most nongovernmental organizations (NGO), MFIs, and microfinance banks are not profitable, and they do not charge interest rates that would support profitable operations, largely because they still receive significant donor and government funded subsidies. Recently in India, competition between subsidy-oriented government programs and MFIs has resulted in coercive pressure by a state government on financially sustainable MFIs to lower interest rates to unsustainable levels. The message this gives to banks that might otherwise consider retail products for microfinance is obvious. Reforms are needed to remove impediments of this kind before a healthy, inclusive financial sector will be able to emerge.

Source: Excerpts from World Bank 2006e.

Endnotes

1. HHI is calculated by squaring the market share of each bank and summing the squares. According to the guidelines, the banking industry is considered as competitive if HHI is less than 1,000, somewhat concentrated if HHI is between 1,000 and 1,800, and highly concentrated if HHI is more than 1,800.

2. SEANZA was formed to promote cooperation among central banks by providing intensive and systematic training courses for central bank staffs. Original members were central banks from Australia, India, New Zealand, Pakistan, and Sri Lanka. The additions were Bangladesh; China; Hong Kong, China; Indonesia; the Islamic Republic of Iran; Japan; the Republic of Korea; Malaysia; Macao, China; Mongolia; Nepal; Papua New Guinea; the Philippines; Singapore; and Thailand.

3. Composite scores range from 0 to 1.

2

The Getting Finance Indicators: Country Perspective

The commercial banking sector is the main financial intermediary in many of these countries, with banking assets accounting for more than 50 percent of the gross domestic product (GDP). This analysis covers six dimensions of the financial sector development over a six-year period from 2001 to 2006. The analysis is further enhanced by the use of benchmarks (for underlying data see appendixes 1, 2, and 3). An update of the major policy developments in prudential regulations covering 2005–06 is also included (see chapter 8). While the previous Financial Performance and Soundness Indicators (FPSI) reports discussed the prudential regulations of each country in detail and benchmarked the prudential norms of South Asian supervisory authorities against international best practices (see World Bank 2004, 2005b, 2006d), this report provides a detailed comparison of benchmark countries with the South Asian group.

Having more than 50 percent of the world's poorest people, South Asia faces the daunting task of developing their economies while eradicating poverty. In terms of income group classification, India, Pakistan, and Sri Lanka are classified as lower-middle-income countries while Bangladesh and Nepal are classified as low-income countries, based on their per capita gross national income (GNI).[1] Populations range from 19 million in Sri Lanka to more than 1 billion in India, which accounts for around 75 percent of the region's population and 80 percent of its GDP. Together, Bangladesh, India, and Pakistan account for around 97 percent of the region's population and GDP (see table 2.1).

Financial sectors in South Asian countries continue to be dominated by their banking sectors. With the exception of India, capital markets are at early stages of development, hence private sectors continue to rely on bank credit rather than bond or equity financing, for their investment requirements. South Asian countries, however, are making considerable efforts to develop their financial sectors.

Bangladesh

With a population of around 144.3 million and a GDP of nearly US$61.96 million (2006 data), Bangladesh is the third largest country in terms of these two measures.

Table 2.1 Key Economic Indicators for South Asian Countries, 2006

	Bangladesh	India	Nepal	Pakistan	Sri Lanka
Population (millions)	144.30	1,109.80	27.70	159.00	19.80
Gross national income (GNI) per capita (Atlas method US$)	490	820	290	800	1,320
Gross domestic product (GDP) (US$ billion)	61.96	906.27	8.05	128.83	26.97
GDP (% annual average growth)	6.70	9.20	2.30	6.60	7.20
Gross dom. investment/GDP	25.00	35.00	30.30	20.00	28.70
Gross national savings/GDP	33.00	33.00[a]	35.00	17.00	24.80
Equity market capitalization (US$ billion)	3.61	818.88	1.31	45.52	7.77
Equity market capitalization (% of GDP)	5.83	90.36	16.31	35.33	28.81
Domestic bonds outstanding (US$ billion)	7.30	325.68	1.22	32.41	13.71
Domestic bonds outstanding (% of GDP)	11.85	35.94	15.09	25.16	50.84
Banking assets (US$ billion)	32.74	587.38	4.33	50.70	10.30
Banking assets (% of GDP)	52.84	64.81	53.82	39.35	38.20
Deposit interest rate (%)	9.11	7.25	2.25	4.94	11.50
Lending interest rate (%)	15.33	14.25	8.00	11.55	14.64
No. of commercial banks	43	85	18	35	23
No. of specialized banks	5	7	46	10	14
No. of nonbank financial institutions (NBFIs)	28	428[b]	134[c]	78[d]	48[e]
Exchange rate/US$ (year end)	69.07	44.25	71.10	60.92	107.71

Sources: World Bank 2007a, 2007b; IMF 2007b; regulatory authorities.
a. 2005 data.
b. Deposit-taking nonbank financial companies (NBFCs).
c. Includes finance companies, savings and credit institutions, and nongovernmental organizations (NGOs).
d. 2004 data.
e. Includes finance companies and leasing companies.

With a GNI of approximately US$490, Bangladesh is classified as a low-income country. The GDP continues to grow at an average annual growth rate of 6.7 percent. Bangladesh continues to be a heavily agrarian economy (19.6 percent of the GDP); however, over the years, the service sector has emerged as the dominant sector in the economy, accounting for more than 52.5 percent of the GDP in 2006. Export of goods and services continues to improve at 19 percent of the GDP. In 2006, Bangladesh had a high gross national savings rate, at 33 percent of GDP, and total debt equaled 35.4 percent of GDP. The market capitalization of listed companies was 6 percent of GDP. The domestic bond outstanding was 11.85 percent of the GDP, at US$7.30 billion.

In Bangladesh, commercial banks dominate the financial sector with banking assets of around 52.84 percent of GDP. The country's four nationalized commercial banks (NCBs) dominate the banking system, accounting for more than 52.21 percent of assets and operating 65 percent of branches (3,384) in March 2007. In addition to the 4 NCBs, Bangladesh's 43 commercial banks in 2006 included 30 private banks and 9 foreign banks. (Bangladesh Bank 2007b).

Figure 2.1 The Bangladesh Banking Sector Demonstrated Lower Concentration

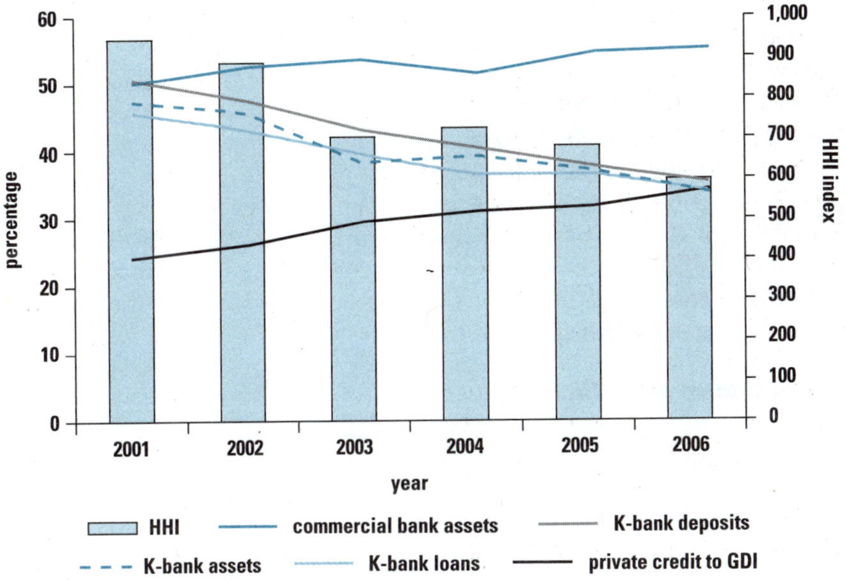

Legend: HHI; commercial bank assets; K-bank deposits; K-bank assets; K-bank loans; private credit to GDI

Source: Data from Bangladesh Bank; see appendix 1, table A1.7.

Analysis of the micro indicators of the Bangladesh commercial banking sector suggests that the main focus should be stability (improving the capital base and provisions, improving credit quality, and tightening underwriting standards to bring down nonperforming loans [NPLs]), performance and evaluation (curtailing operating costs and improving margins), and corporate governance (aligning local accounting and auditing standards with international best practices and improving the corporate governance policy). Banking sector concentration is commendably low on all measures, but higher levels of bank credits and assets denote the competitiveness of the banking sector (see figure 2.1). As with most other South Asian countries, Bangladesh capital markets are still at the developmental stage with a weak bond market and low equity market capitalization. Improvements in the market infrastructure and regulatory aspects would be needed before Bangladesh can reach its full potential as a reliable long-term funding source.

Access to Finance

Financial outreach improved marginally between 2001 and 2006. Demographic branch penetration decreased slightly from 4.83 bank branches per 100,000 people in 2001 to 4.73 in 2006. By the end of 2006, however, demographic automated teller machine (ATM) penetration growth was still low at 0.3 per 100,000 people. The geographic branch penetration hardly changed, whereas ATM penetration increased by nearly 200 percent from 0.91 per 1,000 km^2 to almost 2.71 in 2006. On usage of financial services, deposit accounts rose gradually from 231.97 per 1,000 people in 2001 to 255.23 in 2006, and loan accounts per 1,000 people grew by about 8 percent. The deposit mobilization of commercial banks largely remains an urban phenomenon. The majority of banking deposits are now held by the private banks, which compete closely with public banks for the major share in the lending market. Lending to the private sector showed increased participation by the private banks, hence the growth.

As stated earlier, however, the access to finance measures discussed here applies only to the commercial banking sector. Bangladesh leads microfinance efforts in South Asia with more than 1,000 semiformal microfinance institutions (MFIs) serving more than 22 million people. Funds disbursed through microfinance have reached US$12 billion. These facts underlie the importance of microfinance in the system. The government also has supported this movement in many ways. The establishment of a Microfinance Research and Reference Unit (MRRU) in Bangladesh Bank and the enactment of the Microcredit Regulatory Authority Act (MRAA) are some examples. The MRAA is processing licenses for microcredit institutions to streamline their operations.

Performance and Efficiency

The overall efficiency of the banking system has improved marginally since 2001. Both return on equity (ROE) and return on assets (ROA) initially dropped from 2001 and then improved, except in 2004, when a loss was registered due to the charging of accumulated provisioning shortfall for one nationalized bank. ROE stood at 33.86 percent in 2006, almost a 98 percent increase from the 2001 ratio of 17.12 percent, while ROA almost doubled over the six-year period to reach 1.66 percent at the end of 2006. The improvement in returns was mainly due to the better performance by foreign banks and, to a lesser extent, by private banks.

The banking system appears to have made mixed results in cost-efficiency. The staff cost ratio rose over the years, from 44.75 percent in 2001 to 61.39 percent in 2006. The operating cost ratio fell by almost 136.30 percentage points, from 236.78 percent to 100.48 percent in 2006. Bangladesh has the highest operating cost ratios in the region. Gains in overall operating efficiency were reflected in modest growth in both net interest margin (23 percent) and recurring earnings power (52 percent), over the six-year period. State-owned banks reorganization is a necessary condition to improve the overall performance of the banking sector.

Financial Stability

Over the years, resulting from negative capital position of the state-owned banks, the regulatory capital adequacy ratio (CAR) was below the required level of 8 percent. State-owned banks struggled with provisioning shortfall issues and cumulative losses over the years, which affected the overall capital position of the commercial banking sector. With the restructuring and divesting process under way for the state-owned banks, this trend seemed to have changed in 2006, during which time a 8.33 percent ratio was recorded. The leverage ratio fluctuated around assets at four times its own funds throughout the period, which improved slightly to 5.33 in 2006, denoting improvement in the capital position. In addition, with a view toward strengthening the capital base of banks and aligning the banks for the implementation of Basel II Accord, the regulatory authorities have mandated that banks move toward maintaining a capital to risk-weighted assets ratio of 10 percent at the minimum.

The state-owned banks hold the majority of the NPLs in the banking sector, which is the cause for their continued provisioning shortfall issues. The gross NPL ratio declined considerably, by 58 percent over the period to 13.15 percent in

2006. The provisioning ratio hardly changed over the six-year period and remained around 26 percent. These improvements are caused by proactive loan recovery policies adopted by the banks coupled with more stringent credit requirements. Regulatory authorities have played their part by improving prudential regulation and implementing the NCB reform program.

The liquid assets ratio declined by about 38 percent over the period to 18.67 percent in 2006 from nearly 30.03 percent in 2001, while liquid assets covered the liabilities ratio on almost a one-to-one basis over the years. Liquidity was not an issue for Bangladeshi banks with a Statutory Liquidity Requirement (SLR) of around 20 percent of the deposit base, including a 4 percent Cash Reserve Requirement (CRR).

In keeping with the international trends and guidelines, Bangladesh Bank has decided in principle to adopt the Basel II. Given the complexities involved, however, Bangladesh Bank has adopted a mix of standardized and foundation Internal Rating-Based (IRB) approaches to guide the minimum capital requirement, and the process is ongoing. The bank has already issued guidelines on managing core risks in banks. It is expected that these measures will show results through increased capital positions in the future (see chapter 8 for more details on Basel II adoption by Bangladesh).

Capital Market Development

Capital market development in Bangladesh is still in its early stages. The domestic bond market of Bangladesh is composed almost entirely of government borrowing. This market—which happened to be the smallest in the region—showed to be around 17 percent of GDP throughout the six-year period under consideration. The bond market, at almost three times the size of equity market capitalization, showed that the equity market is still very much in the development stage. Equity market capitalization to GDP had almost doubled over the period from 2.57 percent in 2001 to 5.41 percent in 2006. However, this is the least developed market compared with other stock markets in the region. A market liquidity around 1 percent and low stock market turnover of around 0.20 times denoted the relative inefficiencies inherent in smaller markets. Fewer players, as shown by the high top 10 stocks turnover ratio, dominated stock market. However, this ratio has been declining over the years from 59.16 percent in 2001 to 39.68 percent in 2006, by almost 33 percent.

To achieve diversity in the funding options for the private sector in their investment activities, it is expected that Bangladesh capital markets would grow rapidly in the future. In fact, progress had been made in the stock market in the latter part of 2007. Developing benchmark bonds, expanding the investor base, improving the market infrastructure, streamlining the regulatory framework and guidelines, and managing the market distortions created by government savings schemes are some of the issues that need to be addressed to jumpstart the capital market development process.

Market Concentration and Competitiveness

The banking system had better results in market concentration. All the concentration ratios have declined over the years. The Herfindahl-Hirschman Index (HHI) declined by almost 348.1 points over the six years. Bank concentration ratios on assets, deposits, and loans have all registered significant declines of 29 percent,

30 percent, and 26 percent, respectively. These ratios indicate a lower level of concentration in the market, and therefore, further room for expansion.

On the other hand, private credit extended by the banks increased from 24.33 percent in 2001 to 34.45 percent in 2006. The commercial banking assets-to-GDP ratio has been increasing from 50.35 percent to 55.43 percent in 2006. Because of the disproportionate reliance of bank credit by the private sector, the increase in the bank credit should be monitored carefully.

Corporate Governance

Corporate governance is still in its early stages in Bangladesh as it is for other developing countries. To strengthen corporate governance in banking, Bangladesh Bank issued several prudential regulations and guidelines over the years. Some of the major directives issued cover the following areas:

- Qualifications of bank directors and chief executive officers (CEOs)
- Authorities and responsibilities of the chairman, board of directors, CEO, and advisers
- Limits on the size of the board
- Responsibilities of the board
- Establishment of audit committees
- Disclosure requirements of banks
- Establishment of the Basel II Accord
- Policy on loan classification and provisioning
- Restriction on lending to directors of private banks
- Fit-and-proper test (FPT) for appointment of bank directors
- Policy on large loans, loan rescheduling, loan write-off, and large loan restructuring
- Dividend payments
- Loans against share and debentures
- Management of core risks in banking

These guidelines are still at the development stage. No significant changes are reported from 2005, when the questionnaire was first forwarded to the authorities (see appendix 3.A). Examination of the responses to the questionnaire revealed that more attention is needed in the following areas: the augmentation of guidelines with legal provisions governing beneficial ownership, the remuneration of directors, and the roles and responsibilities of external and internal auditors. Full conformity with international accounting and auditing standards should be pursued. Although the regulatory authorities have started moving ahead with the process, much more needs to be done to infuse the banking system with a corporate governance culture. Given below is the corporate governance analysis of Bangladesh from the previous project.

Some issues relating to ownership structure and the influence of stakeholders have been addressed. No individual or family can hold more than 10 percent of the shares of a banking company, and under the Bank Companies Act, banks must disclose their shareholding structure in their Articles of Association. No legal provision seems to identify a threshold of share ownership to be disclosed to the general public. The government determines the nominations of directors for government-controlled banks, while the central bank regulates the remuneration of directors.

The Companies Act protects the preemption rights of minority shareholders. There are no provisions to establish stakeholders' rights. Nor are there legal provisions governing the disclosure of beneficial ownership by shareholders other than the requirement that shareholders disclose their portfolios in their tax returns.

Investor rights in terms of voting procedures and shareholder meetings appear to be in place. Adequate information is disclosed to shareholders in a timely fashion, and they are able to vote in absentia. No rules govern third-party verification of voting. Shareholders may vote on a range of issues including related-party transactions. Special voting rights of individual shareholders other than the government are capped at 5 percent of the total votes.

In contrast, basic ownership rights need improvement. Shareholders can vote on appointments and dismissals of directors, and in the government-controlled banks it is evident that the government exercises control over such outcomes. A clear dividend policy is in place and structural defenses that can prevent takeover bids are not established. Minority shareholders cannot easily nominate a director, pointing to a need for legal provisions to safeguard their interests in the appointment of directors. Finally, no evidence shows that shareholders exercise any of these basic ownership rights.

Questionnaire responses on transparency and disclosure requirements indicate that financial statements are prepared annually and in accordance with local generally accepted accounting standards, which are in material conformity with international accounting standards. Yet other studies on financial reporting and standards have revealed gaps remaining between the two sets of standards (see World Bank 2003). Preparation of accounting and auditing standards in line with the international standards should be a priority.

In addition, audit functions need to be defined in detail. Banks are required to appoint audit committees, but it is unclear whether the committees' mandate includes determining the process for selecting auditors. Contrary to internationally accepted standards, external auditors can perform other, nonaudit services for banks. And while auditing standards are said to conform with international standards, here again other reports point to areas needing improvement (see World Bank 2003). Moreover, provisions that govern the roles and responsibilities of the internal auditor are not established.

Responses on the structure and effectiveness of boards of directors show that Bangladesh banks follow a unitary structure, with around 13 directors on average. Minimum qualifications for directors are governed by the guidelines for FPTs issued by the central bank. The roles and responsibilities of boards of directors are clearly defined.

Compensation policies need to be reviewed, however. Contrary to accepted standards, shareholders have no say on the remuneration of directors, and the board sets the remuneration of the bank's CEO with approval from the central bank. Provisions for performance-based compensation are not included in the remuneration package of directors. Such provisions are widely accepted as a positive incentive in today's competitive world. In addition, disclosure of the compensation of directors is not required.

India

India is the largest country in terms of its population (1.1 billion) and GDP (US$906.27 billion), which is the highest in the region. India recorded phenomenal growth over the past few years, and as a result, with a GNI per capita at US$820, India was classified as a lower-middle-income country. The economy continued to grow at an impressive average annual growth rate of 9.2 percent. Services dominate the economy at 54.6 percent of the GDP, while industry, agriculture, and manufacturing sectors account for 27.9 percent, 17.5 percent, and 16.1 percent, respectively. India's principal exports are engineering goods, petroleum products, textile, and clothing. As with most other South Asian countries, India also had a high gross national savings rate, at 33 percent of GDP in 2005. In 2006, the market capitalization of listed companies was 90.36 percent of GDP, or US$818.88 billion. The domestic bond outstanding was 35.94 percent of the GDP, or US$325.68 billion. Over the past years, India has remained one of the largest recipients of portfolio investments.

In contrast to other South Asian countries, India has a developed capital market (bond market as well as equity market) and commercial banking system. The Indian banking system plays an important part in economic growth. Banking assets account for more than 80 percent of total financial assets and 64.81 percent of GDP. In 2006, India's 85 commercial banks included 28 public sector banks (8 state and 20 nationalized banks), 28 private sector banks (20 old and 8 new), and 29 foreign banks (Reserve Bank of India 2006a).

This analysis signifies India's superior financial stability in the banking sector (see figure 2.2) and its capital markets development in the region. Among the six dimensions analyzed, India needs to focus on access to finance (mainly to improve physical access) and improve performance and efficiency, especially in the areas of returns and cost-efficiencies. In addition, corporate governance practices between public and private banks should be harmonized.

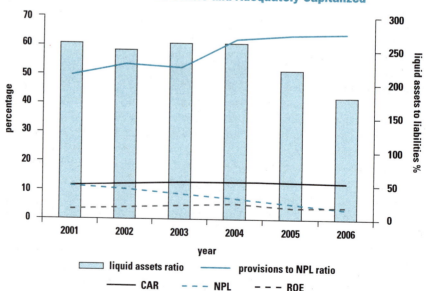

Figure 2.2 Indian Banks Are Stable and Adequately Capitalized

Source: Data from Indian Banks' Association 2006a, 2006b, and 2006c; Reserve Bank of India 2006a, 2006b, 2006c, and 2007; see appendix 1, table A1.8.

Access to Finance

Indian banks have to improve financial outreach to keep pace with the rapid economic growth. Demographic branch penetration dropped marginally to 6.37 branches from 6.42 bank branches per 100,000 people in 2006, while demographic ATM penetration in 2006 was a low 1.93 per 100,000 people. Geographic branch penetration improvement over the six-year period was just over 6 percent, while geographic ATM penetration (data available only for the last two years) showed a higher level of increase of more than 20 percent in just one year.

The usage indicators increased over the period. Deposit accounts per 1,000 people increased slightly from 416.77 to 442.87, indicating just a 6 percent increase, whereas loan accounts per 1,000 people grew by about 53 percent. In 2006, the state bank group dominated the lending and deposit markets with 72.9 percent and 75 percent market share, respectively. Private banks accounted for around 14 percent in both markets, and foreign banks accounted for around 6 percent.

Indian authorities had taken various measures to improve the physical access to financial services. One such measure is a phased-out program permitting foreign banks to open branches in excess of the World Trade Organization (WTO) commitment of 12 branches in a year. In addition, they took steps to simplify the Know Your Customer (KYC) procedures and instructed banks to provide basic no-frills accounts to facilitate financial inclusion. Furthermore, they allowed banks to use NGOs, self-help groups (SHGs), MFIs, and civil society organizations (CSOs) to act as financial intermediaries in providing banking services. These important steps would help the Indian banking sector to match financial outreach with its economic growth.

The microfinance movement that provides financial outreach to many people is not included in this study, and thus the above interpretations are relevant only to the commercial banking sector. As of 2006, more than 2.2 million SHGs were operating in India, and the number of families helped by these groups had reached more than 32.9 million families. Their lending portfolio was greater than US$2.57 billion. India also established other major institutions, such as the National Bank for Agriculture and Rural Development (NABARD), whose primary function is to aid development activities in rural areas. Other institutions, such as rural banks and cooperative credit institutions, also provide financial services, which again are not included in this study.

Performance and Efficiency

Indian banks have shown increased returns and lower costs; however, when compared to the regional performances, India could have performed better given the rapid rates of economic growth the country is experiencing. Returns on both equity and assets increased steadily over the six-year period, except in 2005 when they dropped slightly. In 2006, both returns recorded increases. ROE was 17 percent and ROA was 1.31 percent. This increase was attributed to the high demand for bank credit in 2006, which pushed the interest rates higher.

The staff cost ratio dropped over the years due to lower wage bill possibly resulting from the voluntary retirement scheme offered to the public banks. In 2006, a ratio of 56.9 percent was recorded, which was a 16 percent decline over the years. The operating cost ratio increased over the last year to 75.65 percent. Higher cost of borrowing caused the increase. However, operating cost ratios dropped by about 18 percent over the six years. With regard to the overall operating efficiency,

India recorded high net interest margins over the years. Net interest margin ratio improved marginally by less than 1 percent, with a drop in 2005, to 3.01 percent in 2006. The recurring earning power ratio has increased by nearly 38 percent over the six-year period, to 2.2 in 2006. This is low, however, when compared with the region.

Financial Stability

Among the South Asian banking systems, Indian banks were the most consistent in maintaining the regulatory CAR well above the required 8 percent. In all years, the ratio was maintained above 12 percent. In 2006, the ratio dropped marginally to 12.4 percent. The reasons for this reduction were application of capital charges for market risk, increase in risk-weighted assets due to higher credit growth, and increase in risk weights on certain types of loans by the regulatory authority. The leverage ratio continued to improve, with an average capital of around six times the assets (figure 2.2). These were indicative of India's success and focus on managing the risk portfolio.

The gross NPL ratio continued to reduce over the period, falling by 71 percent, and was at 3.33 percent in 2006. Provisions ratio improved over the period to 64.2 percent at the end of 2006. Improved credit quality plus stringent recovery and provisioning policies are the reason for the improvements recorded over the years. Banks have made healthy progress in protecting their loan portfolios through these measures.

Liquidity was not an issue for Indian banks with the SLR and CRR imposed by the Reserve Bank of India. The liquid assets ratio remained stable at around 40 percent, while the liquid-assets-to-liabilities ratio showed a small reduction.

Overall, Indian banks have consistently performed well in maintaining financial stability through adequate capital base, improved asset quality, and better liquidity management. Regulatory authorities have taken necessary policy decisions to ensure the stability of the banking system. One such measure is the planned adoption of the Basel II Capital Accord.

The Reserve Bank is committed to the adoption of Basel II by the banks. All scheduled commercial banks are encouraged to migrate to the Standardized Approach for credit risk and the Basic Indicator Approach for operational risk under Basel II, no later than March 31, 2009. To move the banks to conform to proposed Basel norms to provide an explicit capital charge for market risk in banking business, banks were advised in January 2002 to build up their investment fluctuation reserves (IFRs) to a minimum of 5 percent of investment in "Held for Trade" and "Available for Sale" categories in the investment portfolio. Furthermore, in 2004, banks were advised to maintain capital charge for market risk in a phased manner over a two-year period ending March 31, 2006. In addition, to facilitate the raising of capital necessary for a smooth transition to Basel II, banks were permitted to augment their capital funds by issue of innovative and hybrid instruments in January 2006. It is, therefore, not surprising that banks are adequately capitalized and stable (see chapter 8 for more details on Basel II adoption by India).

Capital Market Development

India has a well-developed capital market consisting primarily of equity and debt markets, which have played a significant role in the economic development process. The equity market, which is almost three times the size of the bond market, is growing rapidly. The domestic bond market represents around 30 percent of the GDP throughout the six-year period under consideration. The equity market capitalization to GDP has more than doubled over the period, from 29.4 percent in 2001 to 82.6 percent in 2006. Market liquidity decreased initially, showed gradual increase over the period, and was around 67.6 percent in 2006. Stock market turnover dropped sharply from 2.13 times in 2001 to 0.64 times in 2006. This denotes the reduction of market liquidity and reflects negatively on the efficiency of the market. The Indian stock market appears to be a mature market with many players, however, as shown by the top 10 stocks turnover ratio declining over the period from 72.9 percent in 2001 to 32.36 percent in 2006.

Similar to other South Asian countries, government securities accounted for nearly 79 percent of the total bond market, and unlike other South Asian countries, the corporate bond market also had around 21 percent market share. However, while the government securities market is relatively well developed, the corporate bond market lacks in size and depth. While necessary infrastructure systems have been built over a period, which brings in efficiencies and cost reductions, further efforts are necessary to develop the bond market to meet the increasing needs of the private sector more efficiently. For example, simplifying primary issuance processes and costs to encourage corporate bond issues, introducing streamlined disclosures and adopting self-registration process for all corporate debt issuers, relaxing the limits on foreign participation, and relaxing the investment guidelines for banks and key institutional investors to provide flexibility would further stimulate the development process.

Market Concentration and Competitiveness

The Indian banking system proves to be the best in the region on market concentration. All the concentration ratios declined over the years. The HHI declined by almost 24 percent over the six years. Bank concentration ratios on assets, deposits, and loans stabilized around 30 percent.

On the other hand, private credit extended by the banks increased from 21.5 percent in 2001 to 39.4 percent in 2006, and the commercial banking assets-to-GDP ratio also increased from 61.9 percent to 78.9 percent in 2006. An increase in the private credit ratio is a matter of concern for credit risk. Because it is coupled with prudential credit-risk management systems, however, the banking system in India should be able to deal with the expansion.

Corporate Governance

Corporate governance in India has improved over the years. To promote sound corporate governance, the Reserve Bank of India had issued comprehensive guidelines. More recently, in February 2005, the Reserve Bank laid down a comprehensive policy framework for ownership and governance in private sector banks. The broad principles underlying the framework were to ensure that ultimate ownership and control of commercial banks is well diversified, key shareholders and directors and CEOs pass the FPT, and the board observes sound corporate governance principles. These principles have expanded the transparency and disclosure standards gradually.

Corporate governance guidelines should expand further to ensure transparency and fair play. One such area that needs attention is the difference between the governance rules applying to government-controlled banks and those applying to private banks.

Since most of the governance rues and guidelines have not changed since the last report, the analysis of corporate governance guidelines and norms in the last report is given below.

Understanding the importance of corporate governance in banking, the Reserve Bank of India, under the guidance of the government, laid out a comprehensive policy framework for ownership and governance of private banks in February 2005. These, along with a series of legal and regulatory reforms, have increased the responsibility and accountability of banks.

Legal provisions are in place to cover most major issues of ownership structure and stakeholder influence. However, those relating to government ownership and rights and the disclosure of beneficial ownership could be further strengthened. The regulatory guidelines of both the central bank and the stock exchange require disclosure of the shareholdings of promoters as well as the top 10 shareholders in the annual report. The threshold for reporting prescribed by the central bank is 5 percent and over. In addition, private banks are required to disclose holdings of 1 percent and over in their annual reports, to which both shareholders and market participants have access. For public banks, government ownership is disclosed. However, special privileges need not be disclosed because the privileges of the government stem from statute.

For private banks, shareholders select the board of directors. In the case of public banks, the government controls nominations. There are provisions for establishing stakeholders' rights, including representation of labor unions on the board of government-owned banks. The preemption rights of minority shareholders are protected by the Companies Act, with any alteration requiring approval by a supermajority (75 percent).

Legal provisions governing the disclosure of beneficial ownership of shareholders are available, although no thresholds are prescribed. Shareholders are required to disclose such ownership to the company.

Investor rights appear to be in place in terms of voting and shareholder meetings. Adequate information is disclosed to shareholders in a timely fashion. Shareholders can vote in absentia, although electronic voting is not permitted. Third-party verification of voting is done. Shareholders can vote on a range of issues, including related-party transactions. Separate guidelines on disclosure of special voting rights and caps on voting rights are deemed unnecessary, as these are already mandated by the Banking Regulations Act.

Basic ownership rights, however, need improvement. Again, it is the government's control of voting rights that needs to be looked into, along with minority shareholder rights in selecting directors. In private banks, shareholders can vote on appointments and dismissals of directors, while in state-owned banks the government controls the outcomes. A clear dividend policy is in place. Specific structural defenses that can prevent a takeover bid are not established, other than the requirement that any transfer of shares exceeding 5 percent of total paid-up capital is subject to registration and regulatory scrutiny. However, the central bank reserves the right to approve such transfers. No specific provision provides for minority shareholders to elect directors in public banks.

India appears to be doing well overall on transparency and disclosure. But policy improvements are needed on disclosure requirements, audit fees, and the internal audit function. Financial statements are prepared in accordance with generally accepted local accounting principles, which are in material conformity with international accounting standards. Financial reporting is done quarterly, semiannually, and annually. Provisions requiring disclosure of audit fees paid to external auditors are not established.

The Reserve Bank of India has issued clear guidelines on the appointment of audit committees and has clearly delineated their roles and responsibilities. In private banks, these committees control the process of selecting external auditors; for government-owned banks, the central bank appoints the auditors from a preapproved list. External auditors do not perform other nonaudit services for the banks they audit.

The central bank has issued clear guidelines on the roles and responsibilities of internal auditors. The internal audit function is performed by bank staff with the required professional qualifications and work experience. But internal auditors face no requirement to report to the board of directors rather than to management, raising questions about their independence.

Indian banks follow a unitary structure for their boards, with around 8–12 members on average. The Bank Regulations Act governs requirements on the qualifications and experience of board members. The roles and responsibilities of the board are clearly defined. However, tasks and objectives are not individually assigned to board members. Furthermore, no provisions exist to institute formal and systematic training for directors, an issue that warrants attention.

Since our last study, compensation policies have been reviewed. Effective March 2006, executive directors of the banks will be compensated with performance-based compensation for achieving targets. Detailed guidelines need to be issued to harmonize the practices between private and public banks. In private banks, shareholders can vote on the remuneration of the board of directors, while in public banks the government has the right to set remuneration. As in most South Asian countries, performance-based compensation for the board of directors exists only in private banks, not in public ones. In addition, while private banks disclose directors' compensation in detail, public banks disclose only the aggregate compensation.[2]

Nepal

In terms of population, Nepal (27.7 million) was fourth, ahead of Sri Lanka among the five South Asian countries. However, it had the smallest GDP in the group with US$8.05 billion. Nepal was classified as a low-income country with a GNI per capita of US$290, which was well below the low-income country average of US$650. In recent years, the economy was characterized by slow growth (at 2.3 percent in 2006), weak output and exports, and rising inflation. Nepal is primarily an agrarian-based economy with 39.5 percent of GDP in agriculture. Services also commanded 39.5 percent, while industry and manufacturing sectors accounted for 27.1 percent and 7.7 percent, respectively. Exports of goods and services were around 18.6 percent. Nepal had the highest gross national savings rate in 2006, at 35 percent of GDP. The market capitalization of listed companies was 16.31 percent of GDP, or US$1.31 billion. Similarly, the domestic bond outstanding was 15.09 percent of the GDP, equivalent to US$1.22 billion.

With 84.7 percent of total financial assets, the commercial banking system dominated the financial sector. This was 53.82 percent of GDP. The Nepal banking sector consisted of 18 commercial banks—3 public banks, 9 private banks, and 6 foreign banks (Nepal Rastra Bank 2006). The capital markets in Nepal are still at the development stage.

This analysis revealed that Nepal is in need of a focused action plan to enhance the performance of its banking sector so that it can participate more effectively in the economic development process. Capital shortfall is a major concern that permeates into other dimensions of financial sector development—including stability, efficiency, and capital market development. Nepal should improve the credit quality, tighten liquidity management, reduce NPLs, and further improve cost-effectiveness. It should expand financial outreach further so that more people are able to avail themselves to financial services. Furthermore, corporate governance needs attention from Nepal Rastra Bank (NRB), the country's central bank, along with ensuring compliance with and enforcement of applicable rules and regulations. Nepal's bond market is at its infant stage of development and remains dominated by government securities. The equity market is not fully developed. However, it is expected that the regulatory authorities would initiate the development efforts on these areas as well.

Access to Finance

Access indicators have not improved significantly. Between 2001 and 2006, demographic branch penetration declined sharply from 2.09 bank branches per 100,000 people in 2001 to 1.73 in 2006. However, ATM penetration increased markedly from 0.05 per 100,000 people to 0.28. Geographic branch penetration over the six-year period also decreased by about 10 percent, while geographic ATM penetration shows a fivefold increase from 0.08 to 0.48 in 2006. Branch closings due to insurgency situations were the main reasons for the drop in branch penetration indicators, and ATM network expansion is confined mostly to urban areas. With regard to the use of financial services, poor performance can be observed: deposit accounts fell from 111.59 per 1,000 people to 110.4 over the period, and loan accounts per 1,000 people dropped from 19.45 in 2001 to 10.83 in 2006. The access and usage figures remain low when compared with the regional data.

Furthermore, Nepal's microcredit development banks, cooperative banks, and other NGOs that serve the rural poor accounted for around 2.36 percent of the total financial sector assets. These institutions were not included in this study. As of 2006, total deposits and lending by the microcredit development banks amounted to approximately US$12.9 million and US$60.6 million, respectively.

Performance and Efficiency

Profitability of the entire banking sector was affected by the poor performance of the state banks. Except for these state banks, all other commercial banks were profitable. However, the massive losses incurred by the state banks during the period coupled with their huge retained losses, depressed the returns on the entire industry. Thanks to the restructuring process of the public banks initiated by the authorities, during the latter part of 2004, this negative trend reversed and public banks posted profits that affected the returns of the entire industry positively.

ROE was still negative, mainly due to the retained losses, but dropped from −93.62 percent to −43.30 percent—an improvement of 54 percent over the years.

Figure 2.3 Nepal's Banking Sector Needs To Be Capitalized; Operating Costs Are Down

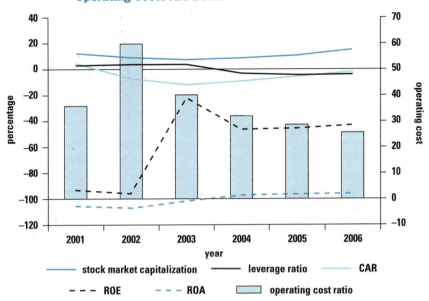

Source: Data from Nepal Rastra Bank, and the Securities Board of Nepal; see appendix 1, table A1.9.

ROA, on the other hand, was positive at 1.90 percent in 2006, which was an increase of almost 162.5 percent over the years.

The staff cost ratio continued to decline over the years by an impressive 41 percent, while the operating cost ratio was at 25.55 percent. Nepal had the lowest operating cost ratios in the region, which is commendable (figure 2.3). In terms of overall operating efficiency, the net interest margin improved by almost 28 percent to 2.26 in 2006, while the recurring earning power ratio almost tripled to 2.39 percent in 2006.

The public bank reform process that brought about increased interest spread and higher cost-efficiencies can be credited for these favorable outcomes, a trend that has to continue to improve the soundness of the commercial banking sector.

Financial Stability

In all six years, the Nepal banking sector was unable to meet the regulatory CAR of 8 percent of risk-weighted assets. The CAR during the last six years was negative. This negative trend can be attributed to the huge retained losses of the public banks as well as increased NPLs that resulted in losses in three of the private banks. Except for these three banks, all others had complied with the regulatory requirement. The capital position improved over the past years, and although it was still negative, the capital shortfall was reduced from negative 7.25 in 2002 to negative 1.75 in 2006, a 75 percent improvement. This favorable trend demonstrated during the latter part of the period under review was partly due to the public bank restructuring process. The banks were able to raise capital from the market through rights issues as well. The leverage ratio movement mirrors this positive movement (figure 2.3).

The gross NPL ratio decreased by almost 52 percent over the period, to 14.22 percent in 2006. Although the total advances increased over the six years, the NPLs have reduced progressively. Once again, the massive NPL portfolio of the public banks was the root cause. The aggressive recovery procedures adopted as a part of the reforms process had shown positive results. However, the available data show that the provisions ratio declined from 30.59 percent in 2001 to just 4.72 percent in 2006, an 85 percent reduction. This is a matter for concern because the banking system still has large amounts of NPLs. Successful loan recoveries were achieved by the two public banks, which were under professional management during the past four years (2003–06).

Banks' liquidity position also poses a concern. The liquid assets ratio dropped over the period from 22.1 percent in 2001 to 9.7 percent in 2006, while the liquid assets-to-liabilities ratio declined during the same period by 60 percent to 19.07 percent in 2006. Because one of the main sources of financial instability stems from the collapse of market liquidity, this declining liquidity position should be monitored with concern.

To promote a healthy and sound financial market, NRB is moving toward the adoption of Basel II. NRB has decided that the Nepalese financial market does not warrant advanced approaches like the IRB Approach or the Standardized Approach. Therefore, NRB intends to start with the Simplified Standardized Approach for credit risk, Basic Indicator Approach for operational risk, and Net Open Exchange Model for the Market Risk. Progress has been made in this process, and NRB has prepared a draft capital adequacy framework with detailed guidelines on each of the three pillars, based on the proposed approach, which has been circulated among the stakeholders for review. It is expected that this Capital Framework will come into effect by 2008 (see chapter 8 for more details on Basel II adoption by Nepal).

Capital Market Development

Nepal's bond market is at its infant stage of development and is dominated by government securities. The sizes of the bond market and equity market are comparable in terms of capitalization. The domestic bond market was around 14 percent of the GDP. Corporate bond market activity is negligible. Equity market capitalization to GDP increased by 30 percent over the period, from 11.76 percent in 2001 to 15.19 percent in 2006. The equity market is also not fully developed. Few players dominate the stock market, as denoted by the high top 10 stocks turnover ratio. However, this had declined over the years from 83.13 percent in 2001 to 66.5 percent in 2006, by almost 20 percent. Market liquidity was low and hardly changed; as denoted by the low value of stocks traded given as a percentage of GDP—0.59 percent in 2001 reduced further to 0.54 percent. Market efficiency was low, as expected; the ratio was less than 1 throughout the period.

Although growth of the capital market would provide additional funding sources to the private sector and therefore aid economic growth, Nepal had not focused on developing the capital markets. Continued political uncertainty had hampered such efforts largely. Nepal will have to (1) develop the infrastructure, investor base, regulatory aspects, and market confidence; and (2) harmonize the tax systems and accounting standards. Having these systems and structures in place would trigger the development process.

Market Concentration and Competitiveness

Markets are somewhat concentrated in Nepal. On a positive note, all the concentration ratios have declined over the years. The HHI was at 949.86, which defines unconcentrated markets by the industry standards, and has declined by almost 613.6 points over the six years. In 2006, bank concentration ratios on assets, deposits, and loans had all registered significant declines. However, nearly 40 percent of assets, deposits, and loans of the banking sector were concentrated in just three banks, which is a matter for concern. It is interesting, however, that more than 62 percent of the deposits and more than 65 percent of the loans were concentrated in private banks. This is a favorable trend because, with economic upturn, private banks tend to improve their outreach and activities far more efficiently than the public banks.

On the other hand, private credit extended by the banks had not changed significantly over the years and remained at 26.98 percent in 2006. The commercial banking assets-to-GDP ratio was constant around 67 percent. These ratios were indicative of the lower level of economic activity in the market.

Corporate Governance

Regulatory authorities of Nepal have identified corporate governance as one of the most important aspects in the health of the financial systems. The awareness on the subject is growing fast. As such, NRB has issued guidelines and its bank supervision department assessed the corporate governance systems of the banks as part of its on-site supervision. As a result, serious lapses of corporate governance were observed in public banks as well as in several private banks. These were identified as contributory factors for the problems faced by the banks; hence, they were placed under close surveillance. Effective from June 2005, the NRB issued guidelines as part of the unified directives relating to banks and financial institutions. Some of the important areas covered are as follows:

- Code of ethics for directors
- Duties and responsibilities of board of directors
- Appointment of the chief executive
- Code of ethics for employees
- Audit committee
- Prohibition to extend credit to the directors, shareholders, employees, and firms related to directors, promoters, and shareholders
- Prohibition against extension of credit on collateral of assets of directors and family members

Despite establishing these directives, the corporate governance situation in Nepal has not changed much since 2005. The issues are the adaptation of the guidelines and effective enforceability. Most of the guidelines should be improved further and banks should strive to incorporate corporate governance as an integral part of their culture. It is hoped that the adoption of Basel II would help strengthen the effectiveness of corporate governance in banks. Important areas for which a greater focus is needed include broadening the investor rights and disclosure rights, improving adherence to international accounting and auditing standards, and strengthening the effectiveness of the board.

Detailed analysis of the corporate governance presented in the last report is given below:

Also needed are greater transparency and disclosure on share ownership and beneficial ownership, and legal provisions for establishing the rights of external stakeholders and minority shareholders. The regulatory guidelines contain no provision relating to disclosure of ownership. Although the central bank requires disclosure of shareholdings above 0.5 percent, this requirement is seldom enforced. Hence, in practice, the public has no access to such information. No provisions establish the rights of external stakeholders, such as whistleblower rules. Rules or regulations to protect the preemption rights of minority shareholders are not established. In addition, legal provisions that govern the disclosure of beneficial ownership of shareholders are not established.

Clear provisions and guidelines establishing shareholders' rights, including their right to attend and vote at shareholder meetings, need to be formalized. It is also important to examine the practices of shareholders to see whether they in fact exercise their rights. Information is disclosed to shareholders in a timely fashion; shareholders can vote in absentia, by proxy or by post; and third-party verification of voting is permitted. However, shareholders are unable to vote on a range of issues, including related-party transactions. Banks are required to disclose special voting rights and caps on voting rights in their Memorandum of Association and Articles of Association.

Shareholders can vote on appointments to the board of directors, though the board itself appoints some members. For the government-controlled banks, the government can appoint directors. A clear dividend policy is not in place; instead, the policy is set by the board and approved by the annual general meeting. Specific structural defenses that can prevent a takeover bid are not established, other than the legal requirement for regulatory approval of any transfer of promoters' shares. There is also no specific provision to ensure that minority shareholders can elect directors.

Banks' financial statements are prepared in accordance with generally accepted local accounting principles. Other studies have revealed that accounting and auditing standards are still being issued and do not yet fully conform to international accounting standards (see World Bank 2005a). Still, to the extent that NRB has issued guidelines, it is safe to conclude that banks are meeting the reporting standards to a certain extent. Financial reporting is done on a quarterly basis, and banks are required to disclose audit fees paid to external auditors.

Nepal's auditing standards appear to be at the development stage, as evidenced by other reports (see World Bank 2005a). It is advisable that NRB issue detailed guidelines on the appointment of both external and internal auditors. The central bank has issued guidelines on the appointment of audit committees as well as on their primary roles and responsibilities. But it is not clear whether the audit committees have control over the selection process of external auditors. Moreover, the guidelines do not cover the frequency of their meetings and other pertinent details. They do, however, prohibit external auditors from performing other, nonaudit services for the banks they audit. External auditors are appointed with the approval of the annual general meeting. Central bank guidelines require the internal auditor to be appointed by management and report to the audit committee.

NRB has issued detailed guidelines on the structure of boards and on directors' roles and responsibilities. These guidelines appear to be adequate as long as they are strictly enforced. Banks in Nepal follow a hybrid structure, with boards having five to nine members on average. The guidelines do not specify detailed requirements for directors' qualifications and experience, although they do outline such requirements for the CEO. Directors are not required to attend any special training on their fiduciary duties and responsibilities. Hence, a systematic training program needs to be developed. Shareholders can vote on the remuneration of directors. Compensation of directors can be performance based and must be disclosed in detail.

NRB has continued to review the relevant legislations and regulations and to improve the financial sector legislative framework. Some new acts, namely, the Bank and Financial Institution Act (2006), Insolvency Act (2006), Secured Transaction Act (2006), and Company Act (2006) have been enacted. Money-laundering Control, and Deposit and Credit Guarantee Acts are to follow. Passing draft legislation that provides authority to key institutions is important. However, the current political uncertainty situation could delay this process.

Pakistan

Pakistan is the second largest country in terms of both population (159 million) and GDP (US$128.83 billion). In 2006, the economy grew at an average annual rate of 6.6 percent. It was classified as a lower-middle-income country with a GNI per capita of US$800. Analysis of the economic structure revealed that services at 53.4 percent of the GDP was the dominant sector in 2006. Industry, manufacturing, and agriculture sectors accounted for 27.2 percent, 19.5 percent, and 19.4 percent, respectively. Export of goods and services was 15.3 percent. Pakistan's gross national savings rate at 17 percent of GDP was the lowest among the five countries. Capital markets are developing fast. In 2006, the market capitalization of listed companies was about 35.33 percent of GDP, amounting to US$45.52 billion. Pakistan had the second largest equity market in the region, after India. The bond market is developing at a lesser pace. The domestic bond outstanding was 25.16 percent of the GDP, equivalent to US$32.41 billion. This consists of mainly government bonds, as the corporate market is yet to develop.

The commercial banking system dominates the financial sector: banking assets were around 53 percent of GDP. Pakistan had 35 commercial banks in 2006: 4 public sector banks, 24 private banks, and 7 foreign banks (State Bank of Pakistan 2006a).

Banking sector reforms implemented by the State Bank of Pakistan (SBP) had resulted in notable improvements in the soundness indicators. Pakistan leads the region in performance and efficiency as well as in corporate governance (figure 2.4). The areas on which Pakistan most needed to focus were access to finance (improving physical access to banking facilities, encouraging the use of financial services provided by commercial banks, and expanding outreach), capital market development, and market concentration.

Access to Finance

Pakistan needs to focus on improving financial outreach through its commercial banking sector. Demographic branch penetration is low, around five bank branches per 100,000 people during the six-year period. ATM penetration increased to 1.25 per 100,000 people in 2006. Even the geographic branch penetration had not

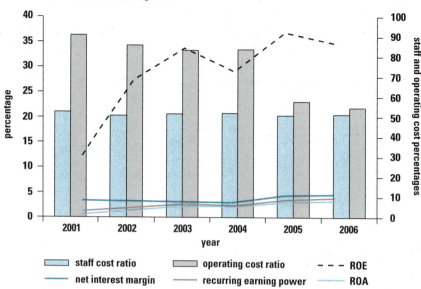

Figure 2.4 Pakistan Banking Sector Demonstrated Better Performance and Efficiency

Source: Data from State Bank of Pakistan, and the Securities and Exchange Commission of Pakistan; see appendix 1, table A1.10.

changed much over the six-year period at nine branches per 1,000 km² in 2006. Geographic ATM penetration was 2.44, which had increased slightly. Although this was high, branch distribution had favored urban settings. Hence, objectives of financial outreach may not be fulfilled. To promote branch openings in rural areas, the SBP has introduced the Annual Branch Licensing Policy, which requires commercial banks with 100 branches or more to open at least 20 percent of their branches outside big cities and set up branches in Tehsil Headquarters, where no branch of any bank exists.

Usage indicators showed mixed results. While deposit accounts dropped from 195.84 per 1,000 people in 2001 to 171.14 in 2006, loan accounts per 1,000 grew by almost 98 percent. One would have expected both ratios to grow, given the economic growth experienced by Pakistan over the last few years. Private sector commercial banks dominate both deposits and loan portfolios with more than 75 percent market share. It is expected, therefore, that private sector banks would spur the growth of deposits and lending to improve the usage of financial services, taking advantage of technological advancements as well as innovative financial products.

SBP had directed all commercial banks to provide basic banking accounts and basic banking facilities to the low-income people in Pakistan. In June 2006, to facilitate the downscaling of financial services of commercial banks, SBP prepared guidelines that include establishing microfinance counters in the existing branches, designating standalone microfinance branches, establishing independent microfinance subsidiaries, and developing linkages with other MFIs.

Pakistan is one of the few countries in the world that has a separate legal and regulatory framework for microfinance banking. Though in Pakistan the potential market size is huge (around 30 million), the penetration remains low. Despite a substantial increase in the number of borrowers (from 60,000 in 1999 to around a million in December 2006), huge portions of this potential market remain underserved (State Bank of Pakistan 2006a).

Realizing the need to improve financial outreach, the SBP has taken several important steps in this direction. SBP has targeted future reforms in the following areas:

- Increasing the geographical outreach of the banking services and target the underserved regions
- Increasing institutional and branch outreach and emphasizing products that meet the unique requirements, and as such, increasing focus on previously underserved sectors such as microfinance, agriculture credit, and small and medium enterprises (SMEs)
- Providing Islamic banking due to its faith-based appeal in increasing the overall penetration of financial services

Performance and Efficiency

Pakistan showed strong performance especially during the latter years. Over the six years, ROE almost tripled to 34.06 percent in 2006 and ROA growth was more than fivefold, from 0.60 percent in 2001 to 3.20 percent in 2006 (figure 2.4). From 2005 to 2006, ROE dropped slightly due to increase in capital requirements for the banks. One reason for the banking sector's high performance was the growth of high-yielding assets in its credit expansion. In addition, tax rate reductions over the last years had reduced the tax burden on banks, and this contributed toward higher returns. Staff costs had not changed over the years and operating costs had dropped to 54.63 percent in 2006, which was almost a 40 percent reduction from the 2001 level.

The overall efficiency of the system would increase with further reduction of the cost ratios. The operating efficiency of the banking system is improving. Both net interest margin and recurring earning power ratios increased steadily over the period and were at 4.41 percent and 3.66 percent, respectively, in 2006. These improvements could be attributed to higher yields and growth in credit. However, high-yielding assets should be monitored with caution to avoid potential credit risk.

Financial Stability

Pakistan banks maintained the regulatory CAR well above 8 percent. Strong returns and fresh capital injections to several banks resulted in this positive trend. Over the six-year period, the ratio increased to 13.33 percent in 2006. Leverage ratio almost doubled to 8.94 percent in 2006.

The gross NPL ratio reduced progressively from 19.6 percent in 2001 to 5.7 percent in 2006. Similarly, the provisions ratio increased to 81.5 percent, which is the highest for the region. Further examination revealed that NPLs of the private banks had decreased, whereas those for public sector banks had increased. Foreign banks have managed their NPLs well and have minimum amounts. Stringent provisioning policies and writing off bad loans had kept the total NPL position in check. On the positive side, because private banks dominated the banking sector in terms of lending (at 75 percent), this positive trend in reduction of NPL is expected to continue. The NPL position of the public bank should be monitored continually, however, because any adverse movements in this sector could have a negative impact on the entire banking industry, as public banks hold a significant share of the lending portfolio.

Banks' liquidity position was relatively stable and had not changed much during the six-year period. The liquid assets ratio declined marginally to around 32 percent. In July 2006, the SBP raised the liquidity requirement to 18 percent from 15 percent (on both the time and demand liabilities) and CRRs changed to 7 percent of the demand liabilities and 3 percent of the time liabilities (previously 5 percent for both). Even so, the liquidity situation recorded a rise in 2006. This situation should be monitored carefully using measures such as maturity gap analysis, to find out the presence of any liquidity mismatches.

One other important step toward improving financial stability is the adoption of Basel II. The SBP issued a road map in March 2005 outlining the implementation process of Basel II. In terms of these guidelines, banks initially adopted the Simplified Standardized Approach and went on a parallel run for one-and-a-half years starting from July 2006. The SBP envisaged adopting different approaches under Basel II—the Standardized Approach for credit risk and the Basic Indicator and Standardized Approaches for operational risk from January 1, 2008. The SBP would adopt the Internal Ratings–Based Approach from January 1, 2010, with banks and development finance institutions (DFIs) permitted to implement it sooner if the SBP approves their internal risk management systems. Banks and DFIs would be required to adopt a parallel run of one-and-a-half years for the Standardized Approach starting July 1, 2006, and two years for the Internal Ratings–Based Approach starting January 1, 2008. The process is ongoing (see chapter 8 for more details on Basel II adoption by Pakistan).

Capital Market Development

The Pakistan bond market is still at its development stage and is dominated by government securities at around 97 percent (see World Bank 2007b). Corporate bonds have yet to become significant. Bond market capitalization has remained largely unaltered over the period, and accounted for little more than half of equity market capitalization (71.2 percent in 2006). The domestic public bonds-to-GDP ratio decreased by about 30 percent over the six-year period. This indicates improved fiscal management by the government. The lack of growth in the bond market should be a concern, however, as this deprives the market of an alternate funding source.

Stock market growth was remarkable, with market capitalization to GDP rising from approximately 8.06 percent in 2001 to more than 35.87 percent by end 2006, equivalent to a 345 percent growth. Pakistan had the second largest equity market in the region, after India. Market liquidity denoted by stock trading value to GDP shows a lower liquidity position around 0.03 percent in 2006. The turnover ratio was less than 1.00, indicating lower efficiency. Improvements in the market infrastructure, regulatory aspects, and corporate governance are needed for the development of capital markets.

Market Concentration and Competitiveness

Market concentration is significant in Pakistan's banking system. On a positive note, all the concentration ratios declined gradually over the years. The HHI declined by almost 307.8 points over the six years, and was at 784.01 in 2006. Bank concentration ratios on assets, deposits, and loans all registered significant declines of 25 percent, 26 percent, and 42 percent, respectively. The continued reduction of concentration had promoted healthy competition and, therefore, efficiency of the banking system. Still, however, nearly 40 percent of assets, deposits, and loans of the banking sector are concentrated in just three banks.

Moreover, private credit extended by the banks increased over the years and was at 29.3 percent in 2006. Expansion of bank credit should be monitored vigilantly to contain credit risk. This is especially important for Pakistan with the recent trend in increased exposure to high-yielding assets. The commercial banking assets-to-GDP ratio also increased by 24 percent, from 43.61 percent in 2001 to 53.96 percent in 2006.

Corporate Governance

Pakistan leads the region in corporate governance scores. The country has taken proactive steps in introducing reforms to improve corporate governance in the banking sector. A handbook of corporate governance had been issued to banks, and Pakistan established the Pakistan Institute of Corporate Governance with the aim of providing training on corporate governance issues and for awareness building.[3]

Recently SBP had amended two components of the code of corporate governance issued to the banks—the FPT criteria for board members, CEOs, presidents, and key executives; and responsibilities of boards of directors and management of banks and DFIs. They key amendments cover the following:

- Broadening the scope of FPT to include sponsors and strategic investors in addition to directors, CEOs, and key executives of banks and DFIs
- Approving the entry of sponsors and strategic investors and appointment of directors and CEO, with prior clearance in writing from SBP
- Seeking prior approval of major shareholders in writing from the SBP for acquiring 5 percent or more shares of a bank or DFI
- Further clarifying the scope of the board of directors and management
- Increasing mandatory requirement of independent directors and restrictions on family and executive directors in banks
- Emphasizing that the board remain independent of the management by focusing on policy making and providing general direction of the bank and DFI to oversee and supervise, rather than get involved in day-to-day operations, including credit decisions

Some of the amendments would improve the self-governance; others, such as seeking SBP approval for 5 percent or more shares, need to be reviewed. Other areas to focus on include greater transparency and disclosure, greater accountability, further disclosures on beneficial ownership, safeguards on stakeholder rights, further improvements to responsibilities of the board, and further emphasis on self-governance for the institutions.

Detailed analysis of the corporate governance in Pakistan reported in phase III is as follows:

Pakistan has legal provisions covering most aspects of banks' ownership structure and the influence of stakeholders, although the provisions relating to beneficial ownership can be further strengthened. The central bank's regulatory guidelines, the Banking Companies Ordinance of 1962, and the Companies Ordinance of 1984 require disclosure of share ownership, with the threshold set at 10 percent, through means available to both the market and the public. In addition, banks must disclose shareholdings of 3 percent or more to the SBP. Share acquisitions of 5 percent or more require the SBP's prior approval. Government ownership is disclosed in the same manner.

Only the board and the company can appoint bank directors, and their remuneration is set at annual general meetings. The government, however, can nominate directors of government-controlled banks. Certain provisions exist for establishing the rights of stakeholders such as labor unions, though no details were available for an assessment. The preemption rights of minority shareholders are protected. The SBP requires disclosure of beneficial ownership of shareholders, with the threshold set at 3 percent. However, this information is not available to the public.

Investor rights relating to voting and shareholder meetings appear to be in place. Adequate information is disclosed to shareholders in a timely fashion before shareholders' meetings. Shareholders can vote in absentia, though postal and electronic voting is not used. Voting is verified by a third party. Shareholders can vote on a normal range of issues, including related-party transactions. Banks are required to disclose special voting rights and caps on voting rights.

Even though basic ownership rights existed, regulatory control over share transactions and management changes need to be reviewed. Appointments and dismissals of directors are subject to vote by shareholders, although the SBP has the power to remove directors and managers. The government can appoint directors to government-controlled banks only by virtue of its shareholdings. A clear dividend policy is in place. Specific structural defenses that can prevent a takeover bid are established, including the requirement that the SBP give prior approval for share acquisitions exceeding 5 percent of total paid-up capital. In addition, the central bank must approve any change in bank management, and in the case of privatization, it assesses prospective investors to determine whether they meet its FPT for owners and managers. All companies are encouraged to protect the interests of minority shareholders.

Provisions for transparency and disclosure have met the main criteria, but the internal audit function has room for further improvement. Banks' financial statements are prepared in accordance with international accounting standards as issued by the International Accounting Standards Committee (IASC) and interpreted by the Standing Interpretation Committee. Financial reporting is done quarterly, semi-annually, and annually. Disclosure of audit fees paid to external auditors is required.

The SBP issued clear guidelines on the appointment of audit committees and clearly outlined their roles and responsibilities, which include controlling the selection of auditors. External auditors were not permitted to perform other, nonaudit services for the banks they audit. The State Bank also issued guidelines relating to internal auditors. Bank staff members who met FPT criteria performed the internal audit function. Internal auditors were independent and reported to the audit committee, though the frequency of such reporting was not defined.

Pakistani banks follow a unitary board structure with a minimum of seven directors. Board members' qualifications and experience are governed by the FPT criteria outlined in prudential guidelines. The board's roles and responsibilities are clearly defined; however, its tasks and objectives are not individually assigned and are left to be defined by the board. While the code of corporate governance issued by the Securities and Exchange Commission (SEC) of Pakistan recommends orientation courses for directors, no formal or systematic training process was established. Developing a systematic training program for directors is thus important.

Remuneration of the board of directors is subject to a shareholder vote at annual general meetings. Provisions for performance-based compensation are not included in the remuneration package of directors. To attract and retain qualified and competent staff, a review of compensation policies is needed. Banks are required to disclose the compensation of directors in detail.

Although the guidelines have been issued, the success of the governance procedure largely depends on commitment by the banks. Their approach to corporate governance should extend beyond simple compliance with legal requirements. This is an evolving process and cannot happen overnight. As such, the regulatory authority surveillance and enforcement is important.

Sri Lanka

Sri Lanka is classified as a lower-middle-income country with a GNI per capita of US$1,350 per month. Sri Lanka has the smallest population in the region at 19.8 million and the fourth largest GDP at US$26.97 billion, in 2006, which grew at an average annual rate of 7.2 percent. Over the six years, the Sri Lankan economy continued to show resilience amid shocks, such as conflicts and the 2004 tsunami. Gross national savings rate was 24.8 percent of GDP. In 2006, the economy was dominated by the services sector with 56.5 percent of the GDP. Industries, agriculture, and manufacturing sectors contributed 27.1 percent, 16.5 percent, and 13.9 percent, respectively. The exports-to-GDP ratio was around 31.6 percent of the GDP.

The Sri Lankan bond market is dominated by government securities, at more than 90 percent of total outstanding bonds. The Sri Lankan stock market is fairly well developed. In 2006, the market capitalization of listed companies was 28.81 percent of GDP, equivalent to US$7.77 billion.

As in most other countries in the region, banks are the main providers of funding to the economy. Commercial banking assets accounted for 34 percent of total financial assets and 38.2 percent of GDP. The Sri Lankan commercial banking system consisted of 2 state banks, 9 private banks, and 12 foreign banks (Central Bank of Sri Lanka 2006b, 2007a).

Sri Lanka leads the region in ranking on access to finance, and the banking sector needs to focus on market concentration, financial stability, and corporate governance. The banking sector in Sri Lanka is highly concentrated with more than 50 percent of assets, deposits, and loans concentrated in three banks. In terms of improving stability, the liquidity position needs careful monitoring. Furthermore, the corporate governance guidelines needs to be expanded,[4] and more important, the banking sector should strive to adopt the guidelines set out by the Central Bank of Sri Lanka (CBSL) at a level beyond simple compliance with legal requirements. On a positive note, the Sri Lankan banking sector has laudable performance in providing physical access and leads the region in this category. Performance and efficiency measures are also improving. Capital markets show good progress on improvements in the regulatory and infrastructure areas.

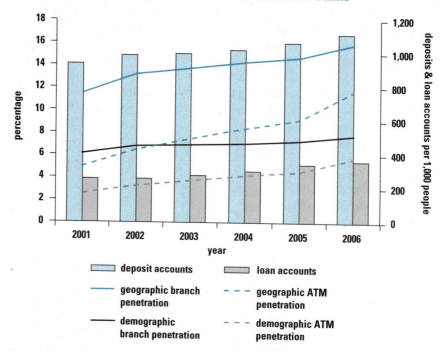

Figure 2.5 Accessibility Is on the Rise in Sri Lankan Banks

Sources: Data from Central Bank of Sri Lanka, Securities and Exchange Commission of Sri Lanka, and the Colombo Stock Exchange; see appendix 1, table A1.11.

Access to Finance

Sri Lanka led the region in providing access to finance through commercial banks. Both demographic branch penetration and ATM penetration expanded over the years and, by the end of 2006, reached 7.69 and 5.67, respectively. Geographic penetration ratios for branches and ATMs also increased over the six-year period by almost 35 percent. On usage, deposit accounts per 1,000 people as well as loan accounts per 1,000 grew by about 35 percent and 42 percent, respectively. Overall, provision of access and usage had improved at a healthy rate (figure 2.5).

In addition to commercial banks, there are 14 specialized banks with a branch network of 415. These include 6 development banks and 4 savings banks that operate with a branch network of 201 and 136, respectively. Two housing finance institutions have 28 branches island-wide. These institutions provide various types of financial services to the public.

Unlike most other South Asian countries, the microfinance industry in Sri Lanka is reasonably commercialized and is channeled mainly through cooperative institutions and Samurdhi Banking Societies. Equity capital as well as member deposits fund these institutions. In view of the large amount of funding channeled through these institutions the CBSL has formulated a Micro-Finance Institutions Act with a view toward establishing a regulatory and supervisory mechanism. It is expected that this act would become law in the near future.

Performance and Efficiency

During the six-year period, returns of the commercial banks continued to increase progressively. ROE increased by about 31 percent over the period. The ROA ratio almost doubled, from 0.84 percent in 2001 to 1.83 in 2006. Higher interest margins and growth in business activities resulted in increased profitability. Performance of the two state banks also contributed significantly toward this increase.

The staff cost ratio declined slightly and was around 41.49 percent in 2006. The operating cost ratio also reduced to 84.68 percent. However, reduction of the cost ratios should improve efficiency further. Overall, operating efficiency is positive with the net interest margin increasing to 4.31 percent in 2006. Recurring earning power shows a slight reduction in the latter part of the six-year period. Interest income is the main source of income for commercial banks. The expansion of credit and the higher interest rate spread contributed toward the progress made. Better management of operational costs would allow the banks to increase efficiency as well as reduce the interest margins. This would allow the banks to reduce intermediary costs and promote economic growth.

Financial Stability

The CAR improved from 8.59 percent in 2001 to 11.82 percent in 2006, an almost 37 percent increase over the six-year period. However, the CAR of one of the state banks was below the regulatory requirement. The CAR of this bank has improved over the years from a negative capital position to a positive level, while still below the regulatory requirement. This situation should be monitored. The ratio dipped slightly in 2006 due to an additional capital charge for market risk that banks had to maintain per guidelines issued by the CBSL. This direction to compute a capital charge for market risk was issued in March 2006, in keeping with current international practices and the requirements of the Basel Committee. The leverage ratio also followed the same pattern indicating adequate capital guidelines followed by the Sri Lankan banking sector.

The NPL ratio decreased over the six-year period by almost 63 percent, from 19.57 percent in 2001 to 7.16 percent in 2006, reflecting the reduction of the perceived credit risk. Provisions increased by well over 53 percent over the period, to 68.12 percent in 2006. The central bank vigilance on NPLs in the banking sector and stringent provisioning requirements resulted in these positive gains in credit quality. Prudential regulations have improved further, and a general provisioning requirement of 1 percent on all performing loans as well as loans in arrears (from three to six months) was introduced in December 2006. Although the provisioning requirements are not in line with the international standards, these improvements are welcome signs. High credit growth and rising interest rates may pose some risks to the banking sector, however.

The liquid assets to total assets ratio declined slightly to 19.00 percent while liquid assets to liabilities ratio also declined. The maturity patterns of the assets and the liabilities of the banking system and the use of the Real-Time Gross Settlement (RTGS) system may have reduced the need to hold excess liquidity in the banking system significantly, but banks should manage the liquidity situation carefully and efficiently.

CBSL has issued a consultative paper on the implementation of Basel II with the computation of credit and market risk on the Standardized Approach and operational risk on the Basic Indicator Approach. Guidelines on integrated risk management systems were issued to banks in March 2006. These guidelines will be refined over the period, based on the results of the test computations during the period of the parallel run. A parallel computation of Basel I and Basel II commenced from the first quarter of 2006, until full implementation of Basel II in the first quarter of 2008. In addition, CBSL is taking necessary steps to shift bank examination from a compliance-based one to risk-based supervision (see chapter 8 for more details on Basel II adoption by Sri Lanka).

Capital Market Development

The Sri Lankan domestic bond market is still at development stages, and it remains dominated by government securities at around 99 percent (see World Bank 2007b). The corporate bond market remains largely underdeveloped. In terms of a percentage of GDP, the Sri Lankan bond market was the largest in the region at 50.84 percent of GDP in 2006, while India was second with 35.94 percent of GDP. The bond market to equity market capitalization ratio declined over the six-year period. The domestic public bonds to GDP ratio almost doubled over the six-year period at 31.62 percent in 2006.

Conversely, stock market growth was remarkable, with market capitalization to GDP rising from approximately 8.81 percent in 2001 to more than 29.8 percent by the end of 2006, equivalent to a 238 percent growth. Market liquidity denoted by stock trading value to GDP showed a healthy liquidity position around 3.75 percent in 2007. The turnover ratio was less than 1, which indicated lower efficiency. Improvements in the market infrastructure, expansion of the investor base, and improvement in legal, regulatory, and corporate governance are needed to develop the capital markets.

Market Concentration and Competitiveness

The Sri Lankan banking system reported the highest market concentration in the region. More than 52 percent of assets, deposits, and loans of the banking sector are concentrated in just three banks. On a positive note, all the concentration ratios declined gradually over the years. The HHI declined by almost 390.94 points over the six years, and was at 1259.88 in 2006. This is still considered moderately concentrated per the international norms. Bank concentration ratios on assets, deposits, and loans registered significant declines. Such concentration could inhibit competition and reduce operational efficiency.

Additionally, private credit extended by the banks increased over the years and remained at 29.30 percent in 2006. The commercial banking assets-to-GDP ratio also increased, by 24 percent, to 53.96 percent in 2006. Expansion of bank credit to the private sector exposes banks to credit risk, and hence prudential credit risk management systems should be in place to contain such risks.

Corporate Governance

CBSL has taken several important steps to ensure better corporate governance in the banking sector. Forthcoming Basel II implementation, proposals to mandate corporate governance standards, and mandated credit ratings to improve better disclosure are some of these steps.

In January 2007, the Central Bank issued new policy guidelines for the regulation of bank ownership. Among these guidelines, one of the most significant was the broad basing of bank ownership by requiring that large ownerships held by single shareholders or groups be reduced to 15 percent within a maximum period of five years. However, the caps on shareholdings in banks are restrictive, and thus create a strong incentive for shareholders to disguise their interests through nominees or associated parties, despite the legal provisions outlawing such agreements. The definition of significant ownership should be broadened to encompass exertion of control irrespective of the size of the shareholding, and a suitability test should be introduced. The Monetary Board (MB) of CBSL should explicitly be empowered to prevent the exercise of voting rights of a party that fails the suitability test.

In August 2007, the CBSL released the comprehensive exposure draft on corporate governance for banks and solicited views, comments, and suggestions from bank stakeholders and the public. The implementation of the code was scheduled for January 1, 2008. The corporate governance directions, which were developed on generally accepted corporate governance principles, mainly cover the broad responsibilities of the board of directors, the board's composition, criteria to assess the fitness and propriety of directors, management functions delegated by the board, separation of duties of the chairman and CEO, board-appointed committees, and disclosure of financial statements. (The direction on corporate governance is available at CBSL 2007c.) The banking sector has a larger responsibility to adopt the guidelines set out by the CBSL not just as guidelines but also as part of the banking culture.

A detailed analysis of the corporate governance standards in Sri Lanka from the previous report is given below along with later adjustments:

In 2002, the CBSL issued a code of corporate governance for banks and other financial institutions for voluntary compliance. This code was compiled by the National Task Force on Corporate Governance in the Financial Sector, set up to promote best practices in corporate governance at the national level. Issuing this code of conduct for banks was a step in the right direction. Yet, disclosure requirements and detailed guidelines are still needed on many issues, such as stakeholder rights, beneficial ownership, special voting rights, rights of shareholders to vote on bank operations, regulatory and government control of share transactions, and minority shareholder rights. These issues should be reviewed, with necessary changes incorporated into regulatory guidelines and legal statutes.

Under the guidelines and regulations issued by the Colombo Stock Exchange, publicly listed companies must disclose the share ownership of their top 20 shareholders in their annual reports, available to both the market and the general public. In addition, banks must disclose holdings of 5 percent and above to the Central Bank. Government ownership is disclosed in the same manner. Only the board of directors and the company can appoint directors and decide on their remuneration at annual general meetings. For government-controlled banks, however, the government can nominate directors. Even though rules protect the preemption rights of minority shareholders, no provisions establish stakeholder rights. Additionally, no rules require disclosure of beneficial ownership of shareholders. The ownership structure, stakeholder rights, and rules governing beneficial ownership should be clearly defined, with legal provisions to ensure proper disclosure.

Investor rights relating to voting procedures and shareholder meetings need further strengthening. Adequate information is disclosed to shareholders in a timely fashion before shareholders' meetings, and shareholders can vote in absentia. Yet, no provisions exist for third-party verification of voting. Shareholders cannot vote on a normal range of issues, including related-party transactions. Disclosure of special voting rights and caps on voting rights is not mandated.

Basic ownership rights also need improvement, particularly with respect to shareholders' right to vote on the operations of banks, regulatory and government control of share transactions, and the rights of minority shareholders. Board appointments and dismissals are not subject to shareholders vote, while the government can control these outcomes in state banks. The ability of minority shareholders to appoint directors depends on banks' internal rules. A clear dividend policy is in place. Additionally structural defenses against takeover bids are established, including the acquisition of a material interest in a bank (10 percent or more of its shares), which requires prior approval of the Central Bank and the Ministry of Finance. In addition, the SEC requires any investor acquiring more than 30 percent of a listed company to make a mandatory offer to all other shareholders.

Banks' financial statements are prepared in accordance with generally accepted local accounting principles, which are in material conformity with international accounting standards. Financial reporting is done monthly, quarterly, and annually, and audit fees paid to external auditors must be disclosed. The Central Bank issued clear guidelines on the appointment of audit committees and defined their roles and responsibilities, although it is unclear whether these committees control the selection of auditors. External auditors are not permitted to perform other, nonaudit services for the banks they audit. Guidelines are issued on internal auditors, but further improvements can be made. Internal auditors are independent, reporting to the audit committee, but the frequency of such reporting is not clearly defined.

Sri Lankan banks follow a hybrid board structure with around 5–11 members on average. Board members' qualifications and experience are governed by the FPT criteria set by prudential guidelines. Board committee requirements are presented only in the SEC Governance Rules and in the voluntary code. The rules require boards to have two committees (the remuneration and the audit committees) that must be composed of at least two independent directors and the chairpersons, nonexecutives in both cases. The roles and responsibilities of boards are clearly defined, and tasks and objectives are defined and individually assigned. In addition, the corporate governance code details the need for systematic training for directors. Banks are permitted to disclose merely the aggregate compensation of their directors in their annual reports. No information is available on whether banks offer performance-based compensation to their directors or whether shareholders can vote on directors' remuneration—both practices that should be incorporated into policy. The board's composition and structure should be enhanced. Concepts such as "independent directorship" and committee structures should be introduced. CBSL should provide clear guidance on their significance and responsibilities, and the key role they play in the governance structure of a financial institution.

Endnotes

1. Using the Atlas method, economies are classified based on their per capita GNI: low-income, US$650 or less; lower-middle-income, US$2,037 or less (see World Bank 2007a for the entire list).

2. Since 2006–07, public sector banks are permitted to pay performance-linked incentives to full-time executive directors of banks (not to nonexecutive directors).

3. The Pakistan Institute of Corporate Governance was incorporated in December 2004 and started to function in 2005.

4. Comprehensive corporate governance rules have been issued with effect from January 1st, 2008.

3

Country Rankings on the Getting Finance Indicators

Analysis of the Getting Finance Indicators confirms that the commercial banking sector in the five South Asian countries have made significant progress under the development dimensions reviewed in this study. The progress made under each dimension varies among the countries. The countries were ranked using a simple-averaged ranking method (for a description of the ranking methodology, see chapter 7). It is anticipated that such rankings would help to understand where performance is strong and where improvements are most needed, and where each country is on the development paradigm.

As with any evaluation system, assessing the health of the financial system based on a limited number of micro indicators imposes many technical as well as practical limitations. And the interpretation of the results reflects these caveats.

To assess the soundness and performance of the financial sector, six development dimensions were used. Six micro indicators were used to represent each of the five financial dimensions—access to finance, performance and evaluation, financial stability, capital market development, and market concentration and competitiveness. For the sixth dimension (corporate governance), a questionnaire was used to assess four key areas. Each of the six dimensions was ranked across the six-year period to arrive at individual composite scores. An overall composite score was computed by averaging the individual composite scores.

Overall Rankings on Development Dimensions

India secured the top rank with an overall composite score of 0.80—emerging as the strongest South Asian commercial banking sector (table 3.1). The Indian commercial banking sector was competitive and financially stable and was ably supported by a well-developed capital market. Pakistan was second (overall composite score of 0.67) with strong performance and quality corporate governance. Sri Lanka secured the third place (overall composite score of 0.65) with healthier financial outreach by the commercial banking sector. Bangladesh was fourth (overall composite score of 0.57) and demonstrated improved access to finance and market concentration, although it did not rank on top. Nepal was ranked fifth

Table 3.1 Getting Finance Indicators for South Asian Countries, 2001–06
(final rankings)

	Bangladesh	India	Nepal	Pakistan	Sri Lanka
Access to finance					
Composite score (total points/180)	0.68	0.66	0.28	0.43	0.93
Indicator rank	2	3	5	4	1
Performance and efficiency					
Composite score (total points/180)	0.42	0.63	0.42	0.80	0.73
Indicator rank	4	3	4	1	2
Financial stability					
Composite score (total points/180)	0.49	0.89	0.24	0.81	0.57
Indicator rank	4	1	5	2	3
Capital market development					
Composite score (total points/180)	0.46	0.91	0.37	0.69	0.58
Indicator rank	4	1	5	2	3
Market concentration and competitiveness					
Composite score (total points/180)	0.71	0.89	0.56	0.44	0.40
Indicator rank	2	1	3	4	5
Corporate governance					
Composite score (total points/40)	0.64	0.80	0.65	0.84	0.67
Indicator rank	5	2	4	1	3
Total points	3.40	4.77	2.52	4.01	3.88
Score (total points/6)	0.57	0.80	0.42	0.67	0.65
Overall Rank	4	1	5	2	3

Source: From table 7.1. Authors' calculations are based on appendixes 1 and 3. Data in appendixes come from South Asian Central Banks, SECs and Boards, and stock exchanges; Indian Banks' Association 2006a, 2006b, and 2006c; Reserve Bank of India 2006a, 2006b, 2006c, and 2007.
Note: The ranking calculation methodology is given in chapter 7.

(overall composite score of 0.45). It has made commendable efforts in certain areas; however, to be comparable, it needs to address many issues to improve its commercial banking system.

All countries have their own strengths and weaknesses. The two radar graphs highlight the key issues that matter to each country in their efforts to develop financial soundness. The first radar graph (figure 3.1) shows India being ahead of other countries with scores ranging from 0.63 on performance and efficiency to 0.91 on capital market development. The range for Pakistan was 0.43 for access to finance and 0.84 for corporate governance. The development dimensions for Sri Lanka ranged between 0.40 for market concentration and 0.93 for access to finance, while the Bangladesh range was between 0.42 for performance and efficiency and 0.71 for market concentration. Nepal had the lowest scores ranging from 0.24 for financial stability and 0.65 for corporate governance.

The second radar graph (figure 3.2) shows how these countries have fared under different dimensions from the dimensions' perspective. All countries had higher performance in corporate governance, ranging from 0.64 in Bangladesh to 0.84 in Pakistan. On the other hand, capital market development showed the least amount of development with scores ranging from 0.30 in Nepal to 0.91 in India. The other four dimensions scored between these two extremes. Access to finance ranged between 0.28 in Nepal to 0.93 in Sri Lanka. Performance and efficiency scores were between 0.42 for both Nepal and Bangladesh, and 0.80 for Pakistan. Financial stability scores were between 0.24 in Nepal and 0.89 in India. Finally, market concentration scores were 0.40 in Sri Lanka to 0.89 in India. These two

Country Rankings on the Getting Finance Indicators   45

Figure 3.1   South Asian Countries: Strengths and Weaknesses of the Commercial Banking Sector

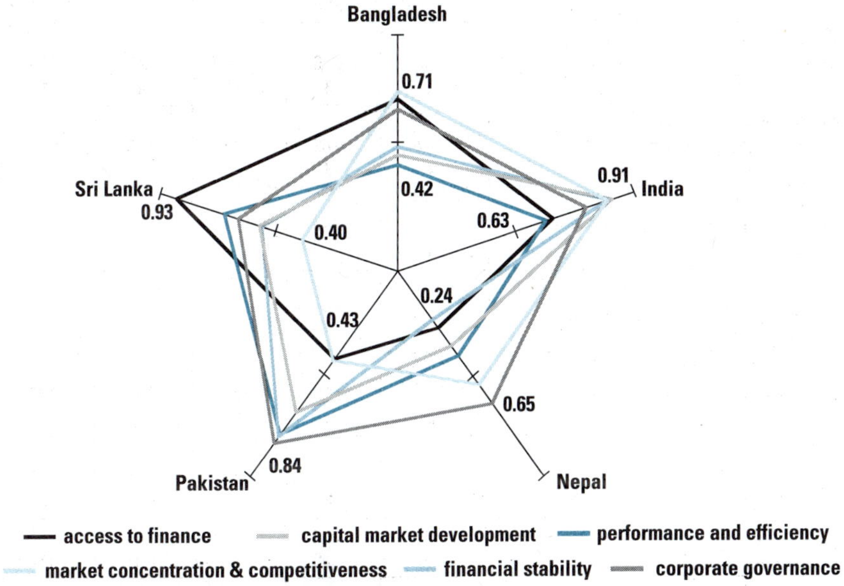

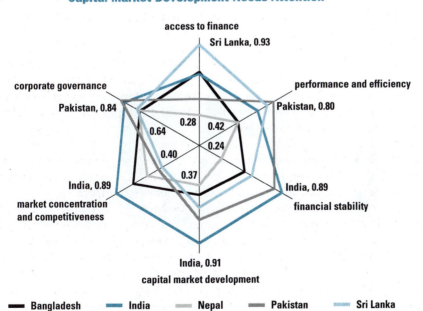

Source: From table 7.1. Data used in table 7.1 calculation come from appendixes 1 and 3, for which the sources are South Asian Central Banks, SECs and Boards, and stock exchanges; Indian Banks' Association 2006a, 2006b, and 2006c; Reserve Bank of India 2006a, 2006b, 2006c, and 2007.

Figure 3.2   South Asian Countries Focused on Corporate Governance; Capital Market Development Needs Attention

Source: From table 7.1. Data used in table 7.1 calculation come from appendixes 1 and 3, for which the sources are South Asian Central Banks, SECs and Boards, and stock exchanges; Indian Banks' Association 2006a, 2006b, and 2006c; Reserve Bank of India 2006a, 2006b, 2006c, and 2007.

graphs show that each country has its own priorities that are different from others, depending on the characteristics of their own financial systems and economic structures and the stage of development they are in as of now.

Individual Rankings on Micro Indicators

The following analysis provides a more comprehensive picture of how each country fared on the micro indicators within each development dimension and thereby key areas on which to focus for each country.

Access to Finance

Sri Lanka leads in the area of access to finance on all indicators except for geographic bank penetration. Its overall access ratios have improved favorably over the period (figure 3.3). Bangladesh has the highest geographic branch penetration. India and Pakistan need to focus on access indicators. Access is lowest in Nepal.

Performance and Efficiency

Pakistan comes first in the performance and efficiency category with superior performance in most micro indicators. India also fares well in all areas. The area that requires Pakistan's focus is operating costs (figure 3.4). Sri Lanka is not far behind, and records the lowest staff cost ratios in the region. Nepal confronts problems of negative capital and low operating efficiency with high staff cost ratios. However, their operating cost ratios are the lowest in the region. Bangladesh must focus on high operating costs and lower net interest margins.

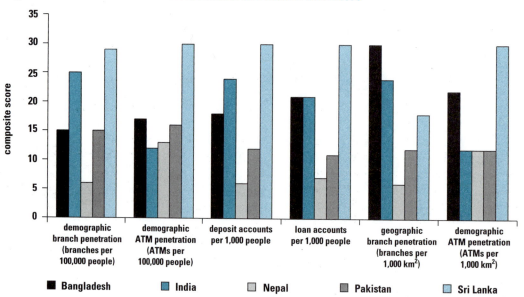

Figure 3.3 Sri Lanka Leads on All Access to Finance Indicators

Source: From table 7.1. Data used in table 7.1 calculation come from appendixes 1 and 3, for which the sources are South Asian Central Banks, SECs and Boards, and stock exchanges; Indian Banks' Association 2006a, 2006b, and 2006c; Reserve Bank of India 2006a, 2006b, 2006c, and 2007.

Financial Stability

India's top performance on stability reflects higher capital adequacy ratios (CARs), lower nonperforming loan (NPL) ratios, and stable liquidity positions (figure 3.5). Pakistan ranks second with higher provisioning ratios; it should focus on its liquidity management. Sri Lanka has improved well in all areas with liquidity as the main area of concern. Bangladesh should improve its capital positions and should focus on NPLs and provisioning. Nepal has negative CARs and lower ratios on all indicators when compared with the region.

Capital Market Development

India fares well with higher market capitalization, liquidity, and lower concentration resulting from having a developed capital market (figure 3.6). All other countries need to concentrate on developing their capital markets. For Pakistan and Sri Lanka, the focus should be on developing their bond markets.

Market Concentration and Competitiveness

The Indian banking system proves to be the best in the region on market concentration (figure 3.7). All the concentration ratios have declined over the years. Bangladesh also fared well in this category. The banking sector in Sri Lanka is highly concentrated, with more than 50 percent of assets, deposits, and loans concentrated in three banks. Most countries should monitor the rapid growth of bank credit to the private sector, with a view to manage credit risk.

Corporate Governance

Pakistan does well in all areas of corporate governance, but the keys to its superior performance are the detailed governance guidelines issued by its regulatory authorities, demonstrating better disclosure and greater shareholder rights (figure 3.8).

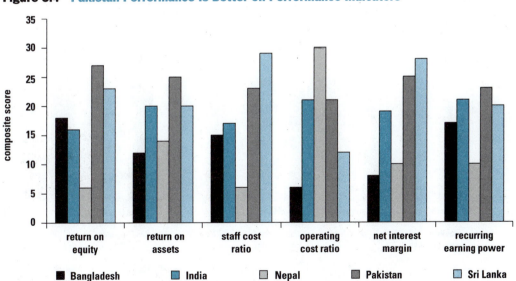

Figure 3.4 Pakistan Performance Is Better on Performance Indicators

Source: From table 7.1. Data used in table 7.1 calculation come from appendixes 1 and 3, for which the sources are South Asian Central Banks, SECs and Boards, and stock exchanges; Indian Banks' Association 2006a, 2006b, and 2006c; Reserve Bank of India 2006a, 2006b, 2006c, and 2007.

Figure 3.5 India Shows Strong Performance on Financial Stability

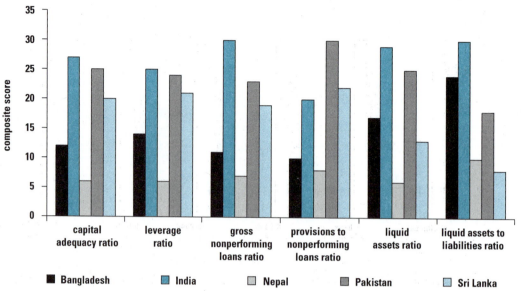

Source: From table 7.1. Data used in table 7.1 calculation come from appendixes 1 and 3, for which the sources are South Asian Central Banks, SECs and Boards, and stock exchanges; Indian Banks' Association 2006a, 2006b, and 2006c; Reserve Bank of India 2006a, 2006b, 2006c, and 2007.

Figure 3.6 India Leads the Region in Capital Market Development Indicators

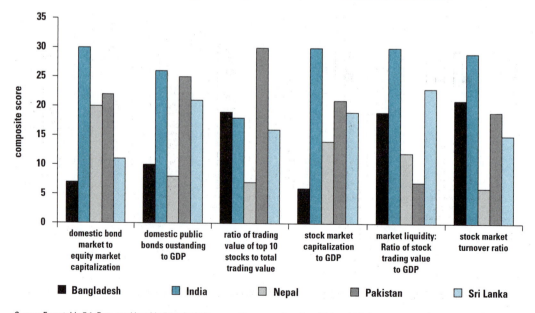

Source: From table 7.1. Data used in table 7.1 calculation come from appendixes 1 and 3, for which the sources are South Asian Central Banks, SECs and Boards, and stock exchanges; Indian Banks' Association 2006a, 2006b, and 2006c; Reserve Bank of India 2006a, 2006b, 2006c, and 2007.

Figure 3.7 India Ranks High on Market Concentration and Competitiveness Indicators

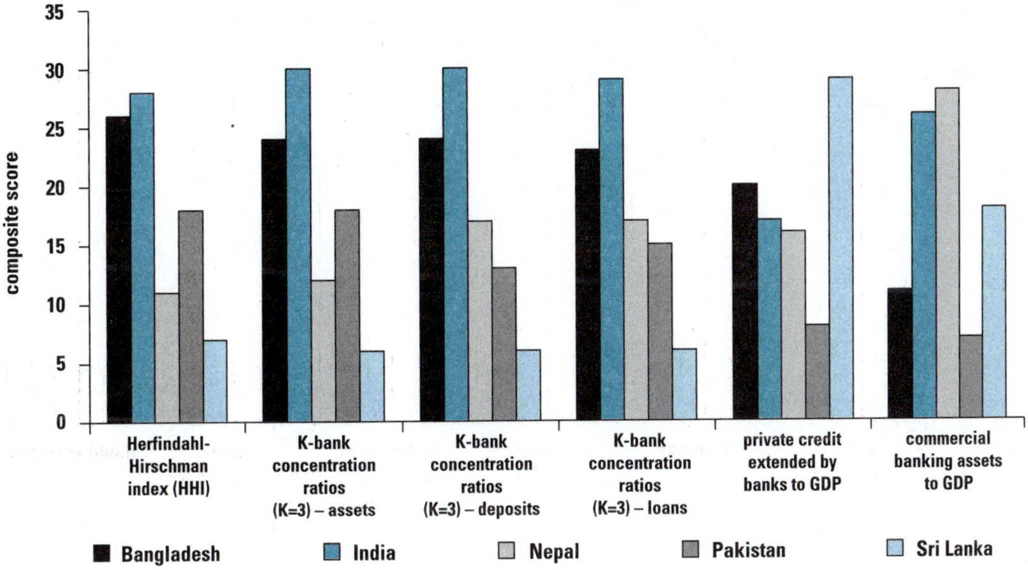

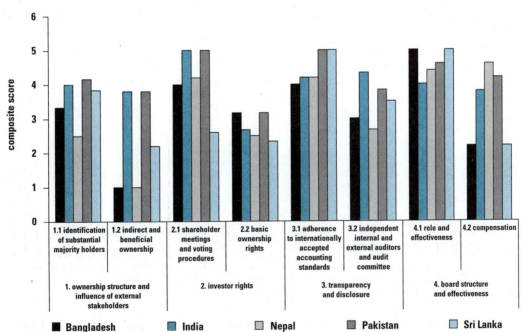

Source: From table 7.1. Data used in table 7.1 calculation come from appendixes 1 and 3, for which the sources are South Asian Central Banks, SECs and Boards, and stock exchanges; Indian Banks' Association 2006a, 2006b, and 2006c; Reserve Bank of India 2006a, 2006b, 2006c, and 2007.

Figure 3.8 Pakistan Leads in Corporate Governance Indicators

Source: From table 7.1. Data used in table 7.1 calculation come from appendixes 1 and 3, for which the sources are South Asian Central Banks, SECs and Boards, and stock exchanges; Indian Banks' Association 2006a, 2006b, and 2006c; Reserve Bank of India 2006a, 2006b, 2006c, and 2007.

India follows closely behind. The other three countries have performed fairly well. All countries appear to have done reasonably well on meetings and voting procedures, board structure, and accounting and auditing standards. All countries need to concentrate on indirect share ownership, basic ownership rights, responsibilities and effectiveness of the boards, and disclosure requirements.

4

An International Perspective

To find out whether South Asian banking systems are comparable to the international systems and to find out how well they compare, comparable data for selected high-income Organisation for Economic Co-operation and Development (OECD) member and nonmember countries—including Australia; Canada; Hong Kong, China; New Zealand; Singapore; the United Kingdom; and the United States—are compiled to serve as the benchmark (for a description of benchmarks, see chapter 1, Development of Benchmarks; for underlying benchmark data, see appendix 2.A; for data sources, see appendix 2.B).

The benchmark ranges (high and low) for each year are compared against the indicators for the five South Asian countries to assess their strengths and weaknesses (see data appendix 1, tables A1.1–1.6 for data comparison of South Asian countries and the benchmark ranges for each year). Comparisons on each micro indicator within the five development dimensions provide a more detailed picture of the comparability and the strong and weak points of each country.

Benchmark Comparison (2006)

Comparative analysis of the 12 micro indicators (under the five dimensions[1]) for 2006 shows that South Asian countries compare well on such ratios as returns, capital adequacy, and market concentration. Areas requiring attention include credit quality issues of nonperforming loans (NPLs) and provisioning. South Asia needs to focus on developing its capital market so that it can meet the long-term finance needs of commerce as well as the portfolio appetite of institutional investors. When comparative data over the six-year period are examined overall, however, it is evident that South Asia is making commendable progress in making their banking systems more efficient and comparable to international standards (for underlying data, see appendix 1, table A1.6).

Access to Finance

South Asian geographic branch penetration figures are significant, especially in Bangladesh (44.53) and India (23.46) and compare well with benchmark range on the higher side. The benchmark countries range from a low of 1 to a high of

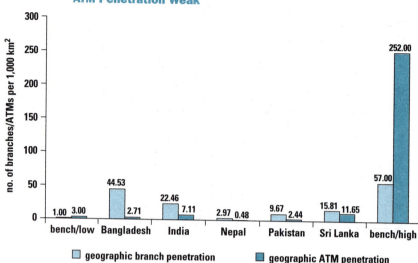

Figure 4.1 Year 2006: South Asian Branch Penetration Is Significant, ATM Penetration Weak

Source: From appendix 1, table A1.6. Data used are from South Asian Central Banks, SECs and Boards, stock exchanges, and publications; Indian Banks' Association 2006a, 2006b, and 2006c; Reserve Bank of India 2006a, 2006b, 2006c, and 2007; and benchmark data sources from appendix 2.B.

57 branches per 1,000 km². Because all of these benchmark countries already use e-banking extensively, the branch network has lesser importance (figure 4.1).

This is confirmed by the geographic automated teller machine (ATM) penetration ratio. The highest South Asian ratio in Sri Lanka at 11.65 ATMs is not significant when compared with the benchmark range between a low of 3 and a high of 252. Technological advancements and infrastructure developments are necessary in South Asia for the region to compare well with the international benchmarks.

Performance and Efficiency

South Asian return-on-equity levels (except for Nepal, with negative returns) are well above the benchmarks. Pakistan and Bangladesh at 34.7 percent and 33.86 percent, respectively, achieved higher returns than the benchmark figures, which range from a high of 18.6 percent to a low of 8.9 percent. India and Sri Lanka achieved returns closer to the benchmark figures at the higher end.

The benchmark returns on assets vary from a high of 1.8 percent to a low of 0.5 percent. Pakistan leads the pack at 3.2 percent, with all countries being able to achieve higher returns than the benchmark countries at the lower end. The high returns are attributable to higher interest spread in South Asian countries (figure 4.2).

Financial Stability

Capital adequacy ratios in most of the South Asian countries are in line with the benchmarks. Pakistan at 13.33 percent is 2.07 percentage points short of the benchmark figure on the higher end of 15.4 percent. India and Sri Lanka have higher than the required norms. Bangladesh, at 8.33 percent, needs to improve its capital adequacy ratio. Nepal has negative capital. The benchmark figure at the lower end is 10.4 percent (figure 4.3).

South Asia needs to exert more effort on reducing NPLs and improving credit quality. The upper and lower benchmarks are just 0.20 percent and 2.40 percent

An International Perspective   53

Figure 4.2 Year 2006: South Asia Beat the Benchmark in Return on Equity

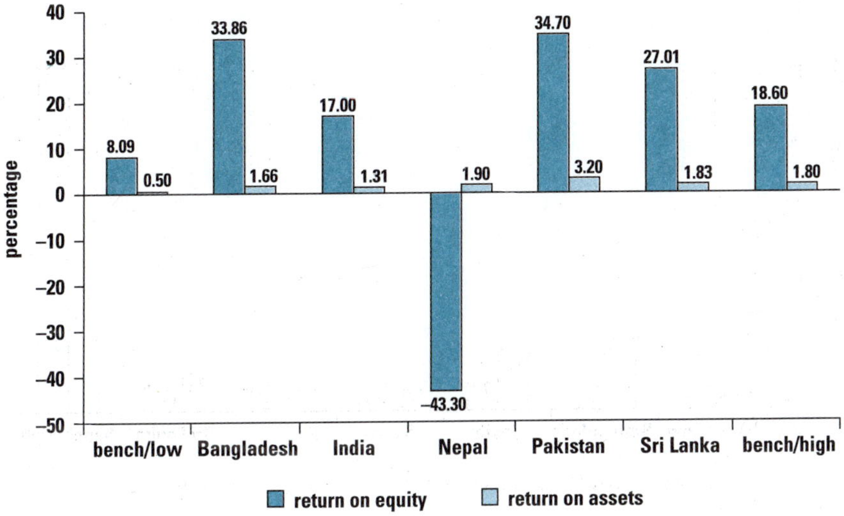

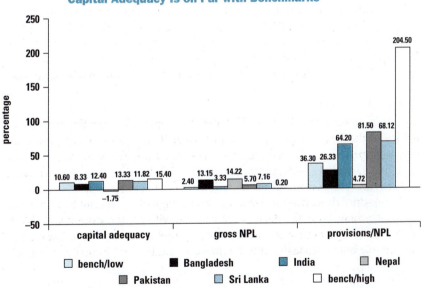

Source: From appendix 1, table A1.6. Data used are from South Asian Central Banks, SECs and Boards, stock exchanges, and publications; Indian Banks' Association 2006a, 2006b, and 2006c; Reserve Bank of India 2006a, 2006b, 2006c, and 2007; and benchmark data sources from appendix 2.B.

Figure 4.3 Year 2006: South Asia Needs to Work on Credit Quality; Capital Adequacy Is on Par with Benchmarks

Source: From appendix 1, table A1.6. Data used are from South Asian Central Banks, SECs and Boards, stock exchanges, and publications; Indian Banks' Association 2006a, 2006b, and 2006c; Reserve Bank of India 2006a, 2006b, 2006c, and 2007; and benchmark data sources from appendix 2.B.

(where 0.2 percent is the high or better benchmark range), while all of South Asian ratios are very much above the benchmark ranges. Nepal has a high NPL level of 14.22 percent of total loans. India has the lowest ratio at 3.33, which is closer to lower level of benchmark range of 2.40 (figure 4.3).

Figure 4.4 Year 2006: For South Asia, Capital Market Development Is a Priority

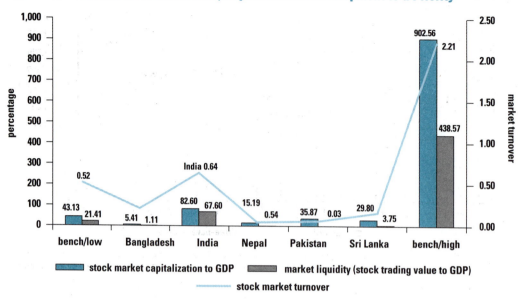

Source: From appendix 1, table A1.6. Data used are from South Asian Central Banks, SECs and Boards, stock exchanges, and publications; Indian Banks' Association 2006a, 2006b, and 2006c; Reserve Bank of India 2006a, 2006b, 2006c, and 2007; and benchmark data sources from appendix 2.B.

Similarly, provisions for NPL ratios of benchmark countries also indicate their finer credit management. The higher end is 204.5 percent while the lower end is 36.3 percent. Other than Nepal, South Asian countries seem to improve their provisioning with policies that are more stringent. Pakistan has the highest ratio in the region, at 81.5 percent (figure 4.3).

Capital Market Development

Except for India, capital markets in all other countries are at the developmental or infant stage, as reflected by comparable data from the benchmark countries. Equity market capitalization varies between 43.13 percent and 903.56 percent, with India at 82.60 percent. Market liquidity indicated by total value of shares traded has a benchmark range of 21.41 percent to 438.57 percent, with India at 67.6 percent. Efficiency of the capital market as measured by stock market turnover has a range of 0.52 times to 2.21 times, and India is 0.64 times (figure 4.4).

Market Concentration and Competitiveness

Overall market concentration is low in South Asia except for Sri Lanka. The Herfindahl-Hirschman Index (HHI) values for benchmark countries range from 563.35 (classified as unconcentrated) to 1,854.41 (highly concentrated). All South Asian countries fall into the category of unconcentrated (HHI less than 1,000) except for Sri Lanka, which at 1,259.88 is classified as moderately concentrated. For the benchmark countries, the three-bank concentration ratio on loans ranges from 31.01 percent to 56.93 percent. All South Asian countries have low concentration ratios (around 30 percent) except Sri Lanka at 52.74 percent (figure 4.5).

Figure 4.5 Year 2006: Market Concentration Is within the Range

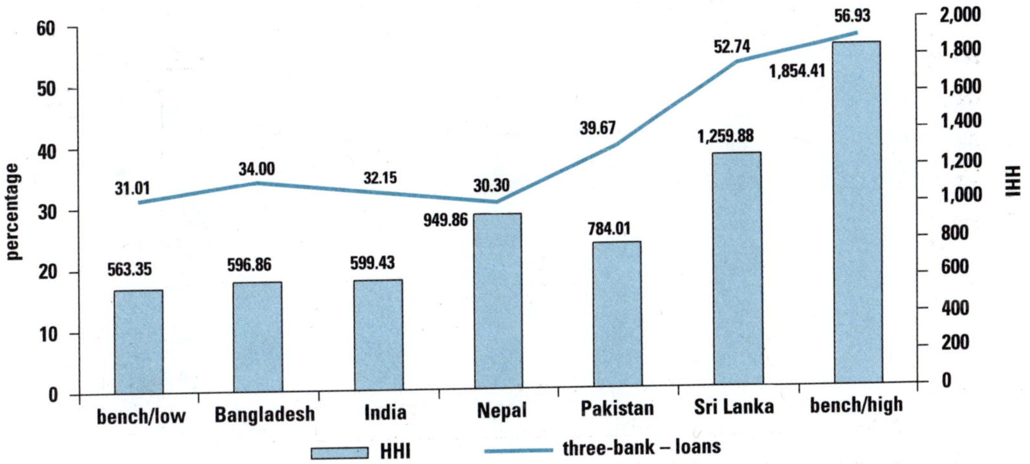

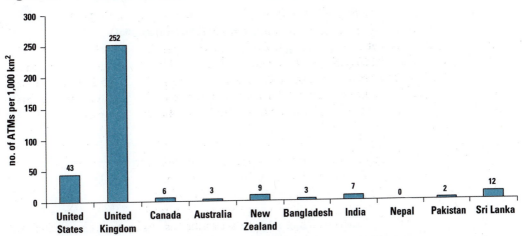

Source: From appendix 1, table A1.6. Data used are from South Asian Central Banks, SECs and Boards, stock exchanges, and publications; Indian Banks' Association 2006a, 2006b, and 2006c; Reserve Bank of India 2006a, 2006b, 2006c, and 2007; and benchmark data sources from appendix 2.B.

International Comparison of Financial Ratios—Benchmark Countries (2006)

The comparative analysis in the preceding section compares South Asian indicators against comparable benchmark ranges. In this section, the performance of South Asian countries on the selected indicators is compared graphically with individual countries in the benchmark group (for underlying data, see appendix 1, table A1.6 and appendix 2.A, table A2.6). Figures 4.6 to 4.10 are self-explanatory.

Figure 4.6 Year 2006: Geographic ATM Penetration, UK Leads

Source: For the five South Asian countries, data are from appendix 1, table A1.6. Data sources include South Asian Central Banks, SECs and Boards, stock exchanges, and publications; Indian Banks' Association 2006a, 2006b, and 2006c: Reserve Bank of India 2006a, 2006b, 2006c, and 2007. For benchmark countries data are from appendix 2.A, table A2.6; data sources are from appendix 2.B.

Figure 4.7 Year 2006: South Asia Better Performances in Return on Equity

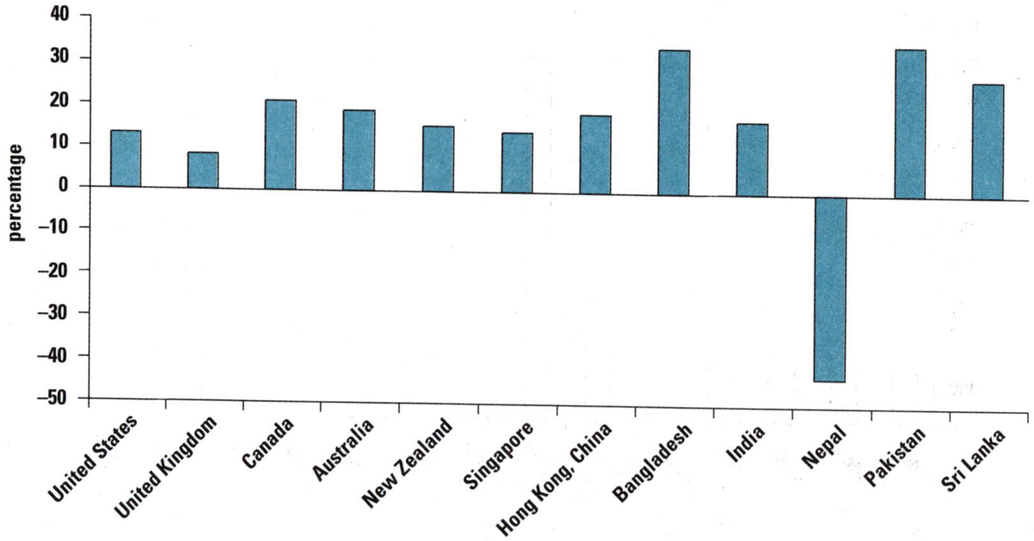

40
30
20
10
0
−10
−20
−30
−40
−50
percentage
United States
United Kingdom
Canada
Australia
New Zealand
Singapore
Hong Kong, China
Bangladesh
India
Nepal
Pakistan
Sri Lanka

Source: For the five South Asian countries, data are from appendix 1, table A1.6. Data sources include South Asian Central Banks, SECs and Boards, stock exchanges, and publications; Indian Banks' Association 2006a, 2006b, and 2006c: Reserve Bank of India 2006a, 2006b, 2006c, and 2007. For benchmark countries data are from appendix 2.A, table A2.6; data sources are from appendix 2.B.

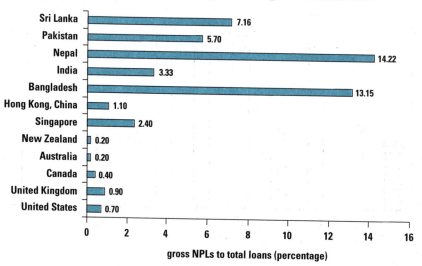

Figure 4.8 Year 2006: Nonperforming Loans Higher in South Asia

Sri Lanka 7.16
Pakistan 5.70
Nepal 14.22
India 3.33
Bangladesh 13.15
Hong Kong, China 1.10
Singapore 2.40
New Zealand 0.20
Australia 0.20
Canada 0.40
United Kingdom 0.90
United States 0.70
0
2
4
6
8
10
12
14
16
gross NPLs to total loans (percentage)

Source: For the five South Asian countries, data are from appendix 1, table A1.6. Data sources include South Asian Central Banks, SECs and Boards, stock exchanges, and publications; Indian Banks' Association 2006a, 2006b, and 2006c: Reserve Bank of India 2006a, 2006b, 2006c, and 2007. For benchmark countries data are from appendix 2.A, table A2.6; data sources are from appendix 2.B.

Figure 4.9 Year 2006: South Asia—Lower Stock Market Capitalization

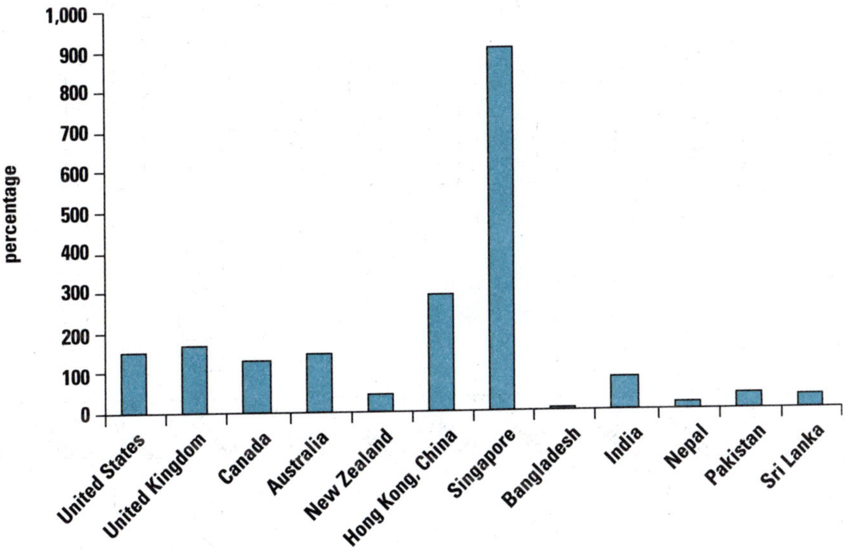

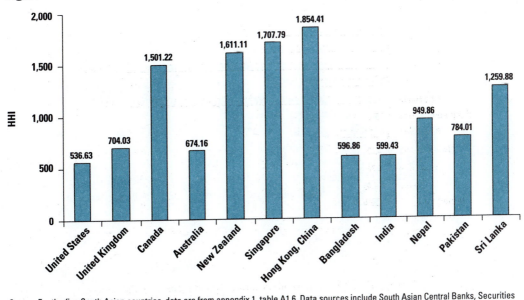

Source: For the five South Asian countries, data are from appendix 1, table A1.6. Data sources include South Asian Central Banks, SECs and Boards, stock exchanges, and publications; Indian Banks' Association 2006a, 2006b, and 2006c: Reserve Bank of India 2006a, 2006b, 2006c, and 2007. For benchmark countries data are from appendix 2.A, table A2.6; data sources are from appendix 2.B.

Figure 4.10 Year 2006: Lower Concentration in South Asia

Source: For the five South Asian countries, data are from appendix 1, table A1.6. Data sources include South Asian Central Banks, Securities Exchange Commissions and Boards, stock exchanges, and publications; Indian Banks' Association 2006a, 2006b, and 2006c: Reserve Bank of India 2006a, 2006b, 2006c, and 2007. For benchmark countries data are from appendix 2.A, table A2.6; data sources are from appendix 2.B.

International Comparison of Financial Ratios—Comparator Groups (2005)

The performance of South Asian countries on selected indicators in 2005 is also compared with that of two comparator groups: a sample of developed countries—Australia, Canada, Japan, New Zealand, the United Kingdom, and the United States—and a peer group in Asia—China; Hong Kong, China; Indonesia; the Republic of Korea; Malaysia; the Philippines; Singapore; and Thailand (for underlying data, see table 4.1).

The results show that the South Asian performance fares well with both groups on some important categories—for example, returns, capital adequacy, and market concentration. Others areas—for example, credit quality, provisioning, and access measures—needed attention. South Asian countries fare poorly in the area of capital market developments.

Access to finance measured by demographic branch and ATM penetration shows that both OECD and selected East Asian peer groups perform better than South Asian countries (figure 4.11).

Under performance and efficiency, the South Asian countries (except for Nepal) record returns on both equity and assets that are comparable to those in the developed countries (figure 4.12).

In the financial stability category, once again, the South Asian group (except for Nepal) is able to match the performance of the two comparator groups, which is an improvement compared with their performances measured in previous studies. The OECD group, however, has significantly lower NPL ratios: the ratios range from 0.2 percent in Australia to 1.8 percent in Japan, whereas those in South Asia range from around 5.13 percent in India to 18.94 percent in Nepal. In the Asian peer group, the ratios are high, ranging from 0.2 in Hong Kong, China to 19.7 in the Philippines (figure 4.13).

The proxies used to measure the capital market development are the domestic public bonds outstanding to GDP ratio and equity market capitalization ratio. For South Asia, with the exception of India, none of these measures compare favorably. Japan recorded the highest bond-to-GDP ratio of 150.6 percent, while Singapore, Malaysia, and the United States recorded significant market capitalization ratios at 152.99 percent, 144 percent, and 135.1 percent, respectively (figure 4.14).

Market concentration was measured by bank asset concentration and private credit-to-GDP ratios. The South Asian group showed lower concentration. Market concentration was highest in Hong Kong, China and Singapore for the Asian peer group, and New Zealand for the OECD group. Private credit was highest in the United Kingdom with 160.48 percent, and for the Asian group, it was highest in Malaysia and the Republic of Korea (around 126 percent) (figure 4.15).

Table 4.1 Financial Ratios for South Asian Countries and Comparator Groups, 2005
(percent)

Economy	Access to finance		Efficiency and performance		Financial stability		Capital market developments		Market concentration and competitiveness	
	D/Branch penetration	D/ATM penetration	Return on equity	Return on assets	Capital adequacy ratio	Gross nonperforming loans	D/Public bonds to GDP	Equity market capitalization	Three-bank assets concentration	Private credit to GDP
South Asia										
Bangladesh	4.64	0.20	28.63	1.30	7.65	13.55	16.75	6.06	37.05	31.87
India	6.33	1.63	16.90	1.30	12.80	5.13	33.00	52.70	32.02	33.30
Nepal	1.67	0.24	−45.87	1.79	−6.07	18.94	16.40	10.49	45.87	27.57
Pakistan	4.82	0.67	36.90	2.90	11.90	6.70	30.90	30.59	40.35	28.83
Sri Lanka	7.20	4.50	27.01	1.70	12.84	8.76	31.77	24.69	53.02	33.87
Asian peer group										
China	1.33[b]	3.80[b]	15.10	0.80	—	9.80	24.60	35.41	66.44	111.80
Hong Kong, China	20	—	11.10	0.70	10.40	0.20	10.07	39.74	73.43	47.84
Indonesia	3.73	4.84[a]	17.50	2.50	19.30	15.60	18.00	27.20	62.28	23.00
Korea, Rep. of	10.50	167.2[b]	22.50	1.30	13.0	1.20	25.40	73.20	50.34	125.80
Malaysia	8.26	16.44[b]	14.10	1.40	13.70	9.60	38.30	144.00	45.31	126.60
Philippines	6.75	5.20	8.70	1.10	17.60	19.70	38.60	35.40	46.23	30.60
Singapore	9	39	11.10	1.20	15.80	3.00	39.78	152.99	98.66	110.21
Thailand	7.37	17.05[c]	14.20	1.90	13.20	9.10	21.20	68.20	53.69	90.50
OECD countries										
Australia	24	115	25.30	1.80	10.40	0.20	15.25	111.27	69.70	109.73
Canada	28	158	14.90	0.70	12.90	0.50	57.38	109.19	58.58	75.65
Japan	45	136	11.30	0.50	12.20	1.80	150.60	106.10	38.66	97.90
New Zealand	28	57	14.54	0.94	10.91	0.30	25.40	39.74	82.67	129.47
United Kingdom	23	97	11.80	0.80	12.80	1.00	28.95	126.22	31.85	160.48
United States	26	134	12.70	1.30	13.00	0.70	47.23	135.10	53.47	47.84

Sources: IMF 2007a, 2007b; regulatory Web sites; Bank for International Settlements 2007; World Bank 2007a; World Federation of Exchanges 2007; supervisory authorities; and staff calculations.
Note: For definitions of acronyms and abbreviations, see the list at the beginning of the report.
a. 2000 data.
b. 2003 data.
c. 2004 data.

Figure 4.11 South Asia Is Not Comparable on Access Indicators

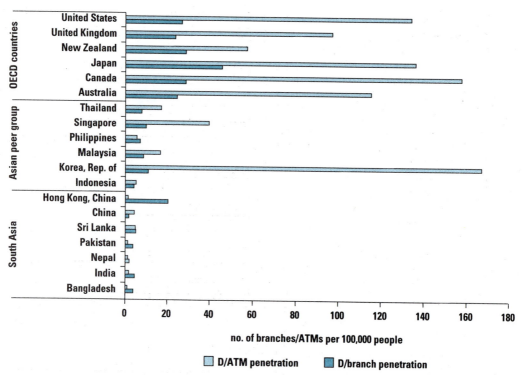

Source: IMF 2007a, 2007b; regulatory Web sites; Bank for International Settlements 2007; World Bank 2007a; World Federation of Exchanges 2007; supervisory authorities; and staff calculations.

Figure 4.12 South Asia Performance Indicators Are Better

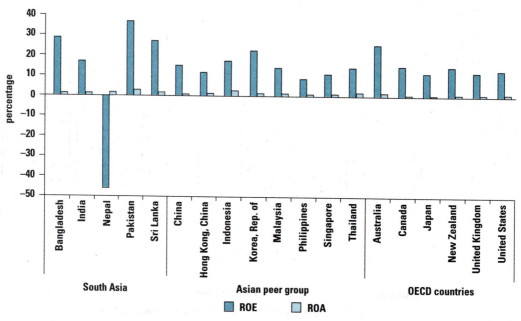

Source: IMF 2007a, 2007b; regulatory Web sites; Bank for International Settlements 2007; World Bank 2007a; World Federation of Exchanges 2007; supervisory authorities; and staff calculations.

Figure 4.13 South Asia Capital Adequacy Is on Par, Nonperforming Loans Are below Peer Groups

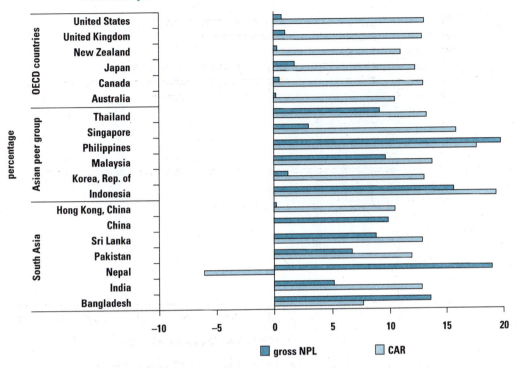

Source: IMF 2007a, 2007b; regulatory Web sites; Bank for International Settlements 2007; World Bank 2007a; World Federation of Exchanges 2007; supervisory authorities; and staff calculations.

Figure 4.14 South Asia Capital Market Development below Peer Groups, except India

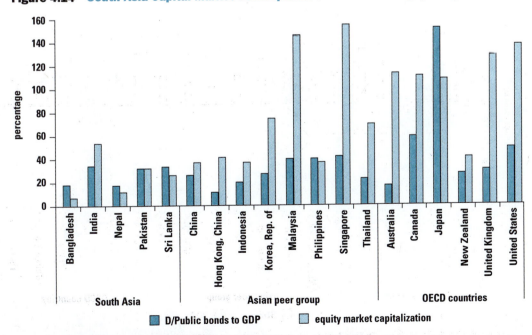

Source: IMF 2007a, 2007b; regulatory Web sites; Bank for International Settlements 2007; World Bank 2007a; World Federation of Exchanges 2007; supervisory authorities; and staff calculations.

Figure 4.15 South Asia Has a Comparatively Low Market Concentration

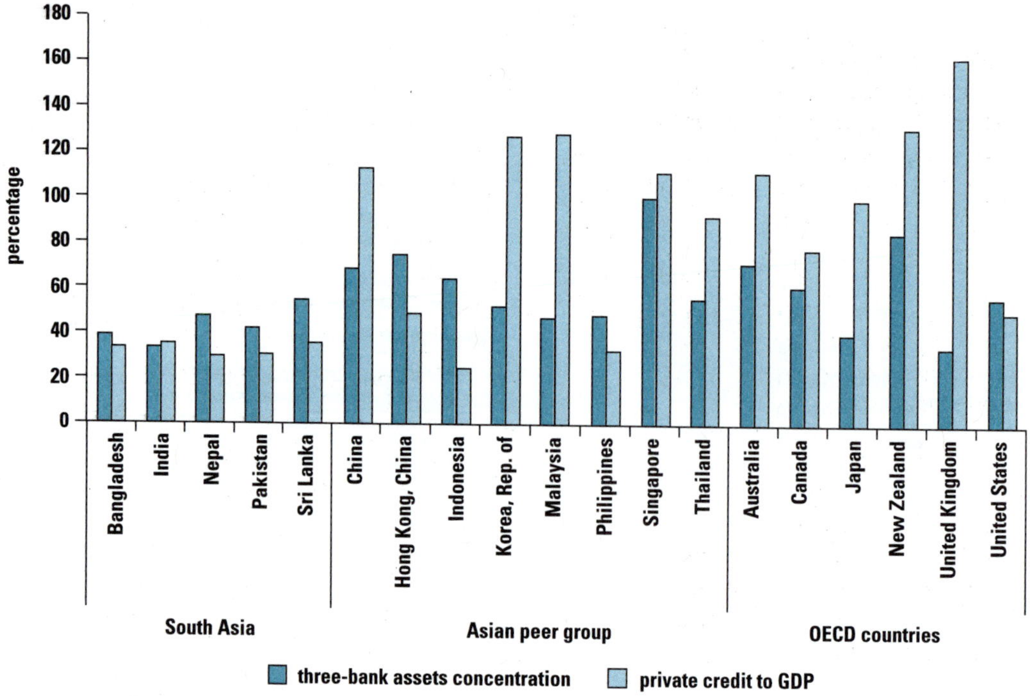

■ three-bank assets concentration   □ private credit to GDP

Source: IMF 2007a, 2007b; regulatory Web sites; Bank for International Settlements 2007; World Bank 2007a; World Federation of Exchanges 2007; supervisory authorities; and staff calculations.

Endnote

1. Corporate governance was not benchmarked.

5
Findings and Observations

Financial sector development affects poverty both directly and indirectly—indirectly by affecting the economic development process, which will increase income-generating capacities, and directly by increasing access to financial services for the underprivileged. Recognizing the importance of financial development to their growth and poverty reduction strategies, South Asian authorities actively pursue financial sector reform measures to build a stable financial system that is resilient to economic shocks. Financial sector development can be observed in many ways, including better allocations of resources, lower intermediation costs, increased efficiencies through technological developments, diversity of the market players, availability of innovative instruments, market-oriented regulatory systems, and better access to finance. Supervisory authorities continue to monitor these developments to spot vulnerabilities and weaknesses and thus take preventive measures. Thus, this report is a useful reference tool in this process.

As stated earlier in the report, findings are confined to the commercial banking sector and should be viewed with the noted technical and practical limitations in mind. These findings and observations are important, however, because the trend analysis of the micro indicators flag areas of strengths and weaknesses. One or even several ratios might be misleading; however, when combined with other observations about the local situation and the industry, they could provide information for the regulatory authorities to focus on in their development efforts.

Access to Finance

South Asian countries need to focus on improving access to finance in the commercial banking sector. When compared with the economic growth and the progress made in other areas such as performance and returns, the provision of financial access has lagged. It is recognized that, in South Asia, other players such as microfinance institutions (MFIs) also play a significant role in providing financial services to the poor, but they are unable to mobilize funds and diversify risks on a large scale as banks do. Hence, it is important that banks play a more active role in financial intermediation so that more people may benefit through increased access to financial services. Among the countries studied, Nepal needs to pay more attention to improve access; in comparison to other countries, Sri Lanka has progressed well.

Performance and Efficiency

South Asia recorded commendable improvements in the performance and efficiency category. Higher interest rate spreads, larger volumes in trade, and more aggressive regulatory measures are instrumental in the banking system, registering improved performance. Higher interest spreads should be monitored and reduced, however, to provide lower intermediary cost to the users. Pakistan leads the South Asian countries in this category. South Asian group have posted returns higher than the high-income Organisation for Economic Co-operation and Development (OECD) member and nonmember benchmark countries as well as the East Asian peer group in this category. Although most of the region's banking sectors have managed to bring down their staff and operating cost ratios considerably, there is room for further improvement.

Financial Stability

Capital adequacy is another area of encouraging performance by South Asian countries, except in Nepal, where negative reserves have affected the capital adequacy ratios (CARs). India ranks high on financial stability ratios. Nepal has a negative capital position that needs to be rectified immediately, and Bangladesh has a CAR below the required level. All countries need to focus on reducing the nonperforming loans (NPLs) further. South Asia lags benchmark countries as well as peer groups in both NPLs and provisioning ratios. Although significant legal and regulatory reforms have taken place, prudential norms should align with international norms so that a sound credit culture can develop. Furthermore, although not an imminent problem, the liquidity situation needs monitoring.

Having recognized the importance of prudent risk management, all South Asian countries have initiated action to implement the Basel II capital framework in their banking systems in the near future. It is encouraging that each country is at various stages of development in this process. Once implemented, this would align the capital needed with the risk profiles. Henceforth, banks would be able to better manage their capital as well as their business risks.

Capital Market Development

Except for India, all other countries are at various levels of development stages in capital market development. Local bond markets are dominated by government borrowing, while most stock markets are concentrated on few players or industries. Improvements in the market infrastructure, regulatory and legal reforms, and governance are needed for the development of capital markets. Authorities have to exercise concerted efforts on capital market development to further improve the financial intermediation options.

Market Concentration and Competitiveness

Market concentration is low in South Asia except for Sri Lanka, where with respect to deposits, loans, and assets, three-bank concentration ratios are more than 50 percent. Further, increases in private credit extended as a percentage of gross domestic product (GDP) ratios need to be monitored carefully by the countries, as increasing volumes of credit pose a major risk if interest margins are to fall. Therefore, countries should tighten up their prudential guidelines as well as evaluate the funding sources to avoid possible maturity mismatches.

Corporate Governance

All the South Asian countries have attempted to incorporate corporate governance guidelines. India, Pakistan, and, more recently, Sri Lanka have issued detailed guidelines. Still, all countries need to review and strengthen their corporate governance guidelines in various areas. Bangladesh and Nepal need to further develop their corporate governance guidelines and work toward improving their accounting and auditing standards to conform to international standards. Sri Lanka needs to improve its corporate governance guidelines mainly as they relate to stakeholders' rights and disclosure of beneficial ownership. India needs to review differences between governance rules applicable to government-controlled banks and those applicable to private banks. In addition, all countries need to improve transparency and disclosure requirements.

It is important to ensure that these guidelines and regulations are enforceable. Finally, banking institutions should strive to be guided in their decisions by the guidelines issued by the regulatory authorities.

Benchmarking and Comparability

Comparison of the performance of South Asian countries with benchmark data—high-income OECD member and nonmember countries and the East Asian peer group—show that South Asian performance fares favorably with both groups on some important categories—for example, returns, capital adequacy, and market concentration. But other categories—for example, credit quality, provisioning, and access measures—need attention. Capital market developments require concerted efforts by policy makers of South Asian countries.

Part II

Indicators

6

Compilation Guide for the Getting Finance Indicators for South Asia

As part of the World Bank's regional initiative to develop standardized indicators to measure the performance and soundness of the financial sector, this report, *Getting Finance in South Asia 2009: Indicators and Analysis of the Commercial Banking Sector*, uses indicators under six categories: (1) access to finance, (2) performance and efficiency, (3) financial stability, (4) capital market development, (5) market concentration and competitiveness, and (6) corporate governance. Initially, these indicators will be computed only for commercial banks.

Interpretation and analysis of these indicators is likely to vary unless banking supervisors adopt a common methodology for computing them. Because most of the indicators take the form of ratios, understanding the nature of the underlying data is imperative. This guide provides common definitions, data sources, and concepts for both compilers and users of the indicators. For indicators appearing in previous FPSI reports, the definitions are the same as those given in the compilation guide issued under those studies.

Access to Finance

In countries seeking to develop financial markets, it is important to monitor and measure the level of access to financial services. This knowledge provides a more balanced picture of financial sector development. It also enables policy makers and regulatory authorities to better target the development efforts. Initially it is expected that access to finance will be analyzed using data relating to providers of finance (supply-side data). Demographic as well as geographic market penetration will be analyzed.

1. Demographic branch penetration

$$\text{Bank branches per 100,000 people} = \frac{\text{Number of bank branches}}{\text{Total population}} \times 100,000$$

Number of bank branches: Number of commercial bank branches in the country at year-end.
Total population: Total population at year-end.

This indicator measures the demographic penetration of the banking sector in terms of access to banks' physical outlets. Higher penetration means more branches and thus easier access.

2. Demographic ATM penetration

$$\text{ATMs per 100,000 people} = \frac{\text{Number of ATMs}}{\text{Total population}} \times 100{,}000$$

Number of automated teller machines (ATMs): Number of ATMs of commercial banks in the country at year-end.
Total population: As defined in eq. (1) above.

This indicator also measures the demographic penetration of the banking sector in terms of access to physical outlets. Higher penetration means more ATMs and thus easier access.

3. Deposit accounts per 1,000 people

$$\text{Number of deposit accounts per 1,000 people} = \frac{\text{Number of deposit accounts}}{\text{Total population}} \times 1{,}000$$

Number of deposit accounts: Number of deposit accounts in commercial banks in the country at year-end.
Total population: As defined in eq. (1) above.

This indicator measures the use of banking services. Higher values mean greater use of services.

4. Loan accounts per 1,000 people

$$\text{Number of loan accounts per 1,000 people} = \frac{\text{Number of deposit accounts}}{\text{Total population}} \times 1{,}000$$

Number of loan accounts: Number of loan accounts granted by commercial banks in the country at year-end.
Total population: As defined in eq. (1) above.

This indicator also measures the use of banking services, with higher values indicating greater use.

5. Geographic branch penetration

$$\text{Bank branches per 1,000 km}^2 = \frac{\text{Number of bank branches}}{\text{Total surface area (km}^2\text{)}} \times 1{,}000$$

Number of bank branches: As defined in eq. (1) above.
Total surface area (km^2): Total surface area of the country as measured by square kilometers.

This measures the geographic penetration of the banking sector in terms of access to the physical outlets of the bank. Higher penetration would indicate easier geographic access of branches.

6. Geographic ATM penetration

$$\text{ATMs per 1,000 km}^2 = \frac{\text{Number of ATMs}}{\text{Total surface area (km}^2)} \times 1{,}000$$

Number of ATMs: As defined in eq. (2) above.
Total surface area (sq. km.): As defined in eq. (5) above.

This measures the geographic penetration of the banking sector in terms of access to the physical outlets of the bank. Higher penetration would indicate easier geographic access to ATMs.

Performance and Efficiency

Bank efficiency has become critically important in an environment of increasingly competitive international markets. Thus, comparative data on the efficiency of banks are important both to regulators and to banks, which can use the data to adjust their operating policies. For this study, two types of efficiencies are analyzed: returns efficiency and cost efficiency.

7. Profits to period-average equity (ROE)

$$\text{Return on equity} = \frac{\text{Net income}}{\text{Average value of total equity}}$$

Net income: Net profit before tax and other extraordinary adjustments.
Average value of total equity: Can be calculated by taking the beginning- and end-period values for total capital (total equity) and finding the average.
Total capital (total equity): Also called regulatory capital funds or own funds. Defined as Tier I (core) capital + Tier II (supplementary) capital.
Tier I capital: Equity capital and disclosed reserves that are freely available to meet claims against the bank. Tier I capital comprises paid-up shares, share premiums, retained earnings, statutory reserves, and general reserves. Goodwill should be deducted because its value may fall during crises. Tier I capital should be at least 50 percent of the total capital funds.
Tier II capital: Undisclosed reserves, revaluation reserves, general loan loss provisions, and hybrid instruments that combine the characteristics of debt and equity and are available to meet losses and unsecured subordinated debt. Tier II capital should be less than or equal to Tier I capital. Subordinated debt should not exceed 50 percent of Tier I capital. Loan-loss provisions should not exceed 1.25 percent of the total risk-weighted assets.

This ratio measures the efficiency with which a bank uses capital and, over time, the sustainability of its capital position.

8. Profits to period-average assets (ROA)

$$\text{Return on assets} = \frac{\text{Net income}}{\text{Average value of total assets}}$$

Net income: As defined in eq. (7) above.
Average value of total assets: Can be calculated by taking the beginning- and end-period values for total assets and finding the average.

This ratio measures the efficiency with which a bank uses assets.

9. Staff cost ratio

$$\text{Staff cost ratio} = \frac{\text{Personnel expenses}}{\text{Operating expenses}}$$

Personnel expenses: Total remuneration payable to employees.
Operating expenses: All expenses other than interest expenses and provisions.

This ratio measures personnel cost as a share of total administrative expenses and reflects cost efficiency.

10. Operating cost ratio

$$\text{Operating cost ratio} = \frac{\text{Operating expenses}}{\text{Net interest earnings}}$$

Operating expenses: As defined in eq. (9) above.
Net interest earnings (net interest income): Interest earned less interest expenses.

This ratio measures efficiency in controlling administrative and operating expenses in relation to net interest income.

11. Net interest margin

$$\text{Net interest margin ratio} = \frac{\text{Net interest earnings}}{\text{Average value of total assets}}$$

Net interest earnings (net interest income): As defined in eq. (10) above.
Average value of total assets: As defined in eq. (8) above.

This ratio measures the overall operating efficiency of the banking sector.

12. Recurring earning power

$$\text{Recurring earning power ratio} = \frac{\text{Preprovision profits}}{\text{Average value of total assets}}$$

Preprovision profits: Profits before tax and loan loss provisions.
Average value of total assets: As defined in eq. (8) above.

This ratio measures the recurring earning strength and efficiency of the banking sector.

Financial Stability

Financial stability means avoiding significant disruptions to the financial system and its functions. It is key to achieving both low inflation and sustainable economic growth. While different indicators measure different aspects of financial sector stability, this study uses capital adequacy, asset quality, and liquidity ratios. The capital adequacy ratios (CARs) measure the capacity of an institution to absorb losses and thus indicate its financial strength. The asset quality and liquidity ratios measure major vulnerabilities relating to credit risk and liquidity risk.

13. Capital adequacy ratio (CAR)

$$\text{Capital adequacy ratio} = \frac{\text{Regulatory capital funds}}{\text{Risk-weighted assets}}$$

Regulatory capital funds: Also called own funds or total capital funds, as defined in eq. (7) above.

Risk-weighted assets: Each class of assets and off–balance sheet exposures are weighted using weights related to the credit risk associated with each type of assets. The standard risk weights used as international best practices (Basel I) are as follows:

- Cash, gold, and government or treasury securities, 0 percent
- Government agencies, 20 percent
- Mortgage loans, 50 percent
- Others, 100 percent

The CAR provides an assessment of how well the capital cushions fluctuations in earnings and supports asset growth. The ratio should be calculated on a consolidated basis. Under international best practice, 8 percent of total risk-weighted assets on a consolidated basis is considered adequate capital.

14. Leverage ratio

$$\text{Leverage ratio} = \frac{\text{Total equity}}{\text{Total on-balance sheet assets}}$$

Total Equity: Total capital funds as defined in eq. (7) above.
Total on-balance sheet assets: Total assets in the balance sheet at the end of period without risk weighting.

This ratio measures the extent to which assets are financed by funds other than own funds; hence, it is a measure of capital adequacy.

15. Gross nonperforming loans ratio

$$\text{Gross nonperforming loans ratio} = \frac{\text{Gross nonperforming loans}}{\text{Total advances}}$$

Gross nonperforming loans (NPLs): The amount of NPLs before specific loan loss provisions are deducted. According to prudential norms, loans are classified as nonperforming when payments of principal and interest are past due by three months.

Total advances: Gross loans and advances, including NPLs before deducting specific loan-loss provisions.

This ratio is a measure of asset quality and indicates the credit quality of a bank's loan portfolio.

16. Provisions to nonperforming loans ratio

$$\text{Provisions to nonperforming loans ratio} = \frac{\text{Loan-loss provisions}}{\text{Gross nonperforming loans}}$$

Loan loss provisions: Specific loan-loss provisions outstanding at the end of the period.

Gross NPLs: As defined in eq. (15) above.

This ratio is a measure of asset quality and identifies the adequacy/shortfall of the specific provisions made in respect of NPLs.

17. Liquid assets ratio

$$\text{Liquid assets ratio} = \frac{\text{Liquid assets}}{\text{Total assets}}$$

Liquid assets: Cash, demand deposits, and other financial assets that are available on demand or within three months or less.

Total assets: As defined in eq. (16) above.

This ratio measures stability. It indicates the liquidity available to meet expected and unexpected short-term demands for cash—and thus the vulnerability of the banking sector to loss of funding sources.

18. Liquid assets to liquid liabilities ratio

$$\text{Liquid assets to liquid liabilities ratio} = \frac{\text{Liquid assets}}{\text{Liquid liabilities}}$$

Liquid assets: As defined in eq. (17) above.

Liquid liabilities: Short-term debt liabilities and the net market value of financial derivatives positions (short term).

This ratio also measures stability. It captures the liquidity mismatch between short-term assets and liabilities and indicates the extent to which a bank can meet its short-term obligations without incurring liquidity problems.

Capital Market Development

The development of capital markets is a powerful indicator of the depth of the financial sector. By allocating funds for viable investment projects, healthy capital markets diversify the channels of financial intermediation. This study uses ratios to measure the size and structure of the stock and bond markets.

19. Domestic bond to equity market capitalization ratio

$$\text{Bond to equity market capitalization ratio} = \frac{\text{Domestic bonds outstanding}}{\text{Equity market capitalization}}$$

Domestic bonds outstanding: Total value of outstanding domestic debt securities issued by private entities as well as public entities, at the end of the period.

Equity (stock) market capitalization: Market value of all outstanding shares calculated by share price times the number of shares outstanding at the end of the period.

This ratio gives an indication of the size and structure of the capital markets. It also reflects financial depth and diversity.

20. Domestic public bonds outstanding to GDP ratio

$$\text{Domestic public bonds to GDP ratio} = \frac{\text{Domestic public bonds outstanding}}{\text{GDP}}$$

Domestic public bonds outstanding: Total outstanding value of domestic debt securities issued by public entities.

Gross domestic product (GDP): This is an aggregate measure of production in the economy equal to the total value added of all residential units engaged in production, for the given period.

This is another measure of the size of the bond market. It reflects the extent to which the public sector preempts resources that would otherwise be available to the private sector.

21. Trading value of top 10 stocks to total trading value ratio

$$\text{Trading value of top 10 stocks ratio} = \frac{\text{Trading value of top 10 stocks}}{\text{Total value of shares traded}}$$

Trading value of top 10 stocks: Total value of top 10 actively traded stocks in the stock exchange for the period under consideration, such as financial year or calendar year.

Total value of share traded: Total value of shares traded in the stock exchange for the period under consideration, such as financial year or calendar year

The ratio measures the degree of concentration of the top 10 firms in the market and reflects the depth of the stock market.

22. Stock market capitalization to GDP ratio

$$\text{Stock market capitalization to GDP ratio} = \frac{\text{Stock market capitalization}}{\text{GDP}}$$

Stock market capitalization: As defined in eq. (19) above.
GDP: As defined in eq. (20) above.

This ratio measures the relative importance of the stock market to the size of the economy.

23. Stock trading value to GDP ratio

$$\text{Stock trading value to GDP ratio} = \frac{\text{Total value of shares traded}}{\text{GDP}}$$

Total value of share traded: As defined in eq. (21) above.
GDP: As defined in eq. (20) above.

This is a measure of activity or liquidity in the stock market and reflects the ease of trading.

24. Stock market turnover ratio

$$\text{Stocket market turnover ratio} = \frac{\text{Total value of shares traded}}{\text{Average market capitalization}}$$

Total value of share traded: As defined in eq. (21) above.
Average market capitalization: Average of the end-period market capitalization values for the current period and the previous period.

This is a measure of efficiency in the stock market.

Market Concentration and Competitiveness

The study examines the market structure of the banking sector to evaluate the banking system's proneness to instability and crises. A high level of concentration in the banking industry, by reducing competition and increasing cost, has a negative impact on efficiency. At the same time, a highly competitive banking sector might be more prone to crisis (due to increased fragility resulting from intense competition) than a more concentrated one.

25. Herfindahl-Hirschman Index (HHI)

$$HHI = \sum_{i=1}^{n} (MS_i)^{\wedge 2}$$

HHI is calculated as the sum of the squares of the market share (in terms of assets) of each bank in the geographic banking market.

This ratio measures the market concentration. A highly concentrated commercial banking sector may lead to lack of competitive pressure.

26. K-bank concentration (assets) ratio

$$\text{K-bank concentration ratio (CR}_k\text{) assets} = \frac{\text{Three largest banks' total assets}}{\text{Total assets of commercial banks}}$$

(CR_k), where k = three largest banks.
Three largest banks' total assets: Calculated as total assets of the three largest banks.
Total assets of commercial banks: Total assets of the commercial banking sector.

This ratio measures the banking concentration in terms of assets.

27. K-bank concentration (deposits) ratio

$$\text{K-bank concentration ratio (CR}_k\text{) deposits} = \frac{\text{Three largest banks' total deposits}}{\text{Total deposits of commercial banks}}$$

(CR_k), where k = three largest banks.
Three largest banks' total deposits: Calculated as total deposits of the three largest banks.
Total deposits of commercial banks: Total deposits of the commercial banking sector.

This ratio measures the banking concentration in terms of deposits.

28. K-bank concentration (loans) ratio

$$\text{K-bank concentration ratio (CR}_k\text{) loans} = \frac{\text{Three largest banks' total loans}}{\text{Total loans of commercial banks}}$$

(CR_k), where k = three largest banks.
Three largest banks' total loans: Calculated as total loans of the three largest banks.
Total loans of commercial banks: Total loans of commercial banking sector.

This ratio measures the banking concentration in terms of loans.

29. Private credit extended by banks to GDP ratio

$$\text{Private credit to GDP ratio} = \frac{\text{Total value of private credit by commercial banks}}{\text{GDP}}$$

Total value of private credit by commercial banks: Claims on the private sector by commercial banks.
GDP: As defined in eq. (20) above.

This ratio measures the relative activity of banks as financial intermediaries in channeling savings to investors.

30. Commercial banking assets to GDP ratio

$$\text{Private credit to GDP ratio} = \frac{\text{Total value of private credit by commercial banks}}{\text{Total loans of commercial banks}}$$

Total commercial banking assets: As defined in eq. (26) above.
GDP: As defined in eq. (20) above.

This ratio measures the relative importance of commercial banking sector to the size of the economy.

Corporate Governance

Sound corporate governance creates an environment that promotes banking efficiency, mitigates financial risks, and increases the stability and, therefore, the credibility of financial institutions. Developing countries have much to gain by improving their corporate governance standards. The basic principles are the same everywhere: fairness, transparency, accountability, and responsibility are the minimum standards that give banks legitimacy, reduce vulnerability to financial crisis, and broaden and deepen access to capital.

Scoring performance on corporate governance is hugely challenging and must be done with care. Unlike other types of financial analysis, where quantitative measures can provide "hard" benchmarks to guide the more qualitative aspects of analysis, assessing corporate governance is a largely qualitative exercise. Because corporate governance is assessed in this study through a series of straightforward questions, no definitions or guidelines are provided here.

7

Methodology

Data Compilation

Annual data on the commercial banking sector in each of the five countries representing South Asia (in this study as well as in the phase I, II, and III studies)—Bangladesh, India, Nepal, Pakistan, and Sri Lanka—were compiled for the six years from 2001 to 2006. The data for the financial indicators were collected using a data collection template (for the results, see appendix 1), while the data on corporate governance were collected through a questionnaire (for the responses, see appendix 3.A). In completing this questionnaire, the supervisory agencies were asked to substantiate their responses with relevant legal references or sources.

The data available in this report (and the previous studies) are unique in that they are comparable data collected directly from the regulatory authorities or their published reports. To ensure the compatibility of the indicators across the region and aid consistent interpretation and analysis, a compilation guide (see chapter 6) was prepared, setting out definitions and underlying concepts for both the compilers and the users.

Choice of Indicators

To provide a more holistic perspective of Getting Finance in South Asia, and to improve the understanding of the financial systems in the regions' countries, indicators under the six categories of access to finance, performance and efficiency, corporate governance, financial stability, capital market development, and market concentration and competitiveness were selected.

The financial indicators selected are based on internationally accepted measures and reflect the structure of financial systems in South Asia, just as in the previous reports. The corporate governance indicators are based primarily on the guidelines issued by the Basel Committee on Banking Supervision, which in turn rely on the principles of corporate governance published by the Organisation for Economic Co-operation and Development (OECD) (see chapter 9).

Although market-based indicators such as credit ratings and market volatility would serve better for macro prudential analysis, such indicators were not selected for this study. The effectiveness of such indicators depends on the quality and depth of the financial markets. In most South Asian countries, these characteristics are directly affected by the ownership structure of the commercial banking sector (with government-owned or government-controlled banks accounting for a large share of banking sector assets) and by the lack of stringent public disclosure requirements (for a detailed discussion of the advantages and disadvantages of macro prudential analysis, see World Bank and IMF 2005). It was therefore believed that micro prudential indicators would be better measures of the soundness of financial sectors in South Asia.

Method for Country Rankings

The ranking of countries by the financial and corporate governance indicators is based on a simple-average ranking system. Given the limited size of the sample, ranking based on percentile averages is not warranted. Simple-average ranking also appears to be appropriate given the lack of sufficiently detailed data to assess the impact of each variable on financial soundness and thus permit different weights to be assigned to the variables (see Djankov, Manraj, McLiesh, and Ramalto 2005). Thus, the use of simple-average ranking has made it possible to overcome some of the shortcomings associated with the type of analysis and indicators used in this report.

Financial Indicator Scores

For the rankings on each financial indicator, for each year each country is ranked relative to the others, with 1 representing the lowest ranking and 5 the highest. The lowest score of 1 is also given for any year for which no data are available (indicated in the data tables in appendix 1, by N/A). Except in instances in which no data are available for more than one country or in which more than one country reports the same ratio, each country receives a different score.

These scores are aggregated across the years to arrive at the score for the six-year period on each indicator—and the scores for the indicators within a category are added to arrive at the aggregate score for that category (access to finance, performance and efficiency, financial stability, capital market development, or market concentration and competitiveness). This aggregate score is then divided by the maximum "possible" total score for the category. That maximum score is 180, derived by multiplying the number of indicators in the category (6) by the highest possible score (5), then multiplying that by the number of years (6). Dividing the aggregate score by the maximum possible total score of 180 gives the composite score for each category. The composite scores range from zero to one. See table 7.1 for the composite scores received by the countries under each category. Also, the ranking of countries under each category is given in table 3.1.

Corporate Governance Scores

For corporate governance, each country is individually ranked on the two major sections of each of the four topics on a scale from 1 (not observed) to 5 (largely observed), based on the responses to the questionnaire (see appendix 3.A), the country's corporate governance guidelines, and various reports. Here again a score of 1 is given if no data are available. Because the countries are not ranked comparatively, more than one country can receive the same score in a category.

Table 7.1 Composite Scores on the Getting Finance Indicators for South Asian Countries

	Indicator	Bangladesh	India	Nepal	Pakistan	Sri Lanka
	Access to finance					
1	Demographic branch penetration (branches per 100,000 people)	15	25	6	15	29
2	Demographic ATM penetration (ATMs per 100,000 people)	17	12	13	16	30
3	Deposit accounts per 1,000 people	18	24	6	12	30
4	Loan accounts per 1,000 people	21	21	7	11	30
5	Geographic branch penetration (branches per 1,000 km^2)	30	24	6	12	18
6	Geographic ATM penetration (ATMs per 1,000 km^2)	22	12	12	12	30
	Total points	123	118	50	78	167
	Composite score (total points/180)	0.68	0.66	0.28	0.43	0.93
	Performance and efficiency					
1	Return on equity	18	16	6	27	23
2	Return on assets	12	20	14	25	20
3	Staff cost ratio	15	17	6	23	29
4	Operating cost ratio	6	21	30	21	12
5	Net interest margin	8	19	10	25	28
6	Recurring earning power	17	21	10	23	20
	Total points	76	114	76	144	132
	Composite score (total points/180)	0.42	0.63	0.42	0.80	0.73
	Financial stability					
1	Capital adequacy ratio	12	27	6	25	20
2	Leverage ratio	14	25	6	24	21
3	Gross nonperforming loans ratio	11	30	7	23	19
4	Provisions to nonperforming loans ratio	10	20	8	30	22
5	Liquid assets ratio	17	29	6	25	13
6	Liquid assets to liabilities ratio	24	30	10	18	8
	Total points	88	161	43	145	103
	Composite score (total points/180)	0.49	0.89	0.24	0.81	0.57
	Capital market development					
1	Domestic bond market to equity market capitalization	7	30	20	22	11
2	Domestic public bonds outstanding to GDP	10	26	8	25	21
3	Ratio of trading value of top 10 stocks to total trading value	19	18	7	30	16
4	Stock market capitalization to GDP	6	30	14	21	19
5	Market liquidity: Ratio of stock trading value to GDP	19	30	12	7	23
6	Stock market turnover ratio	21	29	6	19	15
	Total points	82	163	67	124	105
	Composite score (total points/180)	0.46	0.91	0.37	0.69	0.58

(Table continues on next page)

Table 7.1 Composite Scores on the Getting Finance Indicators for South Asian Countries *(continued)*

	Indicator	Bangladesh	India	Nepal	Pakistan	Sri Lanka
	Market concentration and competition					
1	Herfindahl-Hirschman index (HHI)	26	28	11	18	7
2	K-bank concentration ratio (K=3) – assets	24	30	12	18	6
3	K-bank concentration ratios (K=3) – deposits	24	30	17	13	6
4	K-bank concentration ratios (K=3) – loans	23	29	17	15	6
5	Private credit extended by banks to GDP	20	17	16	8	29
6	Commercial Banking assets to GDP	11	26	28	7	18
	Total points	128	160	101	79	72
	Composite score (total points/180)	0.71	0.89	0.56	0.44	0.40
	Corporate governance					
1	Ownership structure and influence of external stakeholders					
	1.1 Identification of substantial majority holders	3	4	3	4	4
	1.2 Indirect and beneficial ownership	1	4	1	4	2
2	Investor rights					
	2.1 Shareholder meetings and voting procedures	4	5	4	5	3
	2.2 Basic ownership rights	3	3	3	3	2
3	Transparency and disclosure					
	3.1 Adherence to internationally accepted accounting standards	4	4	4	5	5
	3.2 Independent internal and external auditors and audit committee	3	4	3	4	4
4	Board structure and effectiveness					
	4.1 Role and effectiveness	5	4	4	5	5
	4.2 Compensation	2	4	5	4	2
	Total points	26	32	26	34	27
	Composite score (total points/40)	0.64	0.80	0.65	0.84	0.67

Source: Calculations based on appendixes 1 and 3. Underlying data from South Asian Central Banks, SECs and Boards, and stock exchanges; Indian Banks' Association 2006a, and 2006b, and 2006c; Reserve Bank of India 2006a, 2006b, 2006c, and 2007.

With four topics and two major sections in each, and with the highest possible score being 5, the maximum "possible" score on corporate governance is 40. The information on corporate governance gathered in the 2005 study was revised in 2006; however, no significant changes are observed. Because comparable data are not available, the scores cannot be aggregated over the six-year period. Therefore, the total scores of 2006 are simply divided by the maximum possible score to arrive at the composite score for corporate governance. See table 7.1 for the composite scores received by the countries. Also, the ranking of countries under the category is given in table 3.1.

Financial Soundness Ranking

To ease comparison and interpretation, the composite scores range from 0 to 1. The composite scores for each of the six categories of indicators are then averaged for each country. These simple averages are then arranged from the highest to the lowest to identify the overall financial soundness ranking for each country (see table 3.1 for the overall ranking).

8

Major Policy Developments in the Prudential Regulations of South Asia, 2005–06

Bangladesh

Implementation of the New Capital Adequacy Framework (Basel II) in Bangladesh

Bangladesh adopted the 1988 Basel I accord in 1988, which required banks to maintain a minimum capital ratio of not less than 8 percent of the risk-weighted assets. Effective June 2003, all banks operating in Bangladesh had to maintain a minimum capital adequacy ratio (CAR) of not less than 9 percent of their risk-weighted assets with at least 4.5 percent in core capital (Tier I capital). In keeping with international practices, Bangladesh Bank (BB) has decided in principle to adopt the Basel II. Given the complexities involved, however, it has decided on a consultative approach. BB has decided to adopt a mix of Standardized and Foundation Internal Rating-Based (IRB) approaches to guide the minimum capital requirement. To study and guide the banking sector through this process, BB has established the following: a high-level steering committee with representations from the BB, banking industry, and accounting profession; and a mid-level coordination committee to study the risk-based grouping and a Basel II implementation cell. Once the process is identified and realistic timeframes are drawn, it is expected that the implementation of the new accord will take place in 2009. At present, BB is reviewing the existing capacities of the banking sector to undertake more stringent risk management processes that are required. BB is taking steps in this direction by issuing guidelines on managing core risks in banks.

Prudential Regulations

Prudential guidelines issued by Bangladesh Bank in 2005–06 include the following:

2005

- **February:** Accounting of the interest of classified loans: A continuous credit, a demand loan, or a term loan that will remain overdue for a period of 90 days or more will be put into the "Special Mention Account," and interest accrued on such loan will be credited to the Interest Suspense Account instead of crediting the same to the Income Account.

- **April:** In the circular in which qualitative judgment is used as the basis for loan classification, it is stated that if the inspection team of BB classifies any loan, the loan can be declassified with the approval of the board of directors of the bank. However, before placing such a case before the board, the chief executive officer (CEO) and branch manager shall certify that the conditions for declassification have been fulfilled.
- **April:** BB issued a circular revising the policy on single-borrower exposure. Among other things, it has been decided to reduce the single-borrower exposure limit from 50 percent to 35 percent. The total outstanding financing facilities by a bank to any single person or enterprise or organization of a group shall not, at any point in time, exceed 35 percent of the bank's total capital subject to the condition that the maximum outstanding against fund-based financing facilities (funded facilities) does not exceed 15 percent of the total capital. Under the same guidelines, nonfunded credit facilities (for example, a letter of credit or guarantee) can be provided to a single large borrower. But under no circumstances shall the total amount of the funded and nonfunded credit facilities exceed 35 percent of a bank's total capital.
- **April:** For the loans that have already been disbursed with the approval of BB, and that have exceeded the limit as stipulated, banks shall take necessary steps to bring down the loan amount within the specified limit. To meet this condition, banks may, if necessary, arrange partaking with other banks. However, for continuous loans, the limit has to be brought down per Section 02 by December 2005. December 2006 is the deadline for term loans.
- **July:** Banks and financial institutions (FIs) have been instructed to formulate and implement specific programs for performing Know-Your-Customer (KYC) procedures per the specified format supplied by the Anti-Money Laundering Department of BB keeping in line with the Guidance Notes on Prevention of Money Laundering.
- **August:** Some amendments have been made to the policy on loan classification and provisioning. Per the amendments, banks will be required to make General Provision at 5 percent on the outstanding amount of loans kept in the Special Mention Account (SMA) after netting off the amount of Interest Suspense and the status of the SMA loan should be reported to the Credit Information Bureau (CIB) of BB. This instruction will be effective from December 31, 2005.
- **October:** An information technology (IT) guideline of minimum security standards for scheduled banks and FIs has been prepared and forwarded to the banks on CD-ROM. Banks are advised to follow the guideline in their IT area and implement all the security standards by May 15, 2006.
- **December:** With the aim to fully implement a Risk Grading System, an Integrated Credit Risk Grading Manual has been developed and forwarded to the banks on CD-ROM. Banks are advised to implement Credit Risk Grading (as described in the manual) by March 31, 2006, for all exposures (irrespective of amount) other than those covered under Consumer and Small Enterprises Financing Prudential Guidelines and those under the Short-Term Agricultural and Micro-Credit. Banks are also advised to submit a compliance report by

April 15, 2006, to the effect that the Credit Risk Grading has been put in place. The Risk Grading Matrix provided in the manual will be the minimum standard of risk rating and banks may adopt and adapt more sophisticated risk grades in line with the size and complexity of their business. Arrangement will be made by BB, if necessary, to train trainers of the banks in this regard. The BB's on-site inspection teams will monitor the progress of implementation of the manual and guideline during routine inspection.

2006

- **February/March:** Policy for rescheduling of loans has been reviewed and it has been decided that borrowers whose credit facility has been rescheduled will get a new loan facility subject to the fulfillment of the following conditions:
  - The defaulting borrower who has an interest waiver must settle at least 15 percent of the compromise amount (excluding the down payment on rescheduling per the present guidelines) to avail of any further credit facility from any bank. In case of borrowing from other banks, the same rule will be applicable (that is, the borrower will have to submit a no objection certificate [NOC] from the rescheduled bank).
  - Export borrowers may be granted further credit facility (after being identified as not a willful defaulter), if required, subject to at least 7.5 percent of the compromise amount (excluding the down payment on rescheduling as per present guidelines) being paid.
  - Prior approval of BB shall have to be obtained if the loan is related to the director or ex-directors of a Bank Company.
  - Information on the loan accounts rescheduled shall be reported to the CIB of Bangladesh Bank.
  - If any such issue is already there (such fresh facility has already been allowed after allowing for a waiver), the same will not fall under purview of this circular.
- **June:** To strengthen credit discipline and bring classification policy in line with international standards, BB has revised its prudential norms for loan classification and provisioning. As part of the process, a Master Circular was issued on June 5, 2006, to enable the banks to have all existing instructions on the subject at one place. This circular also includes a few new instructions as well as new formats for loan classification and provisioning. More concentration has been given on Short-term Micro-Credit by enhancing its limit from Tk 10,000 to Tk 25,000. Banks with Offshore Banking Units (OBUs) have been brought under the purview of loan classification and provisioning to aid transparency of OBU transactions of EPZ (Export Processing Zone) enterprises and report to the Banking Regulation and Policy Department (BRPD) and the CIB for cross-information purposes.

Other Policy Developments

As part of the restructuring of the nationalized commercial banks (NCBs), the Rupali Bank is under the process of being sold to a foreign buyer.

In March 2007, BB made it mandatory for all banks to get credit rated by a credit rating agency. Banks are advised to have credit ratings in all relevant areas as well as the bank management.

India

Implementation of the New Capital Adequacy Framework (Basel II) in India

The Reserve Bank of India (RBI) released draft guidelines on February 14, 2005, for implementation of Basel II in India. According to the draft guidelines, banks are required to adopt a standardized approach for credit risk and a basic indicator approach for operational risk. Banks would need the approval of RBI for migration to advanced approaches of risk measurement. The RBI is committed to the adoption of Basel II by the banks and had earlier indicated March 31, 2007, as the intended date for adoption by all commercial banks. Taking into account the state of preparedness of the banking system, however, banks were given more time to establish appropriate systems to ensure full compliance with Basel II. Foreign banks operating in India and Indian banks having presence outside India were to migrate to the standardized approach for credit risk and the basic indicator approach for operational risk under Basel II with effect from March 31, 2008. All other scheduled commercial banks are encouraged to migrate to these approaches under Basel II, however, not later than March 31, 2009. The Steering Committee of the banks would continue to interact with banks and the RBI, and guide the smooth implementation of Basel II. The banks are required to follow the Standardized Approach for credit risk and the Basic Indicator approach for operational risk.

Under Basel II, the capital requirements are more sensitive to the level of credit risk; they are also applicable to operational risks. Thus, banks would need to raise additional capital for Basel II requirements, as well as to support the expansion of their balance sheets. To enable smooth transition to Basel II and to provide banks in India additional options for raising capital funds, banks were advised in January 2006 that they could augment their capital funds by issue of the following instruments: (1) innovative perpetual debt instruments (IPDI) eligible for inclusion as Tier I capital; (2) debt capital instruments eligible for inclusion as upper Tier II capital; (3) perpetual noncumulative preference shares eligible for inclusion as Tier I capital; and (4) redeemable cumulative preference shares eligible for inclusion as Tier II capital.

To move the banks to conform to Basel norms for explicit charge for market risk, banks were advised, in January 2002, to build up Investment Fluctuation Reserve (IFR) to a minimum of 5 percent of investment in Held for Trading (HFT) and Available for Sale (AFS) categories in the investment portfolio. Later, in 2004, banks were advised to maintain capital charge for market risk in a phased manner over a two-year period ended March 31, 2006. Banks were allowed to treat the entire balance held in IFR as Tier I capital, provided they maintained a capital of at least 9 percent of the risk-weighted assets for both credit and capital charge for market risk.

Prudential Regulations

The following are among the prudential guidelines issued by the Reserve Bank of India in 2005–06:

2005

- **February:** Detailed prudential guidelines were issued by the RBI to banks on capital adequacy for implementation of the new capital adequacy framework under Basel II. To maintain consistency and harmony with international standards, banks were advised to adopt the Standardized Approach for credit risk and the Basic Indicator Approach effective from April 2006. Under the new approach for operational risk framework, banks adopting the Standardized Approach would use the ratings assigned only by those credit rating agencies that are identified by the RBI. Banks were also required to focus on formalizing and operationalizing their internal Capital Adequacy Assessment Process (CAAP), which would serve as a useful benchmark while undertaking a parallel run beginning April 2006.

- **March:** Draft guidelines on the implementation of the new capital adequacy framework were issued by the RBI for comments on management of operational risk.
- **April:** Banks were advised by the RBI to implement a Business Continuity Plan, including a robust information risk management system within a fixed timeframe.
- **April:** Banks with capital adequacy of 9 percent for both credit risk and market risk for both AFS and HFT may treat the balance in the IFR in excess of 5 percent as part of Tier I capital.
- **April:** A minimum framework was outlined, in respect of disclosures by FIs on their risk exposures in derivatives, to provide a clear picture of their exposure to risks in derivatives, risk management systems, objectives, and policies.
- **May:** Detailed guidelines were issued for merger and amalgamation of private sector banks, laying down the process of merger proposal, determination of swap ratios, disclosures, the stages at which the board will get involved in the merger process, and norms for buying and selling shares by the promoters before and during the process of merger.
- **June:** Banks were advised to have a board-mandated policy in respect of their real estate exposure covering exposure limits, collaterals to be considered, margins to be kept, sanctioning authority and level, and sector to be financed. Banks were directed to report their real estate exposure under certain heads and disclose their gross exposure to the real estate sector and provide details of the breakup in their annual report.
- **July:** The risk weight for credit risk on capital market and commercial real estate exposure increased from 100 percent to 125 percent.
- **July:** Banks were permitted to offer Internet-banking services without the prior approval of the RBI but subject to fulfillment of certain conditions.
- **October:** Banks that have maintained capital of at least 9 percent of the risk-weighted assets for both credit risks and market risks for both AFS and HFT categories as on March 31, 2006, were permitted to treat the entire balance in the IFR as Tier I capital. For this purpose, banks may transfer the entire balance in the IFR below the line in the Profit and Loss Appropriation Account to Statutory Reserve, General Reserve, or balance of the Profit and Loss Account.
- **October:** Revised guidance note on management of operational risk issued by the RBI to banks. The design of a risk management framework should be oriented toward a bank's own requirements, and dictated by the size and complexity of business, risk philosophy, market perception, and the expected level of capital. The risk management systems in the bank should be adaptable to change in business, size, market dynamics, and introduction of innovative products.

- **November:** The general provisioning requirement for standard advances, with the exception of direct advances to agricultural and the small and medium enterprise (SME) sectors, is increased to 0.40 percent from 0.25 percent.
- **November:** With a view toward achieving the objective of greater financial inclusion, all banks were advised to initiate steps within one month, to make available a basic banking no-frills account either with nil or low minimum balances and to report to the RBI on a quarterly basis. Banks were advised to give wide publicity, including on their Web sites, to the facility of such no-frills account, indicating the charges in a transparent manner.
- **November:** Banks were advised to have a well-documented policy and a Fair Practices Code for credit card operations. Guidelines include norms relating to issue of cards; interest rate and other charges; wrongful billing; use of direct selling agents (DSAs), direct marketing agents (DMAs), and other agents; protection of customer rights; right to privacy; customer confidentiality; fair practices in debt collection; redress of grievances; internal control and monitoring system; and right to impose penalty.

2006

- **January:** Banks were advised to augment their capital funds by issue of the following additional instruments:
  - IPDI eligible for inclusion as Tier I capital
  - Debt capital instruments eligible for inclusion as upper Tier II capital
  - Perpetual noncumulative preference shares eligible for inclusion as Tier I capital
  - Redeemable cumulative preference shares eligible for inclusion as Tier II capital
- **February:** The Union Budget, 2006–07, proposed the following measures:
  - Increase in foreign institutional investor (FII) investment limit in the government securities to US$2 billion from US$1.75 billion
  - Increase in FII investment limit in corporate debt to US$1.5 billion from US$0.5 billion
  - Increase in ceiling on aggregate investment by mutual funds in overseas instruments to US$2 billion from US$1 billion and removal of requirement of 10 percent reciprocal share holding
  - Limited number of qualified Indian Mutual Funds (MFs) allowed to invest, cumulatively, up to US$1 billion in overseas exchange traded funds
  - Steps to create a single, unified exchange-traded market for corporate bonds
  - An investor protection fund under the aegis of the Securities and Exchange Board of India (SEBI)
- **March:** SEBI amended the SEBI Disclosure and Investment Protection Guidelines, 2000, with respect to rationalization of disclosure requirements, abridged letter of offer, disclosure of issue price, further issue of shares, and lock-in provisions for listed companies making rights or public issue.
- **April:** SEBI amended the SEBI Discloser and Investment Protection Guidelines, 2000, to permit unlisted companies to opt for grading of initial public offerings (IPOs) from credit rating agencies and to ensure disclosure of all grades, including unaccepted grades.

- **May:** The risk weight on exposure of banks to commercial real estate increased to 150 percent from 125 percent. Furthermore, total exposure of banks to venture capital funds will form a part of its capital market exposure and, henceforth, a higher risk weight of 150 percent will be assigned to these exposures.
- **May:** The general provisioning requirement for banks on standard advances in specific sectors (that is, personal loans, loans and advances qualifying as capital market exposures, residential housing loans beyond Rs 20 lakh, and commercial real estate loans) increased to 1 percent from the present level of 0.40 percent.
- **May:** Banks (excluding Regional Rural Banks [RRBs]) were advised to disclose in the Notes on Account the information providing details of the breakup of provisions and contingencies shown under the head Expenditure in Profit and Loss Account as follows: (1) provisions for depreciation on investment; (2) provision toward nonperforming assets (NPAs); (3) provision toward standard asset; (4) provision made toward income tax; and (5) other provision and contingencies (with details).

Other Policy Developments

In February 2005, the RBI laid down a comprehensive policy framework for ownership and governance in private sector banks. The broad principles underlying the framework were to ensure that ultimate ownership and control of commercial banks is well-diversified, key shareholders and directors and CEO pass the "fit-and-proper" test (FPT), and the board observes sound corporate governance principles.

In March 2005, the RBI set up the Board for Regulation and Supervision of Payment and Settlement Systems (BPSS), as a committee of the Central Board of the Reserve Bank. BPSS is the apex body for giving policy direction in the area of payment and settlement systems.

At present, foreign banks operate in India through only one of the three channels: branches, wholly owned subsidiaries (WOS), or a subsidiary with an aggregate foreign investment up to 74 percent. With a view of delineating the direction and pace of the reform process in the area of foreign ownership in domestic banks, in February 2005, the RBI laid down a road map for the presence of foreign banks in India in two phases. During the first phase, covering the period from 2005 to 2009, foreign banks, existing and new, may be permitted to open branches in excess of the World Trade Organization (WTO) commitment of 12 branches in a year. The existing and new foreign banks may choose either the branch or WOS route. The RBI may prescribe market access and national treatment limitation consistent with WTO and international practices. During this phase, permission for acquisition of shareholdings in Indian private sector banks by eligible foreign banks will be limited to banks identified by the RBI for restructuring.

In the second phase, commencing April 2009, RBI will address the issues of removing limitations on the operations of the WOS and according them treatment on par with domestic banks. This phase will begin after reviewing the experience in Phase I and after due consultations with all stakeholders in the banking sector.

The RBI has been issuing instructions and guidance notes on various risks for the benefit of the banks and to sensitize the banks in regard to the growing need for establishing proper risk management systems. RBI issued a set of instructions to banks on June 29, 2005, for risk management of exposures arising from advance against real estate. In terms of these guidelines, banks must have a board-mandated policy in respect of their real estate exposure and the policy must set limits, establish a risk management system, monitor the exposure to this sensitive sector, and disclose the exposure in their annual report.

In November 2005, as a major step toward setting up and operating a national-level payment system, the National Electronic Fund Transfer (NEFT) was operationalized.

The Banking Companies (Acquisition and Transfer of Undertakings) and Financial Institutions Laws (Amendment) Act, 2005, mainly seeks to amend the Banking Companies (Acquisition and Transfer of Undertakings) Act, 1970, and the Banking Companies (Acquisition and Transfer of Undertakings) Act, 1980.

The implementation of a Cheque Truncation System (CTS) basis in the national capital region of Delhi was introduced as a pilot project at the end of December 2006. The CTS would be implemented in the rest of the country phase by phase.

The Reserve Bank of India Act, 1934, was amended by the Parliament in 2006. This amendment, among other things, has empowered the RBI to determine the Cash Reserve Requirement (CRR) without any ceiling or floor rate.

The RBI had issued draft guidelines on securitizations of standard assets in April 2005. Based on the feedback received from all stakeholders, the final guidelines on securitizations of standard assets were issued on February 1, 2006.

The Government Securities Act, 2006, proposes to consolidate and amend the law relating to issuance and management of government securities by the RBI.

The Payments and Settlements Bill, 2006, was introduced in the Lok Sabha on July 25, 2006. The bill seeks to designate the RBI as the authority to regulate payment and settlement systems.

Nepal

Implementation of the New Capital Adequacy Framework (Basel II) in Nepal

To fall in line with the international best practices and to promote a healthy and sound financial market, Nepal Rastra Bank (NRB) is moving toward the adoption of Basel II. The complexity and sophistication of the Nepalese financial market does not warrant advanced approaches like the IRB Approach or the Standardized Approach. Therefore, NRB intends to start with the Simplified Standardized Approach for credit risk, Basic Indicator Approach for operational risk, and Net Open Exchange Model for market risk.

To facilitate progressing toward implementation of the accord, NRB has set up a "New Capital Accord Implementation Preparatory Committee" and a working-level committee called the Accord Implementation Group (AIG). The AIG consists of officers from the NRB as well as the banking sector. AIG has examined the provisions under Basel II and has conducted a Quantitative Impact Study (QIS) of eight banks based on the assumptions and approach finalized. The impact study indicated a reduction in the risk-weighted exposures in the credit risk of the banks. AIG plans to carry out a second QIS to rationalize the findings. The AIG also prepared a draft capital adequacy framework with detailed guidelines on each of the three pillars, based on the proposed approach, which has been circulated among the stakeholders for review. It is expected that this capital framework will come into effect in 2008.

Prudential Regulations

Prudential guidelines issued by NRB in 2004–05 include the following (2006 guidelines are not available):

2004

- **July:** The rates for refinancing facilities provided by NRB to banks and FIs have been fixed as follows: all previous procedural arrangements relating to refinancing facilities remain unchanged.
    - Rate of Refinance provided under Sick Industries Rehabilitation Program: 1.5 percent
    - Rate of Refinance to Rural Development Banks and Export Credit and Agriculture Credit in local currency: 3 percent
    - All other arrangements except those mentioned in above remain unchanged

  Furthermore, the commercial banks, at the time of making a request for refinance under the Sick Industries Rehabilitation Program, shall provide certification as to the fulfillment of criteria set by the Sick Industries Rehabilitation Main Committee and the rate of interest charged to the borrower be fixed at 4.5 percent.
- **July:** With reference to loan-loss provision to be created for rescheduled and restructured accounts for 2003–04, banks and financial institutions will have to create a loan-loss provision of 1 percent as applicable to the Pass Loans category on the accounts that are restructured or rescheduled with the recovery of all due interests. But the banks and financial institutions taking advantage of this facility shall not be allowed to distribute dividends to the shareholders from the profits arising out of this waiver.
- **July:** In accordance with the provisions of the Monetary Policy, the rate of cash reserve ratio to be maintained by the banks has been revised to 5 percent for 2004–05. All the procedural aspects per the earlier directive of NRB shall remain in place.
- **July:** The interest rate for the refinance loan to be provided to banks and financial institutions has been revised. The new interest rate for the Sick Industries Rehabilitation Program will be 1.50 percent, while the rate for the refinance loan to be provided to rural development banks and to refinance export and agricultural loans to be provided in local currency shall be 3 percent.
- **July:** The CAR to be maintained by the banks and financial institutions for 2004–05 was 12 percent. Because of the prevailing difficult circumstances, the CAR for 2004–05 has been reduced to 11 percent.
- **July:** Banks and FIs were required to divest their investment in shares of other banks and financial institutions by mid-July 2004. In this regard, the investment in shares that were not divested by mid-July 2004 and whose divestment is not restricted by statute shall require a provision of 100 percent in 2004–05.
- **August:** The earlier provision requiring preapproval from NRB to conduct banking transaction in the public holidays and beyond the normal banking hours has been repealed. The banks can now conduct such kind of banking transactions under pre-intimation to NRB.

2005

- **March:** Banks and FIs have been given the minimum guidelines to be incorporated in the formulation of the loan write-off bylaw of the respective banks. Some of the major guidelines are as follows:
  - Banks should develop criteria to identify the loans that are unrecoverable and should formulate the bylaw for the write-off of these accounts with the approval of the board.
  - Banks may write off loans that fall under the loan-loss category per NRB directives with 100 percent loan-loss provision. However, all loans with past dues of more than five years and with 100 percent provision should be compulsorily written off.
  - The borrower and other related parties to the loan must be included on the blacklist of the Credit Information Center.
  - Banks should maintain separate and updated information in relation to the loans written off.
  - Banks should establish a separate unit for the recovery of written-off loans and should continue their efforts for the recovery of such written-off loans.
  - Banks should disclose the details of the loans written off during the year in its annual accounts. They should also submit the details of such loans to the Bank Supervision Department and Credit Information Center within 15 days from the date of fiscal year-end.
- **April:** The procedure for calculation of the cash reserve ratio as defined by the circular of July 28, 2003, has been amended. The new methodology will be based on seven days a week and the basis will be the average weekly deposit of four weeks before that date. The average weekly deposit and the cash reserve will be calculated as the sum of the deposits of the bank and their balance with NRB for the week (Sunday to Saturday) and divided by the number of days, independently. Banks are now required to submit the required information within a fortnight from the end of the week. All other procedural aspects in relation to CRR calculation and penalties remain the same.
- **May:** In case of restructure and reschedule of loans of industries, recommended by the Sick Industries Interim Investigation and Recommendation Committee of the Ministry of Industry, Commerce, and Supply, with the recovery of minimum 12 percent of interest and completion of other formalities, banks will have to create a provision of only 25 percent. But, where the interest recovery has been less than 12 percent, banks will have to create provisions per the existing regulation.
- **May:** Banks should arrange to disclose the permanent account number (PAN) of individuals/firms/companies with registration in the value added tax (VAT), in the credit application.
- **May:** The rate of the refinance for export loans funded in foreign currency was revised to 3.25 percent with effect from May 30, 2005, with all the procedural aspects and the conditions remaining the same.
- **May:** The previous directive on blacklisting issued on June 4, 2004, was retracted and a new one was issued. The directive has made the credit information, in respect of loans and advances above a sum of NRs 2.5 million, mandatory. The new directive is more stringent and makes a distinction between

willful and nonwillful defaulters. This directive includes provisions to blacklist the valuator and to recommend for the action against the Chartered Accountants who certify the false documents of the borrowers. The directive includes provisions to recommend for the seizure of passports of blacklisted borrowers. The new directive covers various areas, including procedures to be followed for inclusion in the blacklist; restrictions on the sanction of loans and facilities; conditions for inclusion in the blacklist; identification of individuals, firms, companies, and other organized institutions qualifying for the blacklist; and conditions in which names can be taken off the blacklist.

- **July:** In the beginning of 2005–06 (Nepali FY 2062–63), all circulars separately issued by NRB for commercial banks, development banks, finance companies and microcredit banks were replaced by a unified directive and were issued by the NRB's Banks and Financial Regulations Department via Bai. Bi. Ni. Bi. 148/1/2062/63/Dated: 2062.4.3/July 18, 2005. These directives came into effect on July 16, 2005.
- **August:** All finance companies licensed by NRB (C category licensed FIs) may, by obtaining a license from the Public Debt Department of NRB, carry out the function of "buying and selling or accepting the bonds issued by His Majesty's Government (HMG) or Nepal Rastra Bank."
- **August:** The bank rate and refinance rate have been fixed as follows: other conditions and procedural arrangements with respect to bank rate and refinance rate facilities to be provided to the bank and FIs by this bank remain unchanged.
  - The existing bank rate of 5.5 percent has been increased to 6 percent
  - The existing refinance rate of 3 percent for export credit and agriculture credit to be availed in local currency has been increased to 3.5 percent
  - Other than the above, all other arrangements remain unchanged
- **August:** The loans provided by any commercial banks, currently under the coordination of the Bank of Kathmandu to the workers going for foreign employment under the HMG Youth Self-Employment and Employment Training Program, as well as the loans extended by any licensed FIs by obtaining loans from the commercial banks for the purpose of providing foreign employment loans, will be considered for inclusion under the Deprived Sector Loans of the respective commercial banks.
- **September:** Additional actions against willful defaulters should be implemented per the provisions of the decision of HMG (Council of Ministers) regarding actions to be initiated against the willful defaulters of banks and FIs.
- **October:** Existing clause 2 of the Consolidated Directives issued by NRB to the banks and FIs concerning the branches and offices is replaced by the following: "The A, B, and C class licensed institutions, fulfilling the minimum paid-up capital as prescribed by Nepal Rastra Bank, shall apply for opening of a branch office within the approved working area with a business plan to Bank and Financial Institutions Regulations Department of NRB."

Other Policy Developments

NRB has continued to review the relevant legislations and regulations in 2005–06 to develop the regulatory framework that meets international standards and resolves the issues of the banking industry. To improve the financial sector legislative framework, some new acts, namely the Bank and Financial Institution Act, 2006; Insolvency Act, 2006; Secured Transaction Act, 2006; and Company Act, 2006, were enacted. Money Laundering Control and Deposit and Credit Guarantee Acts are to follow.

Pakistan

Implementation of the New Capital Adequacy Framework (Basel II) in Pakistan

After conducting several Quantity Impact Studies and theoretical as well as empirical studies in consultation with the industry, the State Bank of Pakistan (SBP) issued a road map in March 2005 outlining the implementation process of Basel II. In terms of these guidelines, banks would initially adopt the simplified Standardized Approach and go on a parallel run for one and half years starting from July 2006. In pursuance of the road map, banks submitted their individual plans mentioning the specific approach (Standardized or IRB) they intend to adopt and their internal arrangements for its implementation. The majority of the banks expressed their intention to first adopt a comparatively simple Standardized Approach, keeping in view the requirement of more sophisticated systems for the advanced approaches. Banks that decide to go for the IRB Approach will first have to seek the approval of SBP. A comprehensive review exercise on the part of SBP culminated in a more specific bank-wise internal plan. To streamline the implementation process and to ensure better coordination, each bank nominated its respective coordinators as the head of the group level along with formulation of Basel II units.

Under the Standardized Approach, the capital requirement against credit risk would be determined based on a risk profile assessment by rating agencies recognized by regulators as External Credit Assessment Institutions (ECAIs). To ensure transparency in the recognition process, the eligibility criteria for recognition of ECAIs was devised in consultation with all stakeholders based on broad guidelines described in Basel II. Scrutiny resulted in granting ECAIs status to two rating agencies (The Pakistan Credit Rating Agency [PACRA] and JCR-VIS Credit Rating Co. Ltd.) as both were meeting the minimum requirements laid out in the criteria. The recognition implies that the banks would use ECAI's risk assessment rating of its portfolio to calculate the capital requirement under Basel II. In this regard, SBP issued detailed Eligibility Criteria for Recognition of ECAIs in July 2005. Banks are required to consider the credit ratings assigned by the SBP-recognized ECAIs only. Mapping of ratings with the appropriate risk weights was finalized in consultation with recognized ECAIs. Detailed instructions for adoption of various approaches to calculate the capital adequacy requirements for credit, market, and operational risk were issued on June 27, 2006. Capital reporting formats under Basel II instructions were prescribed in March 2007. These formats primarily cover capital calculation under Standardized Approaches for credit and market risk and Basic Indicator and Standardized Approaches for operational risk.

The gap between previously adopted disclosure practices and new requirements under the market discipline (Pillar III) of Basel II were identified and detailed requirements for public disclosure were issued in February 2006. These instructions provide for the disclosures to be made by the banks under the different approaches of the Basel II that each adopts. A detailed survey to assess the level of preparedness of the banks regarding Basel II implementation was conducted in February 2007. This survey was in identifying and assessing the issues prevalent in the banking industry at large. Implementation of Basel II poses considerable challenges for the banking system in Pakistan. To meet the gigantic task, the banks and SBP are engaged in capacity building in terms of upgrading their IT systems and enhancing expertise of the human resource base. SBP conducted a number of seminars and workshops on new capital accord and risk management techniques for internal and external stakeholders and remained engaged in improving its IT systems to get extensive regulatory reporting in line with the maximum disclosure requirements under Basel II.

SBP envisaged adopting different approaches under Basel II in the following manner:
- Standardized Approach for credit risk and Basic Indicator and Standardized Approach for operational risk from January 1, 2008
- IRB Approach from January 1, 2010, with banks and development finance institutions (DFIs) permitted to implement it sooner if the State Bank approves their internal risk management systems

Banks and DFIs were required to adopt a parallel run of one and a half years for the Standardized Approach starting July 1, 2006, and two years for IRB Approach starting January 1, 2008.

Prudential Regulations

Among the prudential guidelines issued by the SBP in 2005–06 are the following.

2005
- **January:** Establishment of subsidiaries or brokerage companies by banks and DFIs (BPD Circular 1).
- **March:** Prudential regulations for corporate and commercial banking (BPD Circular 8).
- **March:** Relaxation of the regulatory framework for housing finance (BPD Circular 10).
- **March:** Placement of funds under Fe-25 deposits (BPD Circular 9).
- **April:** Establishment of subsidiaries or brokerage companies by banks and DFIs (BPD Circular 13).
- **April:** Prudential regulations for corporate and commercial banking (BPD Circular 14).
- **April:** Rates of return on deposits (BPD Circular 16).
- **May:** Prudential regulations (BPD Circular 19).
- **July:** Guidelines for infrastructure project financing (BPD Circular 23).
- **September:** Prudential regulations (BPD Circular 25).
- **October:** Classification of dormant or inoperative accounts (BPD Circular 26).
- **October:** Amendment of Regulation M-1 on prudential regulations for corporate and commercial banking (BPD Circular 29).

- **October:** Withdrawal of redundant or old instructions (BPD Circular 28).
- **October:** Prudential regulations for agricultural financing (BPD Circular 27).
- **November:** Guidelines for Higher Education Financing Scheme (BPD Circular 31).
- **November:** Introduction of basic banking account (BPD Circular 30).

2006

- **January:** To encourage transparency and promote consistency in the market-based pricing of loans, Banks and DFIs were directed to use Karachi Inter-bank Offered Rate (KIBOR) as a benchmark for determining the pricing of all rupee corporate and commercial bank lending. It has been observed that some banks are using longer-tenor benchmark rates for shorter-tenor loans. This practice is not correct. It is, therefore, clarified that (1) for fixed-rate time loans, the tenor of the benchmark rate should be the same as the tenor of the fixed loan; (2) for tenors exceeding three years and not covered by KIBOR, banks are advised to use appropriate benchmarks such as secondary market yields on the relevant tenor of Pakistan Investment Bonds; and (3) for floating-rate time loans, the tenor of the benchmark rate should be the same as of repricing tenor set for the floating-rate loan.
- **May:** Banks and DFIs, among other things, were required to classify their existing investment portfolio into HFT, AFS, and Held-to-Maturity categories by September 30, 2004. It has been observed that some of the banks and DFIs have moved their risky portfolio to the Held-to-Maturity category to avoid booking a revaluation deficit and have categorized their good portfolio in the HFT and AFS categories. At the same time, they are using Held-to-Maturity securities to manage liquidity by entering into repossession transactions in the interbank market. To discourage such practices, SBP has decided that the securities classified as Held-to-Maturity by the banks and DFIs should neither be sold nor used for entering into repossession transactions in the interbank market or borrowing under the SBP repossession facility or discount window with effect from July 1, 2006. However, the banks and DFIs are allowed a one-time reclassification of their securities. This process of reclassification should be completed by June 15, 2006. The banks and DFIs shall also ensure that the securities acquired or purchased after June 15, 2006, shall, at the time of their acquisition or purchase, be categorized into any of the three categories and the decision taken to that effect shall be recorded in writing on the investment proposal or deal ticket.
- **June:** SBP has reviewed the Prudential Regulation R-4 for Corporate and Commercial Banking on Clean Exposure that requires the banks and DFIs to ensure that aggregate exposure against all their clean facilities shall not, at any point in time, exceed the amount of their equity. It has been decided to set higher limits for assuming unsecured exposure on a case-by-case basis, taking into account the following factors:
  - Capital adequacy, Asset quality, Management quality, Earnings, and Liquidity (CAMEL) rating of the bank or DFI
  - Quality of unsecured portfolio in terms of percentage of classified advances and write-offs and charge-offs

○ Past track record of dealing in the relevant clean products

  The banks/DFIs that wish to take clean exposure in excess of their equity level will be required to obtain prior approval from SBP, and their requests will be processed in light of the above criteria. All other instructions on the subject will, however, remain unchanged.

- **June:** To facilitate the downscaling financial services of the commercial banks, SBP has prepared guidelines for them to provide microfinance services under four different modes, which include the following:
  ○ Establishment of microfinance counters in the existing branches
  ○ Designating stand alone microfinance branches
  ○ Establishing independent microfinance subsidiary
  ○ Developing linkages with microfinance banks and nongovernmental organizations and microfinance institutions (NGO/MFIs).

  The microfinance operations of commercial banks under Modes I, II, and IV will be subject to Prudential Regulations issued separately under the Banking Companies Ordinance of 1962 (BCO) for commercial banks undertaking microfinance. Microfinance operations under Mode III will be governed under MFIs Ordinance 2001 and Prudential Regulations applicable on microfinance banks.

- **July:** SBP has made the following amendments and additions, in public interest, in the Prudential Regulations for Corporate and Commercial Banking with immediate effect to ensure compliance with Financial Action Task Force recommendations on anti–money laundering, safeguard the interest of depositors from risks arising out of money laundering, and to reinforce the measures being taken by the banks and DFIs for proper management of their institutions:
  ○ KYC
  ○ Anti–money laundering measures
  ○ Suspicious transactions

- **July:** To create awareness and to facilitate the public in making informed decisions, the SBP has decided that, henceforth, banks and DFIs shall make complete disclosure of the lending and deposit rates of all consumer products offered by them by posting this information on their Web site as well as prominently displaying on entrances or window of their branches. Banks and DFIs would also disclose annualized percentage rates on all consumer products. In case of deposits, the expected rate of return under the profit and loss sharing (PLS) system will be clearly indicated for each tenure. For lending products, banks and DFIs shall clearly indicate whether the rate is fixed or floating. In case of floating rate, in addition to mentioning the existing rate, the information regarding the tenure of the benchmark (KIBOR or any other rate plus a predefined spread) used and periodicity of repricing should be disclosed. The banks and DFIs, in addition to the above, will take adequate measures to inform their customers about the intricacies of automated teller machines (ATMs), credit cards, and their charges as well as cardholder obligations.

- **July:** In terms of Section 31 of the BCO all banks and DFIs in Pakistan are required to surrender to SBP all those deposits that have not been operated during the last 10 years, except deposits in the name of a minor or a goverment

or a court of law. To facilitate banks and DFIs, instructions on the following subjects issued since 1968 to date have been reviewed and consolidated:
- Definition of unclaimed deposits and instruments
- Reporting of unclaimed deposits and instruments
- Surrender of unclaimed deposits
- Notice to the holder of unclaimed deposits and instruments
- Preservation of documents
- Information in account opening form (AOF)
- Procedure for refund of unclaimed deposit surrendered to SBP

- **August:** Banks are required to cap their investment in shares at 20 percent of their equity except strategic investment. Strategic investment was defined as "an investment which a bank/DFI makes with the intention to hold it for a longer term of duration and should be marked as such at the time of investment and can only be disposed of with the prior approval of State Bank of Pakistan" (as per BPD circular dated August 1, 2006, State Bank of Pakistan).

Other Policy Developments

In April 2005, the Shariah Board of the SBP approved and incorporated some of the suggestions given by different stakeholders in the Essentials of Islamic Modes of Financing to ensure compliance with minimum Shariah standards by banks conducting Islamic banking in Pakistan. These essentials are issued as General Guidelines to be followed by banking institutions conducting Islamic banking in the country (see the SBP Web site at www.sbp.org.pk/).

To provide regulatory framework for payment systems and electronic fund transfers, the Payment Systems and Electronic Fund Transfers Act was enacted in 2007.

Sri Lanka

Implementation of the New Capital Adequacy Framework (Basel II) in Sri Lanka

In January 2008, the Central Bank of Sri Lanka (CBSL) joined the global trend by implementing the Basel II framework in Sri Lanka. A consultative paper was released to banks providing guidelines on the major areas of the framework in June 2007. These new guidelines replaced the guidelines issued in 2006 on the parallel computation of capital adequacy. The impact of Basel II on the banks' capital was monitored based on the results from the parallel computation of capital adequacy under the new guidelines since June 2007. The Capital Adequacy Computation under Basel I was the effective statutory capital ratio during this period of parallel runs. CBSL has directed that initially, during this period, the CAR under Basel II should be computed on a bank-only (solo) basis. Incorporating the feedback received from the stakeholders on the consultative paper, the Directions on Basel II were issued in December 2007 to banks for implementation of Basel II from January 2008. Accordingly, banks are required to apply the Standardized Approach for credit risk, the Standardized Measurement Method for market risk, and the Basic Indicator Approach for operational risk in computing the capital requirement. The Directions issued contains four parts—that is, the direction, the guidelines, the format for computation of the CAR, and the guidelines on the implementation of IT infrastructure for Basel II.

Prudential Regulations

Among the prudential guidelines issued by the SBCL in 2005–06 are the following.

2005
- **January:** Licensed specialized banks: deposit direction (amendment).
- **February:** Direction under section 46 (1) of the Banking (Amendment) Act.
- **February:** Order published under section 47 (4) of the Banking Act.
- **February:** Security to be obtained for an accommodation granted to a director.
- **February:** Banking (Amendment) Act: Issue of directions, and so on.
- **February:** Public disclosure by publication of bank accounts in the press.
- **February:** Submission of the monthly and quarterly compliance reports.
- **March:** Banking Act (Single-Borrower Limit) Direction No. 2 of 2005.
- **March:** Accommodation to directors and related companies.
- **March:** Banking Act (Single-Borrower Limit [SBL]) Direction No. 3 of 2005.
- **March:** Affidavit to be submitted under section 42 (2) of the Banking Act.
- **March:** Appointment of directors of banks (amendment).
- **March:** Declaration to be submitted by person proposed as a director.
- **April:** Enhancement of minimum capital requirement for banks (licensed commercial banks).
- **April:** Enhancement of minimum capital requirement for banks (licensed specialized banks).
- **May:** Introduction of products based on Islamic principles.
- **July:** Request to maintain capital in foreign currency.
- **August:** Annual license fee for licensed specialized banks.
- **August:** SBL Direction No. 4 of 2005.
- **August:** Request to maintain capital of banks in foreign currency.
- **September:** Publication of quarterly financial statements of banks in the press.
- **September:** Imposing a Default Charge on Failure to Maintain Adequate Funds in RTGS (real-time gross settlement) Settlement Accounts for Settlement of Net Clearing Obligations of Licensed Commercial Bank.
- **October:** Banking Act: SBL.

2006
- **January:** Publication of Quarterly Financial Statements of Banks in the Press.
- **February:** Submission of Audited Financial Statements by Banks.
- **February:** Publication of Audited Financial Statements of Banks in the Press.
- **March:** Reporting of Post-Tsunami Remittances received through NGOs and non-NGOs to the Central Bank of Sri Lanka.
- **March:** Inadequate and Incorrect Disclosures and Press Statements by banks.
- **March:** Banking Act—Direction on the Prudential Norms for Classification, Valuation, and Operation of the Bank's Investment Portfolio.
- **March:** Banking Act—Determination on the Computation of a Capital Charge for Market Risk.

- **March:** Parallel Computation of Basel I and Basel II.
- **March:** Reversal of unearned income and classification of advances as nonperforming.
- **March:** Guidelines on Business Continuity Planning.
- **May:** Implementation of the Provisions of Part IX (Sections 72 to 76) of the Banking Act on Abandoned Property.
- **May:** Classification of Banking Outlets.
- **May:** Conduct of NGO Accounts by Licensed Banks.
- **May:** Amendment to LankaSettle System Rules: August 2003 (as amended) Daily Operating Schedule of the LankaSettle System.
- **May:** General Direction—Payment and Settlement Systems Act No. 28 of 2005.
- **June:** Draft Guidelines on the Computation of the Capital Ratio under Basel II.
- **June:** Prevention of Frauds using Electronic Cards.
- **June:** Conduct of NGO Accounts by Licensed Banks (second Direction is issued).
- **June:** Payment of Taxes by the Banking and Financial Sector.
- **June:** SBL—Compliance with the Aggregate Exposure Limit.
- **August:** SBL Direction No. 2 of 2005 as amended by Direction No. 4 of 2005 (for Licensed Commercial Banks incorporated outside Sri Lanka).
- **November:** Banking Act—Amendments to the Direction on Maintenance of the CAR.
- **November:** Banking Act—Amendment to the Determination and Notice on Maintenance of the CAR.
- **December:** Banking Act—Amendments to the Direction on Requirement to Maintain a General Provision for Advances.
- **December:** Minimum Capital Requirement of Licensed Commercial Banks.
- **December:** Standard Times for Settlement of Inter-participant Transactions in the LankaSettle System.

Other Policy Developments

In 2005, the Payment and Settlement Systems Act No. 28 of 2005 was enacted to provide for the regulation of payment, clearing, and settlement systems; for the disposition of securities in the books of the Central Bank; for the regulation of providers of money services; and for the electronic presentment of checks.

In addition to the Convention on the Suppression of the Financing of Terrorism Act, enacted in September 2005, two laws were passed in early 2006 to deal with prevention of money laundering.

The Prevention of Money Laundering Act (PMLA) introduced the offense of money laundering to the laws of the country, but the Financial Transactions Reporting Act (FTRA) provides for the mechanism to monitor and report financial transactions to ensure that the offenses of terrorist financing and money laundering are dealt with strongly.

To give effect to the FTRA, a Financial Intelligence Unit was established in March 2006 in the CBSL and is now fully functional.

In March 2006, CBSL formed the National Payments Council (NPC), the highest decision-making body of the country with regard to the Payment Settlement Systems (PSS) in Sri Lanka (including representatives of all major stakeholders). The CBSL has prepared a PSS policy in consultation with the NPC. The proposed policy, which is planned for the next four-year period (2007–10), provides a framework to mitigate risks and increase efficiency, as well as a road map with measurable action points.

During the first half of 2006, provisions of the Banking Act, No. 30 of 1988, were amended to address several deficiencies in the act.

In March 2006, the Parliament passed the Monetary Law (Amendment) Act, No. 6 of 2006, thus strengthening the powers of the Monetary Board in relation to credit operations of the commercial banks and specialized banks.

With a view to deterring illegal and hazardous practices relating to payment devices, the Payment Devices Frauds Act (No. 30 of 2006) was enacted by the Parliament in September 2006. This act prohibits fraudulent and unauthorized production, trafficking, possession, and use of payment devices.

In August 2007, the Central Bank released the exposure draft on corporate governance for banks soliciting the views, comments, and suggestions from the stakeholders of banks and the general public. Based on these suggestions, comprehensive corporate governance rules have been issued with effect from January 1, 2008.

In December 2007, CBSL issued directions with regard to board committees, independent directors, roles and responsibilities of the board, and so on. A few of the major points relevant to comments made in the report are summarized below:

- Board Committees: Each bank should have at least four board committees, that is, audit, human resources and remuneration, nomination, and integrated risk management committees. The board shall present a report of the performance on each committee, as well as on their duties and roles, at the annual general meeting.
- Internal Audit Committee: Each bank should have an internal audit committee with broad responsibilities for (1) the appointment of the external auditor for audit services to be provided in compliance with the relevant statutes; (2) the implementation of the Central Bank guidelines issued to auditors from time to time; (3) the application of the relevant accounting standards; and (4) the service period, audit fee, and any resignation or dismissal of the auditor, provided that the engagement of the audit partner shall not exceed five years and that the particular audit partner is not reengaged for the audit before the expiry of three years from the date of the completion of the previous term.
- Board Composition: The number of directors on the board shall not be fewer than 7 and not more than 13. The period of service of a director is 9 years and the maximum age is 70 years. The number of executive directors shall not exceed one-third of the number of directors of the board. The board shall have at least three independent nonexecutive directors or one-third of the total number of directors, whichever is higher. Detailed criteria have been set to determine the independence of a director.

Sources: Information available from the regulatory authorities of the five countries and their official Web sites; Indian Banks' Association 2006a, 2006b, and 2006c; and Reserve Bank of India 2006a, 2006b, 2006c, and 2007.

9

International Best Practices in Corporate Governance

Organisation for Economic Co-operation and Development

Corporate governance refers to the structures and processes for the direction and control of companies. It is concerned with the relationships among the management, board of directors, controlling shareholders, minority shareholders, and other stakeholders. Good corporate governance contributes to sustainable economic development by enhancing the performance of companies and increasing their access to outside capital.

The *Organisation for Economic Co-operation and Development Principles of Corporate Governance* (OECD 2004) provides the framework for the work of the World Bank Group in this area and identifies the key practical issues: the rights and equitable treatment of shareholders and other financial stakeholders, the role of nonfinancial stakeholders, disclosure and transparency, and the responsibilities of the board of directors (World Bank 2003). The good governance practices outlined by the OECD also serve as the basis for the questionnaire developed to assess the corporate governance of South Asian countries in this report (see table 9.1).

Basel Committee on Banking Supervision

In February 2006, the Basel Committee on Banking Supervision issued eight principles-based corporate governance schemes to enhance corporate governance for banking organizations, indicating the need for the adoption of corporate governance principles in banks.

Table 9.1 OECD Principles Applied in the Corporate Governance Questionnaire

Principle	Explanation
1. The rights of the shareholder	A corporate governance framework should protect shareholders' rights.
2. The equitable treatment of shareholders	All shareholders, including minority and foreign shareholders, should be treated equally.
3. The role of the stakeholders in corporate governance	Good corporate governance recognizes that it is in the long-term interest of the corporation to respect the rights and interests of the stakeholders.
4. Disclosure and transparency	There is a need to ensure timely and accurate disclosure of all material matters regarding the corporation, including financial aspects, performance, ownership, and governance.
5. The responsibilities of the board	The board is key to the strategic guidance of the company and the effective monitoring of the management. It should be fully able to undertake its tasks and responsibilities and be fully accountable to shareholders.

Source: Enterprise Development Impact Assessment Information Service 2003.

Table 9.2 Sound Corporate Governance Principles

Principle 1	Board members should be qualified for their positions, have a clear understanding of their role in corporate governance, and be able to exercise sound judgment about the affairs of the bank.
Principle 2	The board of directors should approve and oversee the bank's strategic objectives and corporate values that are communicated throughout the banking organization.
Principle 3	The board of directors should set and enforce clear lines of responsibility and accountability throughout the organization.
Principle 4	The board should ensure that there is appropriate oversight by senior management consistent with board policy.
Principle 5	The board and senior management should effectively utilize the work conducted by the internal audit function, external auditors, and internal control functions.
Principle 6	The board should ensure that compensation policies and practices are consistent with the bank's corporate culture, long-term objectives and strategy, and control environment.
Principle 7	The bank should be governed in a transparent manner.
Principle 8	The board and senior management should understand the bank's operational structure, including where the bank operates in jurisdictions, or through structures, that impede transparency (i.e., "know-your-structure").

Source: Bank for International Settlements 2006.

Table 9.3 South Asia Corporate Governance Status, 2006

Bangladesh	Bangladesh Bank has issued guidelines for banks. However, these guidelines are still at the development stage, with room for improvement. In particular, the guidelines need to be augmented by legal provisions governing beneficial ownership, minority shareholders' rights, remuneration of directors, and roles and responsibilities of external and internal auditors. Bangladesh also needs to work toward full conformity with international accounting and auditing standards.
India	Reserve Bank of India has issued guidelines that are both comprehensive and commendable. Yet several areas need further review, the main one being the harmonization needed on the governance rules applicable to government-controlled banks and those applicable to private banks. Minority shareholders' rights also should be revisited.
Nepal	Nepal Rastra Bank has issued detailed guidelines on corporate governance for banks. They need to broaden these guidelines, however, to include investor rights and disclosure rights, beneficial ownership, and the responsibilities of the auditors. A key improvement would be better adherence to international accounting and auditing standards.
Pakistan	The State Bank of Pakistan has issued a comprehensive handbook of corporate governance for banks. In addition, in late 2005 Pakistan established the Pakistan Institute of Corporate Governance to further strengthen the corporate governance culture by providing training and awareness. Still, some areas need review, including further disclosures on beneficial ownership, safeguards on stakeholders' rights, transfer of ownership and management, and competitive compensation packages.
Sri Lanka	The Central Bank of Sri Lanka has issued a code of corporate governance for banks and other financial institutions. Yet disclosure requirements and detailed guidelines are needed on many issues, such as stakeholder rights, beneficial ownership, special voting rights, rights of shareholders to vote on bank operations, regulatory and government control of share transactions, and minority shareholder rights. In August 2007, the Central Bank released the exposure draft on corporate governance for banks soliciting the views, comments, and suggestions from the stakeholders of banks and the public. The implementation of the code is scheduled for January 2008.

Source: Corporate governance responses received from the supervisory authorities; Indian Banks' Association 2006a, 2006b, and 2006c; Reserve Bank of India 2006a, 2006b, 2006c, and 2007.

Appendixes

Appendix 1. Getting Finance Indicators for South Asia, by Country and Year

Table A1.1 Getting Finance Indicators for South Asian Countries, 2001

Indicator	Bangladesh	India	Nepal	Pakistan	Sri Lanka	Benchmark
Access to finance						
Demographic branch penetration (branches per 100,000 people)	4.83	6.42	2.09	4.88	6.03	12–29
Demographic ATM penetration (ATMs per 100,000 people)	0.10	N/A	0.05	N/A	2.55	43–115
Deposit accounts per 1,000 people	231.97	416.77	111.59	195.84	939.32	976–2,418
Loan accounts per 1,000 people	56.56	50.99	19.07	16.04	256.88	248–776
Geographic branch penetration (branches per 1,000 km^2)	42.5	22.18	3.29	8.77	11.68	1–61
Geographic ATM penetration (ATMs per 1,000 km^2)	0.91	N/A	0.08	N/A	4.93	1–152
Performance and efficiency						
Return on equity (percent)	17.12	13.80	−93.62	12.20	20.57	7.70–23.38
Return on assets (percent)	0.74	0.90	−3.04	0.60	0.84	0.50–1.40
Staff cost ratio (percent)	44.75	68.10	194.25	52.58	46.21	35.51–44.55
Operating cost ratio (percent)	236.78	92.33	35.87	90.91	118.66	49.86–149.64
Net interest margin (percent)	1.66	2.98	1.76	3.24	3.30	1.81–3.55
Recurring earning power (percent)	1.70	1.60	0.86	1.17	1.64	1.21–2.22
Financial stability						
Capital adequacy ratio (percent)	7.02	11.40	4.00	11.30	8.59	(not lower than 8% of RWA-Based) 10.40–18.20
Leverage ratio (times)	4.17	4.96	3.27	4.58	3.90	6.58–15.01
Gross nonperforming loans ratio (percent)	31.49	11.40	29.31	19.60	19.57	0.60–8.00
Provisions to nonperforming loans ratio (percent)	25.36	49.70	30.59	53.20	44.43	25.40–128.80
Liquid assets ratio (percent)	30.03	48.20	22.10	39.90	22.80	7.42–40.44
Liquid assets to liabilities ratio (percent)	122.90	260.00	47.88	56.25	26.30	2.83–42.20

Appendix 1. Getting Finance Indicators for South Asia, by Country and Year

Capital market development						
Domestic bond market to equity market capitalization (percent)	663.50	117.85	129.55	537.75	659.05	8.90–108.70
Domestic public bonds outstanding to GDP (percent)	16.17	26.80	14.50	38.90	16.28	8.83–58.69
Ratio of trading value of top 10 stocks to total trading value (percent)	59.16	72.90	83.13	22.52	54.37	15.55–57.00
Stock market capitalization to GDP (percent)	2.57	29.40	11.76	8.06	8.81	35.58–350.02
Market liquidity: Ratio of stock trading value to GDP (percent)	1.28	112.00	0.59	0.02	0.99	16.21–290.00
Stock market turnover ratio (times)	0.50	2.13	0.05	0.12	0.13	0.34–1.99
Market concentration and competitiveness						
Herfindahl-Hirschman index (HHI)	944.90	784.67	1,563.48	1,091.80	1,650.62	[HHI < 1,000 unconcentrated; 1,000 < HHI < 1,800 moderately concentrated; HHI > 1,800 highly concentrated] 498.54–1,658.53
K-bank concentration ratio (K=3) – assets (percent)	47.38	33.80	58.02	50.30	63.09	27.04–61.19
K-bank concentration ratios (K=3) – deposits (percent)	50.55	33.98	51.73	53.23	62.02	27.44–60.18
K-bank concentration ratios (K=3) – loans (percent)	45.76	33.04	52.06	50.86	65.16	27.02–66.30
Private credit extended by banks to GDP (percent)	24.33	21.50	26.95	16.29	28.19	42.00–157.85
Commercial Banking assets to GDP (percent)	50.35	61.90	63.83	43.61	56.80	44.90–174.28

Sources: South Asian Central Banks, SECs and Boards, and stock exchanges; Indian Banks' Association 2006a, 2006b, and 2006c; Reserve Bank of India 2006a, 2006b, 2006c, and 2007.
Note: All benchmark indicators are in respect of selected high-income OECD member and nonmember countries (Australia; Canada; Hong Kong, China; New Zealand; Singapore; the United Kingdom; and the United States).

Table A1.2 Getting Finance Indicators for South Asian Countries, 2002

Indicator	Bangladesh	India	Nepal	Pakistan	Sri Lanka	Benchmark
Access to finance						
Demographic branch penetration (branches per 100,000 people)	4.74	6.33	1.85	4.73	6.70	11–29
Demographic ATM penetration (ATMs per 100,000 people)	0.14	N/A	0.06	N/A	3.27	37–128
Deposit accounts per 1,000 people	234.75	420.84	123.21	194.87	989.94	976–2,418
Loan accounts per 1,000 people	57.14	53.93	14.92	14.93	257.66	248–776
Geographic branch penetration (branches per 1,000 km²)	42.26	22.26	2.96	8.72	13.17	1–60
Geographic ATM penetration (ATMs per 1,000 km²)	1.22	N/A	0.10	N/A	6.43	2–169
Performance and efficiency						
Return on equity (percent)	12.40	17.30	−96.16	27.50	25.71	6.10–25.51
Return on assets (percent)	0.54	1.10	−3.37	1.50	1.11	0.40–1.50
Staff cost ratio (percent)	66.53	64.70	185.00	50.75	47.62	33.35–44.36
Operating cost ratio (percent)	187.63	85.38	59.78	85.81	99.80	53.39–138.44
Net interest margin (percent)	1.04	2.66	0.92	3.10	3.78	1.83–3.55
Recurring earning power (percent)	1.50	2.00	0.21	2.00	2.07	1.18–2.39
Financial stability						
Capital adequacy ratio (percent)	7.60	12.00	−7.25	12.60	10.35	[not lower than 8% of RWA-Basel] 9.60–16.90
Leverage ratio (times)	4.34	5.24	3.71	4.11	4.71	6.92–14.64
Gross nonperforming loans ratio (percent)	28.10	10.40	30.41	17.70	19.09	0.70–7.70
Provisions to nonperforming loans ratio (percent)	25.30	53.40	29.98	58.20	50.38	37.50–123.70
Liquid assets ratio (percent)	25.84	47.40	18.16	48.10	18.80	7.07–31.70
Liquid assets to liabilities ratio (percent)	121.46	250.00	41.33	68.95	21.70	2.99–39.60

Appendix 1. Getting Finance Indicators for South Asia, by Country and Year

Capital market development						
Domestic bond market to equity market capitalization (percent)	735.42	118.92	212.14	278.47	585.08	10.06–145.00
Domestic public bonds outstanding to GDP (percent)	17.53	29.80	17.40	37.80	21.94	9.33–56.57
Ratio of trading value of top 10 stocks to total trading value (percent)	51.64	62.93	81.89	21.89	57.70	17.55–78.70
Stock market capitalization to GDP (percent)	2.61	27.40	8.54	9.15	10.28	33.14–304.85
Market liquidity: Ratio of stock trading value to GDP (percent)	1.28	36.00	0.38	0.15	1.91	12.47–244.23
Stock market turnover ratio (times)	0.49	0.88	0.04	0.90	0.21	0.38–2.03
Market concentration and competitiveness						
Herfindahl-Hirschman index (HHI)	886.66	741.50	1,574.76	1,052.12	1,528.39	*[HHI < 1,000 unconcentrated; 1,000 <HHI < 1,800 moderately concentrated; HHI > 1,800 highly concentrated]* 484.12–1,869.49
K-bank concentration ratio (K=3) – assets (percent)	45.77	33.67	58.68	49.71	60.88	30.03–63.79
K-bank concentration ratios (K=3) – deposits (percent)	47.55	33.26	49.62	51.76	62.43	29.72–62.26
K-bank concentration ratios (K=3) – loans (percent)	43.22	31.92	49.34	47.00	60.02	28.95–62.38
Private credit extended by banks to GDP (percent)	26.32	23.80	27.21	16.90	28.09	42.30–154.98
Commercial Banking assets to GDP (percent)	52.78	67.30	67.69	47.72	54.51	45.23–172.93

Sources: South Asian Central Banks, SECs and Boards, and stock exchanges; Indian Banks' Association 2006a, 2006b, and 2006c; Reserve Bank of India 2006a, 2006b, 2006c, and 2007.
Note: All benchmark indicators are in respect of selected high-income OECD member and nonmember countries (Australia; Canada; Hong Kong, China; New Zealand; Singapore; the United Kingdom; and the United States).

Table A1.3 Getting Finance Indicators for South Asian Countries, 2003

Indicator	Bangladesh	India	Nepal	Pakistan	Sri Lanka	Benchmark
Access to finance						
Demographic branch penetration (branches per 100,000 people)	4.67	6.25	1.85	4.61	6.85	10–30
Demographic ATM penetration (ATMs per 100,000 people)	0.14	N/A	0.08	0.37	3.69	37–139
Deposit accounts per 1,000 people	234.60	418.67	102.43	190.55	1,000.53	976–2,418
Loan accounts per 1,000 people	56.87	55.84	12.96	18.86	279.15	248–776
Geographic branch penetration (branches per 1,000 km2)	42.25	22.41	3.04	8.66	13.63	1–59
Geographic ATM penetration (ATMs per 1,000 km2)	1.26	N/A	0.14	0.69	7.34	3–192
Performance and efficiency						
Return on equity (percent)	12.39	21.00	−22.33	33.70	26.33	8.60–25.27
Return on assets (percent)	0.59	1.50	−0.85	2.10	1.36	0.60–1.90
Staff cost ratio (percent)	64.53	62.10	306.16	51.48	49.58	36.65–45.76
Operating cost ratio (percent)	161.86	80.71	40.14	83.20	94.02	49.20–146.08
Net interest margin (percent)	1.09	2.85	1.58	2.98	4.16	1.70–3.37
Recurring earning power (percent)	1.68	2.50	−0.01	2.57	2.58	1.18–2.30
Financial stability						
Capital adequacy ratio (percent)	8.42	12.70	−11.74	11.10	10.31	[not lower than 8% of RWA-Basel] 10.00–17.90
Leverage ratio (times)	4.77	5.75	3.87	5.03	5.53	6.01–15.39
Gross nonperforming loans ratio (percent)	22.13	8.80	28.80	13.70	16.36	0.30–6.70
Provisions to nonperforming loans ratio (percent)	18.35	52.40	7.55	64.80	58.74	43.50–140.40
Liquid assets ratio (percent)	24.67	48.70	12.49	46.10	17.30	7.59–29.99
Liquid assets to liabilities ratio (percent)	127.19	260.00	27.03	63.44	20.00	2.46–36.66

Appendix 1. Getting Finance Indicators for South Asia, by Country and Year

Capital market development						
Domestic bond market to equity market capitalization (percent)	435.22	72.77	240.19	186.41	389.76	6.46–123.27
Domestic public bonds outstanding to GDP (percent)	16.73	31.60	18.50	36.70	27.43	9.94–54.63
Ratio of trading value of top 10 stocks to total trading value (percent)	51.55	55.42	58.35	19.18	60.83	16.42–74.00
Stock market capitalization to GDP (percent)	2.43	22.50	8.05	15.31	14.92	34.61–382.10
Market liquidity: Ratio of stock trading value to GDP (percent)	1.02	37.70	0.13	0.13	4.18	13.17–214.19
Stock market turnover ratio (times)	0.42	1.08	0.02	0.54	0.35	0.38–1.21
Market concentration and competitiveness						
Herfindahl-Hirschman index (HHI)	702.04	734.59	1,468.53	976.81	1,455.81	[HHI < 1,000 unconcentrated; 1,000 < HHI < 1,800 moderately concentrated; HHI > 1,800 highly concentrated] 459.53–1,864.85
K-bank concentration ratio (K=3) – assets (percent)	38.33	33.49	56.67	47.47	58.19	29.64–64.41
K-bank concentration ratios (K=3) – deposits (percent)	43.27	32.76	46.80	48.93	60.89	29.96–62.80
K-bank concentration ratios (K=3) – loans (percent)	39.57	31.60	44.64	43.58	56.81	27.11–60.04
Private credit extended by banks to GDP (percent)	29.42	25.90	27.80	21.06	29.50	43.11–153.39
Commercial Banking assets to GDP (percent)	53.84	68.80	69.84	50.10	56.06	45.80–172.10

Sources: South Asian Central Banks, SECs and Boards, and stock exchanges; Indian Banks' Association 2006a, 2006b, and 2006c; Reserve Bank of India 2006a, 2006b, 2006c, and 2007.
Note: All benchmark indicators are in respect of selected high-income OECD member and nonmember countries (Australia; Canada; Hong Kong, China; New Zealand; Singapore; the United Kingdom; and the United States).

Table A1.4 Getting Finance Indicators for South Asian Countries, 2004

Indicator	Bangladesh	India	Nepal	Pakistan	Sri Lanka	Benchmark
Access to finance						
Demographic branch penetration (branches per 100,000 people)	4.67	6.26	1.71	4.64	7.06	9–28
Demographic ATM penetration (ATMs per 100,000 people)	0.17	N/A	0.11	0.52	4.16	38–152
Deposit accounts per 1,000 people	233.63	426.11	115.88	180.28	1,023.58	976–2,418
Loan accounts per 1,000 people	60.24	61.88	11.97	24.51	304.11	248–776
Geographic branch penetration (branches per 1,000 km^2)	42.71	22.57	2.87	8.84	14.20	1–58
Geographic ATM penetration (ATMs per 1,000 km^2)	1.55	N/A	0.18	0.99	8.37	3–225
Performance and efficiency						
Return on equity (percent)	−13.39	23.00	−46.42	29.00	25.62	10.90–22.80
Return on assets (percent)	−0.63	1.70	1.47	2.00	1.43	0.70–1.70
Staff cost ratio (percent)	66.24	60.17	181.18	51.97	46.98	38.44–56.30
Operating cost ratio (percent)	141.89	77.05	31.93	83.62	95.66	59.57–154.30
Net interest margin (percent)	1.97	3.07	1.99	2.87	3.97	1.45–3.12
Recurring earning power (percent)	1.86	2.90	1.81	2.26	2.33	1.07–1.97
Financial stability						
Capital adequacy ratio (percent)	7.41	12.90	−9.07	11.40	10.29	[not lower than 8% of RWA-Basel] 10.40–16.10
Leverage ratio (times)	4.16	5.90	−3.00	6.45	5.63	6.41–15.18
Gross nonperforming loans ratio (percent)	17.63	7.20	22.77	9.00	11.29	0.20–4.00
Provisions to nonperforming loans ratio (percent)	19.15	62.00	3.82	72.40	68.29	34.20–182.90
Liquid assets ratio (percent)	23.50	48.70	13.61	37.00	20.30	7.50–31.54
Liquid assets to liabilities ratio (percent)	121.94	260.00	27.30	51.88	23.10	2.49–24.43

Appendix 1. Getting Finance Indicators for South Asia, by Country and Year

Capital market development							
Domestic bond market to equity market capitalization (percent)	239.99	64.33	204.93	108.60	299.80	5.58–118.07	
Domestic public bonds outstanding to GDP (percent)	16.57	33.40	17.30	33.00	31.70	9.67–55.10	
Ratio of trading value of top 10 stocks to total trading value (percent)	46.67	44.86	86.25	16.01	42.92	15.29–75.60	
Stock market capitalization to GDP (percent)	4.28	41.90	8.72	24.07	18.83	38.71–486.34	
Market liquidity: Ratio of stock trading value to GDP (percent)	0.74	57.80	0.45	0.19	2.92	15.45–269.33	
Stock market turnover ratio (times)	0.23	1.10	0.06	0.50	0.18	0.40–1.41	
Market concentration and competitiveness							
Herfindahl-Hirschman index (HHI)	724.09	677.93	1,245.62	903.97	1,377.33	*[HHI < 1,000 unconcentrated; 1,000 < HHI < 1,800 moderately concentrated; HHI > 1,800 highly concentrated]* 345.65–1,449.90	
K-bank concentration ratio (K=3) – assets (percent)	39.33	33.17	52.88	43.95	55.68	21.16–53.39	
K-bank concentration ratios (K=3) – deposits (percent)	40.31	31.29	44.00	45.55	58.25	21.84–52.37	
K-bank concentration ratios (K=3) – loans (percent)	36.54	30.97	42.14	42.56	53.28	21.90–50.16	
Private credit extended by banks to GDP (percent)	30.96	27.50	28.95	25.86	31.26	44.00–147.61	
Commercial Banking assets to GDP (percent)	51.82	71.20	71.55	52.07	56.92	46.22–166.75	

Sources: South Asian Central Banks, SECs and Boards, and stock exchanges; Indian Banks' Association 2006a, 2006b, and 2006c; Reserve Bank of India 2006a, 2006b, 2006c, and 2007.

Note: All benchmark indicators are in respect of selected high-income OECD member and nonmember countries (Australia; Canada; Hong Kong, China; New Zealand; Singapore; the United Kingdom; and the United States).

Table A1.5 Getting Finance Indicators for South Asian Countries, 2005

Indicator	Bangladesh	India	Nepal	Pakistan	Sri Lanka	Benchmark
Access to finance						
Demographic branch penetration (branches per 100,000 people)	4.64	6.33	1.67	4.82	7.20	9–28
Demographic ATM penetration (ATMs per 100,000 people)	0.20	1.63	0.24	0.67	4.50	39–158
Deposit accounts per 1,000 people	237.32	432.11	113.58	173.15	1,066.24	976–2,418
Loan accounts per 1,000 people	60.45	71.42	11.30	30.57	344.17	248–776
Geographic branch penetration (branches per 1,000 km^2)	43.41	22.99	2.87	9.22	14.64	1–57
Geographic ATM penetration (ATMs per 1,000 km^2)	1.84	5.93	0.41	1.29	9.15	3–241
Performance and efficiency						
Return on equity (percent)	28.63	16.90	−45.87	36.90	27.01	11.10–25.30
Return on assets (percent)	1.30	1.30	1.79	2.90	1.70	0.70–1.80
Staff cost ratio (percent)	65.00	58.29	135.35	50.73	44.53	23.00–52.71
Operating cost ratio (percent)	107.91	74.32	28.55	57.73	87.70	65.19–168.99
Net interest margin (percent)	2.38	3.07	2.22	4.11	4.05	1.17–3.13
Recurring earning power (percent)	2.36	2.40	2.33	3.35	2.26	0.82–2.06
Financial stability						
Capital adequacy ratio (percent)	7.65	12.80	−6.07	11.90	12.84	(not lower than 8% of RWA-Basel)/10.40–15.80
Leverage ratio (times)	4.42	6.35	−4.65	7.64	6.93	6.32–15.25
Gross nonperforming loans ratio (percent)	13.55	5.13	18.94	6.70	8.76	0.20–3.00
Provisions to nonperforming loans ratio (percent)	24.31	63.50	11.49	80.40	72.05	38.20–203.00
Liquid assets ratio (percent)	20.61	44.20	9.33	33.90	19.60	7.30–31.26
Liquid assets to liabilities ratio (percent)	104.60	220.00	20.34	52.77	22.10	2.47–23.26

Appendix 1. Getting Finance Indicators for South Asia, by Country and Year

Capital market development						
Domestic bond market to equity market capitalization (percent)	259.28	50.46	142.69	73.94	216.69	4.95–123.66
Domestic public bonds outstanding to GDP (percent)	16.75	33.00	16.40	30.90	31.77	10.07–47.23
Ratio of trading value of top 10 stocks to total trading value (percent)	41.89	41.66	83.96	20.48	43.10	15.88–43.80
Stock market capitalization to GDP (percent)	6.06	52.70	10.39	30.59	24.69	39.74–499.21
Market liquidity: Ratio of stock trading value to GDP (percent)	2.03	53.30	0.77	0.11	4.84	16.92–294.85
Stock market turnover ratio (times)	0.41	0.75	0.09	0.22	0.24	0.41–1.45
Market concentration and competitiveness						
Herfindahl-Hirschman index (HHI)	679.31	642.38	1,019.21	805.61	1,279.44	[HHI < 1,000 unconcentrated; 1,000 < HHI < 1,800 moderately concentrated; HHI > 1,800 highly concentrated] 475.57–1,447.54
K-bank concentration ratio (K=3) – assets (percent)	37.05	32.02	45.87	40.35	53.02	21.30–54.23
K-bank concentration ratios (K=3) – deposits (percent)	37.72	31.09	41.73	41.49	56.30	19.93–53.53
K-bank concentration ratios (K=3) – loans (percent)	36.46	30.84	37.28	41.96	50.44	18.39–50.48
Private credit extended by banks to GDP (percent)	31.87	33.30	27.57	28.83	33.87	47.84–160.48
Commercial Banking assets to GDP (percent)	54.93	73.00	70.25	53.89	61.79	46.50–167.76

Sources: South Asian Central Banks, SECs and Boards, and stock exchanges; Indian Banks' Association 2006a, 2006b, and 2006c; Reserve Bank of India 2006a, 2006b, 2006c, and 2007.

Note: All benchmark indicators are in respect of selected high-income OECD member and nonmember countries (Australia; Canada; Hong Kong, China; New Zealand; Singapore; the United Kingdom; and the United States).

Table A1.6 Getting Finance Indicators for South Asian Countries, 2006

Indicator	Bangladesh	India	Nepal	Pakistan	Sri Lanka	Benchmark
Access to finance						
Demographic branch penetration (branches per 100,000 people)	4.73	6.37	1.73	4.96	7.69	9–28
Demographic ATM penetration (ATMs per 100,000 people)	0.29	1.93	0.28	1.25	5.67	39–167
Deposit accounts per 1,000 people	255.23	442.87	110.40	171.14	1,117.82	976–2,418
Loan accounts per 1,000 people	61.11	78.00	10.83	31.78	364.22	248–776
Geographic branch penetration (branches per 1,000 km2)	44.53	23.46	2.97	9.67	15.81	1–57
Geographic ATM penetration (ATMs per 1,000 km2)	2.71	7.11	0.48	2.44	11.65	3–252
Performance and efficiency						
Return on equity (percent)	33.86	17.00	–43.30	34.70	27.01	8.09–18.60
Return on assets (percent)	1.66	1.31	1.90	3.20	1.83	0.50–1.80
Staff cost ratio (percent)	61.39	56.90	114.32	51.22	41.49	41.86–51.90
Operating cost ratio (percent)	100.48	75.65	25.55	54.63	84.68	62.65–157.59
Net interest margin (percent)	2.04	3.01	2.26	4.41	4.31	1.04–2.93
Recurring earning power (percent)	2.59	2.20	2.39	3.66	2.03	0.81–2.03
Financial stability						
Capital adequacy ratio (percent)	8.33	12.40	–1.75	13.33	11.82	[not lower than 8% of RWA-Basel] 10.60–15.40
Leverage ratio (times)	5.33	6.57	–4.14	8.94	6.78	6.02–14.37
Gross nonperforming loans ratio (percent)	13.15	3.33	14.22	5.70	7.16	0.20–2.40
Provisions to nonperforming loans ratio (percent)	26.33	64.20	4.72	81.50	68.12	36.30–204.50
Liquid assets ratio (percent)	18.67	38.40	9.70	32.20	19.00	9.41–34.13
Liquid assets to liabilities ratio (percent)	116.27	180.00	19.07	55.13	21.90	1.82–22.31

Capital market development

Domestic bond market to equity market capitalization (percent)	316.64	39.77	92.96	71.2	136.68	2.97–145.36
Domestic public bonds outstanding to GDP (percent)	17.13	29.60	14.10	27.46	31.62	9.49–48.57
Ratio of trading value of top 10 stocks to total trading value (percent)	39.68	31.36	66.50	20.02	57.13	14.46–82.10
Stock market capitalization to GDP (percent)	5.41	82.60	15.19	35.87	29.80	43.13–903.56
Market liquidity: Ratio of stock trading value to GDP (percent)	1.11	67.60	0.54	0.03	3.75	21.41–438.57
Stock market turnover ratio (times)	0.20	0.64	0.04	0.06	0.15	0.52–2.21

Market concentration and competitiveness

Herfindahl-Hirschman index (HHI)	596.86	599.43	949.86	784.01	1,259.88	[HHI < 1,000 unconcentrated; 1,000 < HHI < 1,800 moderately concentrated; HHI > 1,800 highly concentrated] 563.35–1,854.41
K-bank concentration ratio (K=3) – assets (percent)	33.70	31.97	43.58	38.96	52.79	30.98–58.29
K-bank concentration ratios (K=3) – deposits (percent)	35.29	30.74	38.16	40.04	55.56	36.51–58.58
K-bank concentration ratios (K=3) – loans (percent)	34.00	32.15	30.30	39.67	52.74	31.01–56.93
Private credit extended by banks to GDP (percent)	34.45	39.40	26.98	29.30	35.45	88.16–193.60
Commercial Banking assets to GDP (percent)	55.43	78.90	67.32	53.96	63.61	46.50–167.76

Sources: South Asian Central Banks, SECs and Boards, and stock exchanges; Indian Banks' Association 2006a, 2006b, and 2006c; Reserve Bank of India 2006a, 2006b, 2006c, and 2007.
Note: All benchmark indicators are in respect of selected high-income OECD member and nonmember countries (Australia; Canada; Hong Kong, China; New Zealand; Singapore; the United Kingdom; and the United States).

Table A1.7 Getting Finance Indicators for Bangladesh, 2001–06

Indicator	2001	2002	2003	2004	2005	2006	Benchmark
Access to finance							
Demographic branch penetration (branches per 100,000 people)	4.83	4.74	4.67	4.67	4.64	4.73	9–30
Demographic ATM penetration (ATMs per 100,000 people)	0.10	0.14	0.14	0.17	0.20	0.29	37–167
Deposit accounts per 1,000 people	231.97	234.75	234.60	233.63	237.32	255.23	976–2,418
Loan accounts per 1,000 people	56.56	57.14	56.87	60.24	60.45	61.11	248–776
Geographic branch penetration (branches per 1,000 km²)	42.5	42.26	42.25	42.71	43.41	44.53	1–61
Geographic ATM penetration (ATMs per 1,000 km²)	0.91	1.22	1.26	1.55	1.84	2.71	1–252
Performance and efficiency							
Return on equity (percent)	17.12	12.40	12.39	–13.39	28.63	33.86	6.10–25.51
Return on assets (percent)	0.74	0.54	0.59	–0.63	1.30	1.66	0.40–1.90
Staff cost ratio (percent)	44.75	66.53	64.53	66.24	65.00	61.39	23.00–56.30
Operating cost ratio (percent)	236.78	187.63	161.86	141.89	107.91	100.48	49.20–157.59
Net interest margin (percent)	1.66	1.04	1.09	1.97	2.38	2.04	1.04–3.55
Recurring earning power (percent)	1.70	1.50	1.68	1.86	2.36	2.59	0.81–2.39
Financial stability							
Capital adequacy ratio (percent)	7.02	7.60	8.42	7.41	7.65	8.33	(not lower than 8% of RWA-Basel)/9.60–18.20
Leverage ratio (times)	4.17	4.34	4.77	4.16	4.42	5.33	6.01–15.39
Gross nonperforming loans ratio (percent)	31.49	28.10	22.13	17.63	13.55	13.15	0.20–8.00
Provisions to nonperforming loans ratio (percent)	25.36	25.30	18.35	19.15	24.31	26.33	25.40–204.50
Liquid assets ratio (percent)	30.03	25.84	24.67	23.50	20.61	18.67	7.07–40.44
Liquid assets to liabilities ratio (percent)	122.90	121.46	127.19	121.94	104.60	116.27	1.82–42.20

Appendix 1. Getting Finance Indicators for South Asia, by Country and Year

Capital market development							
Domestic bond market to equity market capitalization (percent)	663.5	735.42	435.22	239.99	259.28	316.64	2.97–145.36
Domestic public bonds outstanding to GDP (percent)	16.17	17.53	16.73	16.57	16.75	17.13	8.83–58.69
Ratio of trading value of top 10 stocks to total trading value (percent)	59.16	51.64	51.55	46.67	41.89	39.68	14.46–82.10
Stock market capitalization to GDP (percent)	2.57	2.61	2.43	4.28	6.06	5.41	33.14–903.56
Market liquidity: Ratio of stock trading value to GDP (percent)	1.28	1.28	1.02	0.74	2.03	1.11	12.47–438.57
Stock market turnover ratio (times)	0.50	0.49	0.42	0.23	0.41	0.20	0.34–2.21
Market concentration and competitiveness							
Herfindahl-Hirschman index (HHI)	944.90	886.66	702.04	724.09	679.31	596.86	*[HHI < 1,000 unconcentrated; 1,000 < HHI < 1,800 moderately concentrated; HHI > 1,800 highly concentrated]* 345.65–1,869.49
K-bank concentration ratio (K=3) – assets (percent)	47.38	45.77	38.33	39.33	37.05	33.70	21.30–64.41
K-bank concentration ratios (K=3) – deposits (percent)	50.55	47.55	43.27	40.31	37.72	35.29	19.93–62.80
K-bank concentration ratios (K=3) – loans (percent)	45.76	43.22	39.57	36.54	36.46	34.00	18.39–66.30
Private credit extended by banks to GDP (percent)	24.33	26.32	29.42	30.96	31.87	34.45	42.00–193.60
Commercial Banking assets to GDP (percent)	50.35	52.78	53.84	51.82	54.93	55.43	44.90–174.28

Sources: Bangladesh Bank; World Bank 2007a; IMF 2007b (stock market capitalization/GDP for 2001); and Beck, Demirgüç-Kunt, and Levine 2000 (private credit to GDP for 2001 and 2002).
Notes: 2006 (provisional data). All benchmark indicators are in respect of selected high-income OECD member and nonmember countries (Australia; Canada; Hong Kong, China; New Zealand; Singapore; the United Kingdom; and the United States).

Table A1.8 Getting Finance Indicators for India, 2001–06

Indicator	2001	2002	2003	2004	2005	2006	Benchmark
Access to finance							
Demographic branch penetration (branches per 100,000 people)	6.42	6.33	6.25	6.26	6.33	6.37	9–30
Demographic ATM penetration (ATMs per 100,000 people)	N/A	N/A	N/A	N/A	1.63	1.93	37–167
Deposit accounts per 1,000 people	416.77	420.84	418.67	426.11	432.11	442.87	976–2,418
Loan accounts per 1,000 people	50.99	53.93	55.84	61.88	71.42	78.00	248–776
Geographic branch penetration (branches per 1,000 km^2)	22.18	22.26	22.41	22.57	22.99	23.46	1–61
Geographic ATM penetration (ATMs per 1,000 km^2)	N/A	N/A	N/A	N/A	5.93	7.11	1–252
Performance and efficiency							
Return on equity (percent)	13.80	17.30	21.00	23.00	16.90	17.00	6.10–25.51
Return on assets (percent)	0.90	1.10	1.50	1.70	1.30	1.31	0.40–1.90
Staff cost ratio (percent)	68.10	64.70	62.10	60.17	58.29	56.90	23.00–56.30
Operating cost ratio (percent)	92.33	85.38	80.71	77.05	74.32	75.65	49.20–157.59
Net interest margin (percent)	2.98	2.66	2.85	3.07	3.07	3.01	1.04–3.55
Recurring earning power (percent)	1.60	2.00	2.50	2.90	2.40	2.20	0.81–2.39
Financial stability							
Capital adequacy ratio (percent)	11.40	12.00	12.70	12.90	12.80	12.40	[not lower than 8% of RWA-Basel]/9.60–18.20
Leverage ratio (times)	4.96	5.24	5.75	5.90	6.35	6.57	6.01–15.39
Gross nonperforming loans ratio (percent)	11.40	10.40	8.80	7.20	5.13	3.33	0.20–8.00
Provisions to nonperforming loans ratio (percent)	49.70	53.40	52.40	62.00	63.50	64.20	25.40–204.50
Liquid assets ratio (percent)	48.20	47.40	48.70	48.70	44.20	38.40	7.07–40.44
Liquid assets to liabilities ratio (percent)	260.00	250.00	260.00	260.00	220.00	180.00	1.82–42.20

Appendix 1. Getting Finance Indicators for South Asia, by Country and Year

Capital market development							
Domestic bond market to equity market capitalization (percent)	117.85	118.92	72.77	64.33	50.46	39.77	2.97–145.36
Domestic public bonds outstanding to GDP (percent)	26.80	29.80	31.60	33.40	33.00	29.60	8.83–58.69
Ratio of trading value of top 10 stocks to total trading value (percent)	72.90	62.93	55.42	44.86	41.66	31.36	14.46–82.10
Stock market capitalization to GDP (percent)	29.40	27.40	22.50	41.90	52.70	82.60	33.14–903.56
Market liquidity: Ratio of stock trading value to GDP (percent)	112.00	36.00	37.70	57.80	53.30	67.60	12.47–438.57
Stock market turnover ratio (times)	2.13	0.88	1.08	1.10	0.75	0.64	0.34–2.21
Market concentration and competitiveness							
Herfindahl-Hirschman index (HHI)	784.67	741.50	734.59	677.93	642.38	599.43	*[HHI < 1,000 unconcentrated; 1,000 < HHI < 1,800 moderately concentrated; HHI > 1,800 highly concentrated]* 345.65–1,869.49
K-bank concentration ratio (K=3) – assets (percent)	33.80	33.67	33.49	33.17	32.02	31.97	21.30–64.41
K-bank concentration ratios (K=3) – deposits (percent)	33.98	33.26	32.76	31.29	31.09	30.74	19.93–62.80
K-bank concentration ratios (K=3) – loans (percent)	33.04	31.92	31.60	30.97	30.84	32.15	18.39–66.30
Private credit extended by banks to GDP (percent)	21.50	23.80	25.90	27.50	33.30	39.40	42.00–193.60
Commercial Banking assets to GDP (percent)	61.90	67.30	68.80	71.20	73.00	78.90	44.90–174.28

Sources: Indian Banks' Association 2006a, 2006b, and 2006c; Reserve Bank of India 2006a, 2006b, 2006c, and 2007.
Note: All benchmark indicators are in respect of selected high-income OECD member and nonmember countries (Australia; Canada; Hong Kong, China; New Zealand; Singapore; the United Kingdom; and the United States).

Table A1.9 Getting Finance Indicators for Nepal, 2001–06

Indicator	2001	2002	2003	2004	2005	2006	Benchmark
Access to finance							
Demographic branch penetration (branches per 100,000 people)	2.09	1.85	1.85	1.71	1.67	1.73	9–30
Demographic ATM penetration (ATMs per 100,000 people)	0.05	0.06	0.08	0.11	0.24	0.28	37–167
Deposit accounts per 1,000 people	111.59	123.21	102.43	115.88	113.58	110.40	976–2,418
Loan accounts per 1,000 people	19.07	14.92	12.96	11.97	11.30	10.83	248–776
Geographic branch penetration (branches per 1,000 km^2)	3.29	2.96	3.04	2.87	2.87	2.97	1–61
Geographic ATM penetration (ATMs per 1,000 km^2)	0.08	0.10	0.14	0.18	0.41	0.48	1–252
Performance and efficiency							
Return on equity (percent)	–93.62	–96.16	–22.33	–46.42	–45.87	–43.30	6.10–25.51
Return on assets (percent)	–3.04	–3.37	–0.85	1.47	1.79	1.90	0.40–1.90
Staff cost ratio (percent)	194.25	185.00	306.16	181.18	135.35	114.32	23.00–56.30
Operating cost ratio (percent)	35.87	59.78	40.14	31.93	28.55	25.55	49.20–157.59
Net interest margin (percent)	1.76	0.92	1.58	1.99	2.22	2.26	1.04–3.55
Recurring earning power (percent)	0.86	0.21	–0.01	1.81	2.33	2.39	0.81–2.39
Financial stability							
Capital adequacy ratio (percent)	4.00	–7.25	–11.74	–9.07	–6.07	–1.75	(not lower than 8% of RWA-Basel) 9.60–18.20
Leverage ratio (times)	3.27	3.71	3.87	–3.00	–4.65	–4.14	6.01–15.39
Gross nonperforming loans ratio (percent)	29.31	30.41	28.80	22.77	18.94	14.22	0.20–8.00
Provisions to nonperforming loans ratio (percent)	30.59	29.98	7.55	3.82	11.49	4.72	25.40–204.50
Liquid assets ratio (percent)	22.10	18.16	12.49	13.61	9.33	9.70	7.07–40.44
Liquid assets to liabilities ratio (percent)	47.88	41.33	27.03	27.30	20.34	19.07	1.82–42.20

Capital market development

Domestic bond market to equity market capitalization (percent)	129.55	212.14	240.19	204.93	142.69	92.96	2.97–145.36
Domestic public bonds outstanding to GDP (percent)	14.50	17.40	18.50	17.30	16.40	14.10	8.83–58.69
Ratio of trading value of top 10 stocks to total trading value (percent)	83.13	81.89	58.35	86.25	83.96	66.50	14.46–82.10
Stock market capitalization to GDP (percent)	11.76	8.54	8.05	8.72	10.49	15.19	33.14–903.56
Market liquidity: Ratio of stock trading value to GDP (percent)	0.59	0.38	0.13	0.45	0.77	0.54	12.47–438.57
Stock market turnover ratio (times)	0.05	0.04	0.02	0.06	0.09	0.04	0.34–2.21

Market concentration and competitiveness

Herfindahl-Hirschman index (HHI)	1,563.48	1,574.76	1,468.53	1,245.62	1,019.21	949.86	[HHI < 1,000 unconcentrated; 1,000 < HHI < 1,800 moderately concentrated; HHI > 1,800 highly concentrated] 345.65–1,869.49
K-bank concentration ratio (K=3) – assets (percent)	58.02	58.68	56.67	52.88	45.87	43.58	21.30–64.41
K-bank concentration ratios (K=3) – deposits (percent)	51.73	49.62	46.80	44.00	41.73	38.16	19.93–62.80
K-bank concentration ratios (K=3) – loans (percent)	52.06	49.34	44.64	42.14	37.28	30.30	18.39–66.30
Private credit extended by banks to GDP (percent)	26.95	27.21	27.80	28.95	27.57	26.98	42.00–193.60
Commercial Banking assets to GDP (percent)	63.83	67.69	69.84	71.55	70.25	67.32	44.90–174.28

Sources: Nepal Rastra Bank; the Securities Board of Nepal; World Bank 2007a; IMF 2007b (stock market capitalization/GDP for 2001); and Beck, Demirgüç-Kunt, and Levine 2000 (private credit to GDP for 2001 and 2002).

Note: All benchmark indicators are in respect of selected high-income OECD member and nonmember countries (Australia; Canada; Hong Kong, China; New Zealand; Singapore; the United Kingdom; and the United States).

Table A1.10 Getting Finance Indicators for Pakistan, 2001–06

Indicator	2001	2002	2003	2004	2005	2006	Benchmark
Access to finance							
Demographic branch penetration (branches per 100,000 people)	4.88	4.73	4.61	4.64	4.82	4.96	9–30
Demographic ATM penetration (ATMs per 100,000 people)	N/A	N/A	0.37	0.52	0.67	1.25	37–167
Deposit accounts per 1,000 people	195.84	194.87	190.55	180.28	173.15	171.14	976–2,418
Loan accounts per 1,000 people	16.04	14.93	18.86	24.51	30.57	31.78	248–776
Geographic branch penetration (branches per 1,000 km^2)	8.77	8.72	8.66	8.84	9.22	9.67	1–61
Geographic ATM penetration (ATMs per 1,000 km^2)	N/A	N/A	0.69	0.99	1.29	2.44	1–252
Performance and efficiency							
Return on equity (percent)	12.20	27.50	33.70	29.00	36.90	34.70	6.10–25.51
Return on assets (percent)	0.60	1.50	2.10	2.00	2.90	3.20	0.40–1.90
Staff cost ratio (percent)	52.58	50.75	51.48	51.97	50.73	51.22	23.00–56.30
Operating cost ratio (percent)	90.91	85.81	83.20	83.62	57.73	54.63	49.20–157.59
Net interest margin (percent)	3.24	3.10	2.98	2.87	4.11	4.41	1.04–3.55
Recurring earning power (percent)	1.17	2.00	2.57	2.26	3.35	3.66	0.81–2.39
Financial stability							
Capital adequacy ratio (percent)	11.30	12.60	11.10	11.40	11.90	13.33	[not lower than 8% of RWA-Basel] 9.60–18.20
Leverage ratio (times)	4.58	4.11	5.03	6.45	7.64	8.94	6.01–15.39
Gross nonperforming loans ratio (percent)	19.60	17.70	13.70	9.00	6.70	5.70	0.20–8.00
Provisions to nonperforming loans ratio (percent)	53.20	58.20	64.80	72.40	80.40	81.50	25.40–204.50
Liquid assets ratio (percent)	39.90	48.10	46.10	37.00	33.90	32.20	7.07–40.44
Liquid assets to liabilities ratio (percent)	56.25	68.95	63.44	51.88	52.77	55.13	1.82–42.20

Appendix 1. Getting Finance Indicators for South Asia, by Country and Year

Capital market development

Indicator						
Domestic bond market to equity market capitalization (percent)	537.75	278.47	186.41	108.60	73.94	71.20	2.97–145.36
Domestic public bonds outstanding to GDP (percent)	38.90	37.80	36.70	33.00	30.90	27.46	8.83–58.69
Ratio of trading value of top 10 stocks to total trading value (percent)	22.52	21.89	19.18	16.01	20.48	20.02	14.46–82.10
Stock market capitalization to GDP (percent)	8.06	9.15	15.31	24.07	30.59	35.87	33.14–903.56
Market liquidity: Ratio of stock trading value to GDP (percent)	0.02	0.15	0.13	0.19	0.11	0.03	12.47–438.57
Stock market turnover ratio (times)	0.12	0.90	0.54	0.50	0.22	0.06	0.34–2.21

Market concentration and competitiveness

Indicator						
Herfindahl-Hirschman index (HHI)	1,091.80	1,052.12	976.81	903.97	805.61	784.01	[HHI < 1,000 unconcentrated; 1,000 < HHI < 1,800 moderately concentrated; HHI > 1,800 highly concentrated] 345.65–1,869.49
K-bank concentration ratio (K=3) – assets (percent)	50.30	49.71	47.47	43.95	40.35	38.96	21.30–64.41
K-bank concentration ratios (K=3) – deposits (percent)	53.23	51.76	48.93	45.55	41.49	40.04	19.93–62.80
K-bank concentration ratios (K=3) – loans (percent)	50.86	47.00	43.58	42.56	41.96	39.67	18.39–66.30
Private credit extended by banks to GDP (percent)	16.29	16.90	21.06	25.86	28.83	29.30	42.00–193.60
Commercial Banking assets to GDP (percent)	43.61	47.72	50.10	52.07	53.89	53.96	44.90–174.28

Sources: State Bank of Pakistan and the SEC of Pakistan.
Note: All benchmark indicators are in respect of selected high-income OECD member and nonmember countries (Australia; Canada; Hong Kong, China; New Zealand; Singapore; the United Kingdom; and the United States).

Table A1.11 Getting Finance Indicators for Sri Lanka, 2001–06

Indicator	2001	2002	2003	2004	2005	2006	Benchmark
Access to finance							
Demographic branch penetration (branches per 100,000 people)	6.03	6.70	6.85	7.06	7.20	7.69	9–30
Demographic ATM penetration (ATMs per 100,000 people)	2.55	3.27	3.69	4.16	4.50	5.67	37–167
Deposit accounts per 1,000 people	939.32	989.94	1,000.53	1,023.58	1,066.24	1,117.82	976–2,418
Loan accounts per 1,000 people	256.88	257.66	279.15	304.11	344.17	364.22	248–776
Geographic branch penetration (branches per 1,000 km^2)	11.68	13.17	13.63	14.20	14.64	15.81	1–61
Geographic ATM penetration (ATMs per 1,000 km^2)	4.93	6.43	7.34	8.37	9.15	11.65	1–252
Performance and efficiency							
Return on equity (percent)	20.57	25.71	26.33	25.62	27.01	27.01	6.10–25.51
Return on assets (percent)	0.84	1.11	1.36	1.43	1.70	1.83	0.40–1.90
Staff cost ratio (percent)	46.21	47.62	49.58	46.98	44.53	41.49	23.00–56.30
Operating cost ratio (percent)	118.66	99.80	94.02	95.66	87.70	84.68	49.20–157.59
Net interest margin (percent)	3.30	3.78	4.16	3.97	4.05	4.31	1.04–3.55
Recurring earning power (percent)	1.64	2.07	2.58	2.33	2.26	2.03	0.81–2.39
Financial stability							
Capital adequacy ratio (percent)	8.59	10.35	10.31	10.29	12.84	11.82	(not lower than 8% of RWA-Basel)/9.60–18.20
Leverage ratio (times)	3.90	4.71	5.53	5.63	6.93	6.78	6.01–15.39
Gross nonperforming loans ratio (percent)	19.57	19.09	16.36	11.29	8.76	7.16	0.20–8.00
Provisions to nonperforming loans ratio (percent)	44.43	50.38	58.74	68.29	72.05	68.12	25.40–204.50
Liquid assets ratio (percent)	22.80	18.80	17.30	20.30	19.60	19.00	7.07–40.44
Liquid assets to liabilities ratio (percent)	26.30	21.70	20.00	23.10	22.10	21.90	1.82–42.20

Appendix 1. Getting Finance Indicators for South Asia, by Country and Year

Capital market development							
Domestic bond market to equity market capitalization (percent)	659.05	585.08	389.76	299.80	216.69	136.68	2.97–145.36
Domestic public bonds outstanding to GDP (percent)	16.28	21.94	27.43	31.70	31.77	31.62	8.83–58.69
Ratio of trading value of top 10 stocks to total trading value (percent)	54.37	57.70	60.83	42.92	43.10	57.13	14.46–82.10
Stock market capitalization to GDP (percent)	8.81	10.28	14.92	18.83	24.69	29.80	33.14–903.56
Market liquidity: Ratio of stock trading value to GDP (percent)	0.99	1.91	4.18	2.92	4.84	3.75	12.47–438.57
Stock market turnover ratio (times)	0.13	0.21	0.35	0.18	0.24	0.15	0.34–2.21
Market concentration and competitiveness							
Herfindahl-Hirschman index (HHI)	1,650.62	1,528.39	1,455.81	1,377.33	1,279.44	1,259.88	[HHI < 1,000 – unconcentrated; 1,000 < HHI < 1,800 moderately concentrated; HHI > 1,800 highly concentrated] 345.65–1,869.49
K-bank concentration ratio (K=3) – assets (percent)	63.09	60.88	58.19	55.68	53.02	52.79	21.30–64.41
K-bank concentration ratios (K=3) – deposits (percent)	62.02	62.43	60.89	58.25	56.30	55.56	19.93–62.80
K-bank concentration ratios (K=3) – loans (percent)	65.16	60.02	56.81	53.28	50.44	52.74	18.39–66.30
Private credit extended by banks to GDP (percent)	28.19	28.09	29.50	31.26	33.87	35.45	42.00–193.60
Commercial Banking assets to GDP (percent)	56.80	54.51	56.06	56.92	61.79	63.61	44.90–174.28

Sources: Central Bank of Sri Lanka, SEC of Sri Lanka, and the Colombo Stock Exchange.
Note: 2006 data are unaudited and provisional.
All benchmark indicators are in respect of selected high-income OECD member and nonmember countries (Australia; Canada; Hong Kong, China; New Zealand; Singapore; the United Kingdom; and the United States).

Appendix 2A Getting Finance Indicators for benchmark countries, 2001–06

Table A2.1 Benchmark Indicators, 2001

Reference	Indicator	United States	United Kingdom	Canada	Australia	New Zealand	Singapore	Hong Kong, China	Benchmark
	Access to finance								
1	Demographic branch penetration (branches per 100,000 people)	24	25	29	25	21	12	24	12–29
2	Demographic ATM penetration (ATMs per 100,000 people)	114	62	115	68	47	43	—	43–115
3	Deposit accounts per 1,000 people			different countries used (976–2,418)					976–2,418
4	Loan accounts per 1,000 people			different countries used (248–776)					248–776
5	Geographic branch penetration (branches per 1,000 km²)	8	61	1	1	3	710	1,575	1–61
6	Geographic ATM penetration (ATMs per 1,000 km²)	35	152	4	1	7	2,632	—	1–152
	Performance and efficiency								
7	Return on equity (percent)	13.00	7.70	13.90	20.10	23.38	9.70	17.90	7.70–23.38
8	Return on assets (percent)	1.10	0.50	0.70	1.30	1.06	1.00	1.40	0.50–1.40
9	Staff cost ratio (percent)	35.51	41.88	44.55	41.98	42.88	36.93	43.86	35.51–44.55
10	Operating cost ratio (percent)	106.82	109.90	149.64	118.64	82.78	49.86	52.22	49.86–149.64
11	Net interest margin (percent)	3.55	1.89	2.23	2.09	2.10	1.81	2.53	1.81–3.55
12	Recurring earning power (percent)	2.22	1.21	1.29	1.55	1.52	1.31	1.93	1.21–2.22
	Financial stability								
13	Capital adequacy ratio (percent)	12.90	13.20	12.30	10.40	10.79	18.20	16.50	10.40–18.20
14	Leverage ratio (times)	10.74	8.64	7.08	9.32	6.58	15.01	9.50	6.58–15.01
15	Gross nonperforming loans ratio (percent)	1.30	2.60	1.50	0.60	1.20	8.00	6.50	0.60–8.00
16	Provisions to nonperforming loans ratio (percent)	128.80	72.20	44.00	107.10	25.40	60.10	59.20	25.40–128.80
17	Liquid assets ratio (percent)	16.77	22.22	18.95	13.33	7.42	40.44	35.64	7.42–40.44
18	Liquid assets to liabilities ratio (percent)	21.24	22.28	2.83	8.89	7.21	30.18	42.20	2.83–42.20
	Capital market development								
19	Domestic bond market to equity market capitalization (percent)	108.70	30.95	86.90	45.48	77.70	42.28	8,908.90	8,908.90–108.70
20	Domestic public bonds outstanding to GDP (percent)	41.92	29.58	58.69	18.16	27.18	32.11	8.83	8.83–58.69
21	Ratio of trading value of top 10 stocks to total trading value (percent)	15.55	37.00	37.30	50.40	57.00	27.90	44.70	15.55–57.00
22	Stock market capitalization to GDP (percent)	145.98	169.59	110.52	102.22	35.58	160.80	350.02	35.58–350.02
23	Market liquidity: Ratio of stock trading value to GDP (percent)	290.00	130.77	65.53	65.31	16.21	74.68	120.25	16.21–290.00
24	Stock market turnover ratio (times)	1.99	0.77	0.59	0.64	0.46	0.47	0.34	0.34–1.99
	Market concentration and competitiveness								
25	Herfindahl-Hirschman index (HHI)	498.54	514.28	1,375.15	952.49	924.28	1,658.53	1,192.77	498.54–1,658.53
26	K-bank concentration ratio (K=3) – assets (percent)	34.88	27.04	51.56	41.19	33.40	61.19	52.29	27.04–61.19
27	K-bank concentration ratios (K=3) – deposits (percent)	36.16	27.44	51.31	40.20	34.72	60.18	51.01	27.44–60.18
28	K-bank concentration ratios (K=3) – loans (percent)	30.41	27.02	50.19	37.54	34.73	66.30	45.10	27.02–66.30
29	Private credit extended by banks to GDP (percent)	42.00	131.95	66.98	87.65	108.07	112.28	157.85	42.00–157.85
30	Commercial banking assets to GDP (percent)	44.90	131.69	76.98	91.13	113.33	136.51	174.28	44.90–174.28

Appendix 2. Getting Finance Indicators for benchmark countries, 2001–06   133

Table A2.2 Benchmark Indicators, 2002

Reference	Indicator	United States	United Kingdom	Canada	Australia	New Zealand	Singapore	Hong Kong, China	Benchmark
	Access to finance								
1	Demographic branch penetration (branches per 100,000 people)	25	24	29	25	28	11	23	11–29
2	Demographic ATM penetration (ATMs per 100,000 people)	122	69	128	83	48	37	—	37–128
3	Deposit accounts per 1,000 people			different countries used (976–2,418)				976–2,418
4	Loan accounts per 1,000 people			different countries used (248–776)				248–776
5	Geographic branch penetration (branches per 1,000 km²)	8	60	1	1	4	650	1,470	1–60
6	Geographic ATM penetration (ATMs per 1,000 km²)	38	169	4	2	7	2,266	—	2–169
	Performance and efficiency								
7	Return on equity (percent)	14.10	6.10	9.30	20.20	25.51	7.60	17.20	6.10–25.51
8	Return on assets (percent)	1.30	0.40	0.40	1.40	1.25	0.80	1.50	0.40–1.50
9	Staff cost ratio (percent)	35.62	39.19	43.05	41.91	44.36	33.35	43.5933	35–44.36
10	Operating cost ratio (percent)	102.21	106.29	138.44	115.74	75.00	62.27	53.3953	39–138.44
11	Net interest margin (percent)	3.55	1.83	2.45	2.09	2.26	2.01	2.36	1.83–3.55
12	Recurring earning power (percent)	2.39	1.18	1.24	1.53	1.77	1.54	1.83	1.18–2.39
	Financial stability								
13	Capital adequacy ratio (percent)	13.00	13.10	12.40	9.60	11.08	16.90	15.80	9.60–16.90
14	Leverage ratio (times)	10.66	8.47	6.92	9.18	7.19	14.64	9.79	6.92–14.64
15	Gross nonperforming loans ratio (percent)	1.40	2.60	1.60	0.40	0.70	7.70	5.00	0.70–7.70
16	Provisions to nonperforming loans ratio (percent)	123.70	75.00	41.10	106.20	37.50	61.20	62.9337	50–123.70
17	Liquid assets ratio (percent)	16.75	22.16	19.24	13.66	7.07	31.70	30.92	7.07–31.70
18	Liquid assets to liabilities ratio (percent)	21.34	22.61	2.99	9.15	6.65	31.39	39.60	2.99–39.60
	Capital market development								
19	Domestic bond market to equity market capitalization (percent)	145.00	40.99	109.42	55.10	84.40	52.99	10.0610	.06–145.00
20	Domestic public bonds outstanding to GDP (percent)	42.26	28.52	56.57	16.55	26.99	35.53	9.33	9.33–56.57
21	Ratio of trading value of top 10 stocks to total trading value (percent)	17.55	36.40	28.60	48.40	78.70	22.20	46.4017	.55–78.70
22	Stock market capitalization to GDP (percent)	120.61	131.72	88.65	92.86	33.14	124.91	304.8533	14–304.85
23	Market liquidity: Ratio of stock trading value to GDP (percent)	244.23	174.36	56.00	72.13	12.47	63.58	131.8812	.47–244.23
24	Stock market turnover ratio (times)	2.03	1.32	0.63	0.78	0.38	0.51	0.43	0.38–2.03
	Market concentration and competitiveness								
25	Herfindahl-Hirschman index (HHI)	484.12	560.56	1,386.29	927.66	907.04	1,869.49	1,136.5048	4.12–1,869.49
26	K-bank concentration ratio (K=3) – assets (percent)	33.75	30.03	51.88	40.18	34.37	63.79	50.7830	.03–63.79
27	K-bank concentration ratios (K=3) – deposits (percent)	36.17	29.72	51.14	39.56	35.09	62.26	49.0329	.72–62.26
28	K-bank concentration ratios (K=3) – loans (percent)	28.95	30.95	50.34	37.56	35.47	62.38	43.1128	.95–62.38
29	Private credit extended by banks to GDP (percent)	42.30	135.94	67.88	89.79	111.18	111.81	154.9842	.30–154.98
30	Commercial banking assets to GDP (percent)	45.23	136.53	78.39	92.17	116.62	138.06	172.9345	.23–172.93

Table A2.3 Benchmark Indicators, 2003

Reference	Indicator	United States	United Kingdom	Canada	Australia	New Zealand	Singapore	Hong Kong, China	Benchmark
	Access to finance								
1	Demographic branch penetration (branches per 100,000 people)	30	24	29	24	28	10	21	10–30
2	Demographic ATM penetration (ATMs per 100,000 people)	128	78	139	102	47	37	—	37–139
3	Deposit accounts per 1,000 people	different countries used (976–2,418)							976–2,418
4	Loan accounts per 1,000 people	different countries used (248–776)							248–776
5	Geographic branch penetration (branches per 1,000 km^2)	8	59	1	1	4	592	1,375	1–59
6	Geographic ATM penetration (ATMs per 1,000 km^2)	40	192	5	3	7	2,275	—	3–192
	Performance and efficiency								
7	Return on equity (percent)	15.00	8.60	14.70	24.20	25.27	10.10	17.80	8.60–25.27
8	Return on assets (percent)	1.40	0.60	0.70	1.60	1.15	1.10	1.90	0.60–1.90
9	Staff cost ratio (percent)	38.29	39.90	45.76	43.44	40.59	36.65	44.3036.55	45.76
10	Operating cost ratio (percent)	105.72	106.24	146.08	113.93	76.14	49.20	57.2149.20	146.08
11	Net interest margin (percent)	3.37	1.70	2.36	2.02	2.28	2.08	2.11	1.70–3.37
12	Recurring earning power (percent)	2.30	1.18	1.25	1.63	1.82	1.62	1.72	1.18–2.30
	Financial stability								
13	Capital adequacy ratio (percent)	13.00	13.00	13.40	10.00	10.30	17.90	15.3010.00	17.90
14	Leverage ratio (times)	10.57	8.64	6.63	9.71	6.01	15.39	8.88	6.01–15.39
15	Gross nonperforming loans ratio (percent)	1.10	2.50	1.20	0.30	0.30	6.70	3.90	0.30–6.70
16	Provisions to nonperforming loans ratio (percent)	140.40	71.20	43.50	131.80	45.40	64.90	64.0343.50	140.40
17	Liquid assets ratio (percent)	16.73	22.35	21.64	13.76	7.59	29.66	29.99	7.59–29.99
18	Liquid assets to liabilities ratio (percent)	21.46	24.87	2.46	9.39	7.41	29.25	36.66	2.46–36.66
	Capital market development								
19	Domestic bond market to equity market capitalization (percent)	123.27	33.60	88.23	51.92	71.46	39.98	6.466.46	123.27
20	Domestic public bonds outstanding to GDP (percent)	44.17	27.68	54.63	15.46	26.55	38.43	9.94	9.94–54.63
21	Ratio of trading value of top 10 stocks to total trading value (percent)	16.42	35.50	26.00	44.80	74.00	31.70	38.2016.42	74.00
22	Stock market capitalization to GDP (percent)	117.25	120.03	86.18	93.04	34.61	64.90	382.1034.61	382.10
23	Market liquidity: Ratio of stock trading value to GDP (percent)	142.20	120.11	54.61	70.88	13.17	95.12	214.1913.17	214.19
24	Stock market turnover ratio (times)	1.21	1.00	0.63	0.76	0.38	0.71	0.56	0.38–1.21
	Market concentration and competitiveness								
25	Herfindahl-Hirschman index (HHI)	459.53	553.58	1,470.51	926.74	898.85	1,864.85	1,140.87459.53	1,864.85
26	K-bank concentration ratio (K=3) – assets (percent)	32.58	29.64	53.50	39.43	34.43	64.41	50.6929.54	64.41
27	K-bank concentration ratio (K=3) – deposits (percent)	35.03	29.96	53.09	38.07	35.52	62.80	48.5629.96	62.80
28	K-bank concentration ratio (K=3) – loans (percent)	27.11	30.91	51.57	35.76	35.77	60.04	43.6227.11	60.04
29	Private credit extended by banks to GDP (percent)	43.11	140.53	67.96	95.43	113.13	107.83	153.3943.11	153.39
30	Commercial banking assets to GDP (percent)	45.80	141.35	78.28	96.59	119.00	135.21	172.1045.80	172.10

Appendix 2. Getting Finance Indicators for benchmark countries, 2001–06   135

Table A2.4 Benchmark Indicators, 2004

Reference	Indicator	United States	United Kingdom	Canada	Australia	New Zealand	Singapore	Hong Kong, China	Benchmark
	Access to finance								
1	9–28				25	23	28	24	28
20	Demographic branch penetration (branches per 100,000 people)								
2	Demographic ATM penetration (ATMs per 100,000 people)			different countries used (976–2,418)				—	38–152
3	Deposit accounts per 1,000 people								976–2,418
4	Loan accounts per 1,000 people			different countries used (248–776)					248–776
5	Geographic branch penetration (branches per 1,000 km²)	8	58	1	1	4	583	1,352	1–58
6	Geographic ATM penetration (ATMs per 1,000 km²)	42	225	5	3	8	2,357	—	3–225
	Performance and efficiency								
7	Return on equity (percent)	13.20	10.90	16.70	22.80	15.59	11.80	20.30	10.90–22.80
8	Return on assets (percent)	1.30	0.70	0.80	1.50	0.98	1.30	1.70	0.70–1.70
9	Staff cost ratio (percent)	38.44	43.05	48.36	44.98	39.68	43.85	56.30	38.44–56.30
10	Operating cost ratio (percent)	109.56	106.25	154.30	126.78	78.19	59.57	63.01	59.57–154.30
11	Net interest margin (percent)	3.12	1.45	2.19	1.85	2.04	1.82	1.78	1.45–3.12
12	Recurring earning power (percent)	1.97	1.07	1.26	1.40	1.43	1.38	1.55	1.07–1.97
	Financial stability								
13	Capital adequacy ratio (percent)	13.20	12.70	13.30	10.40	10.84	16.10	15.40	10.40–16.10
14	Leverage ratio (times)	10.93	7.89	6.41	10.12	8.16	15.18	8.38	6.41–15.18
15	Gross nonperforming loans ratio (percent)	0.80	1.90	0.70	0.20	0.30	4.00	2.30	0.20–4.00
16	Provisions to nonperforming loans ratio (percent)	168.10	64.50	47.70	182.90	34.20	76.00	88.43	34.20–182.90
17	Liquid assets ratio (percent)	16.45	27.22	21.04	12.99	7.50	31.54	31.53	7.50–31.54
18	Liquid assets to liabilities ratio (percent)	21.36	13.32	2.49	8.45	7.55	21.89	24.43	2.49–24.43
	Capital market development								
19	Domestic bond market to equity market capitalization (percent)	118.07	36.96	74.57	45.85	56.55	38.58	5.58	5.58–118.07
20	Domestic public bonds outstanding to GDP (percent)	45.38	27.82	55.10	14.65	24.40	38.22	9.67	9.67–55.10
21	Ratio of trading value of top 10 stocks to total trading value (percent)	15.29	32.80	24.30	42.50	75.60	40.90	39.50	15.29–75.60
22	Stock market capitalization to GDP (percent)	131.62	122.96	106.37	108.40	38.71	149.04	486.34	38.71–486.34
23	Market liquidity: Ratio of stock trading value to GDP (percent)	165.81	173.37	66.73	81.46	15.45	76.00	269.33	15.45–269.33
24	Stock market turnover ratio (times)	1.26	1.41	0.63	0.75	0.40	0.51	0.55	0.40–1.41
	Market concentration and competitiveness								
25	Herfindahl-Hirschman index (HHI)	517.74	345.65	1,449.90	820.08	1,172.17	1,093.98	627.51	345.65–1,449.90
26	K-bank concentration ratio (K=3) – assets (percent)	35.07	21.16	53.39	35.58	46.59	38.04	35.35	21.16–53.39
27	K-bank concentration ratios (K=3) – deposits (percent)	37.20	21.84	52.37	34.97	44.08	38.96	34.73	21.84–52.37
28	K-bank concentration ratios (K=3) – loans (percent)	28.39	21.90	50.16	33.19	44.66	37.03	31.97	21.90–50.16
29	Private credit extended by banks to GDP (percent)	44.00	147.61	69.59	100.94	116.56	101.38	141.34	44.00–147.61

Table A2.5 Benchmark Indicators, 2005

Reference	Indicator	United States	United Kingdom	Canada	Australia	New Zealand	Singapore	Hong Kong, China	Benchmark
	Access to finance								
1	Demographic branch penetration (branches per 100,000 people)	26	23	28	24	28	9	20	9–28
2	Demographic ATM penetration (ATMs per 100,000 people)	134	97	158	115	57	39	—	39–158
3	Deposit accounts per 1,000 people			different countries used (976–2,418)					976–2,418
4	Loan accounts per 1,000 people			different countries used (248–776)					248–776
5	Geographic branch penetration (branches per 1,000 km²)	8	57	1	1	4	580	1,338	1–57
6	Geographic ATM penetration (ATMs per 1,000 km²)	43	241	6	3	9	2,487	—	3–241
	Performance and efficiency								
7	Return on equity (percent)	12.70	11.80	14.90	25.30	14.54	11.10	19.10	11.10–25.30
8	Return on assets (percent)	1.30	0.80	0.70	1.80	0.94	1.20	1.70	0.70–1.80
9	Staff cost ratio (percent)	40.00	42.69	44.97	42.26	23.00	43.23	52.71	23.00–52.71
10	Operating cost ratio (percent)	108.06	110.00	168.99	101.14	112.46	66.94	65.19	65.19–168.99
11	Net interest margin (percent)	3.13	1.17	1.95	1.98	2.82	1.80	1.84	1.17–3.13
12	Recurring earning power (percent)	2.06	0.82	1.09	1.51	1.39	1.33	1.49	0.82–2.06
	Financial stability								
13	Capital adequacy ratio (percent)	13.00	12.80	12.90	10.40	10.91	15.80	15.30	10.40–15.80
14	Leverage ratio (times)	11.68	6.58	6.32	9.31	8.03	15.25	8.13	6.32–15.25
15	Gross nonperforming loans ratio (percent)	0.70	1.00	0.50	0.20	0.30	3.00	1.40	0.20–3.00
16	Provisions to nonperforming loans ratio (percent)	155.00	56.10	49.30	203.00	38.20	80.90	81.34	38.20–203.00
17	Liquid assets ratio (percent)	15.81	30.94	22.59	10.10	7.30	29.87	31.26	7.30–31.26
18	Liquid assets to liabilities ratio (percent)	20.36	11.78	2.47	5.65	5.81	13.21	23.26	2.47–23.26
	Capital market development								
19	Domestic bond market to equity market capitalization (percent)	123.66	32.79	63.76	45.84	57.43	32.78	4.95	4.95–123.66
20	Domestic public bonds outstanding to GDP (percent)	47.23	28.95	57.38	15.25	25.40	39.78	10.07	10.07–47.23
21	Ratio of trading value of top 10 stocks to total trading value (percent)	15.88	29.60	23.00	38.60	76.40	39.20	43.80	15.88–43.80
22	Stock market capitalization to GDP (percent)	135.10	126.22	109.19	111.27	39.74	152.99	499.21	39.74–499.21
23	Market liquidity: Ratio of stock trading value to GDP (percent)	181.53	189.80	73.06	89.17	16.92	83.20	294.85	16.92–294.85
24	Stock market turnover ratio (times)	1.30	1.45	0.65	0.77	0.41	0.52	0.57	0.41–1.45
	Market concentration and competitiveness								
25	Herfindahl-Hirschman index (HHI)	526.01	596.43	1,447.54	475.57	877.84	1,139.75	1,033.59	475.57 – 1,447.54
26	K-bank concentration ratio (K=3) – assets (percent)	35.24	32.87	54.23	21.30	38.83	41.05	47.56	21.30–54.23
27	K-bank concentration ratios (K=3) – deposits (percent)	37.26	35.10	53.53	19.93	37.05	42.32	48.75	19.93–53.53
28	K-bank concentration ratios (K=3) – loans (percent)	28.72	30.54	50.48	18.39	36.72	40.35	42.37	18.39–50.48
29	Private credit extended by banks to GDP (percent)	47.84	160.48	75.65	109.73	129.47	110.21	160.18	47.84–160.48
30	Commercial banking assets to GDP (percent)	46.50	149.40	79.80	102.30	121.91	127.37	167.76	46.50–167.76

Table A2.6 Benchmark Indicators, 2006

Reference	Indicator	United States	United Kingdom	Canada	Australia	New Zealand	Singapore	Hong Kong, China	Benchmark
	Access to finance								
1	Demographic branch penetration (branches per 100,000 people)	26	23	28	25	28	9	20	9–28
2	Demographic ATM penetration (ATMs per 100,000 people)	134	101	167	120	56	39	—	39–167
3	Deposit accounts per 1,000 people[a]			different countries used (976–2,418)					976–2,418
4	Loan accounts per 1,000 people[a]			different countries used (248–776)					248–776
5	Geographic branch penetration (branches per 1,000 km²)[b]	8	57	1	1	4	580	1,338	1–57
6	Geographic ATM penetration (ATMs per 1,000 km²)[b]	43	252	6	3	9	2,487	—	3–252
	Performance and efficiency								
7	Return on equity (percent)	12.80	8.09	20.90	18.60	14.88	13.70	18.17	8.09–18.60
8	Return on assets (percent)	1.30	0.50	1.00	1.12	0.98	1.40	1.80	0.50–1.80
9	Staff cost ratio (percent)	41.86	45.21	48.82	51.90	43.44	48.36	50.93	41.86–51.90
10	Operating cost ratio (percent)	108.66	117.05	157.59	89.65	70.85	63.28	62.65	62.65–157.59
11	Net interest margin (percent)	2.93	1.04	1.76	2.03	2.07	1.83	1.90	1.04–2.93
12	Recurring earning power (percent)	2.03	0.81	1.30	1.46	1.44	1.62	1.65	0.81–2.03
	Financial stability								
13	Capital adequacy ratio (percent)	13.10	12.90	12.60	10.60	10.67	15.40	15.00	10.60–15.40
14	Leverage ratio (times)	11.77	6.02	6.49	8.50	7.70	14.37	8.69	6.02–14.37
15	Gross nonperforming loans ratio (percent)	0.70	0.90	0.40	0.20	0.20	2.40	1.10	0.20–2.40
16	Provisions to nonperforming loans ratio (percent)	148.40	63.54	55.30	204.50	36.30	86.90	80.56	36.30–204.50
17	Liquid assets ratio (percent)	16.65	34.13	23.96	10.88	9.41	29.61	30.80	9.41–34.13
18	Liquid assets to liabilities ratio (percent)	21.64	17.80	1.82	3.48	6.39	8.47	22.31	1.82–22.31
	Capital market development								
19	Domestic bond market to equity market capitalization (percent)	145.36	32.62	57.90	41.67	45.56	20.61	2,972.97	145.36
20	Domestic public bonds outstanding to GDP (percent)	48.57	35.84	48.52	12.95	19.69	43.03	9.49	9.49–48.57
21	Ratio of trading value of top 10 stocks to total trading value (percent)	14.46	28.10	26.20	—	82.10	37.60	35.30	14.46–82.10
22	Stock market capitalization to GDP (percent)	148.25	164.97	130.82	142.65	43.13	290.69	903.56	43.13–903.56
23	Market liquidity: Ratio of stock trading value to GDP (percent)	259.09	329.20	98.60	111.89	21.41	136.34	438.57	21.41–438.57
24	Stock market turnover ratio (times)	1.85	2.21	0.81	0.90	0.52	0.56	0.60	0.52–2.21
	Market concentration and competitiveness								
25	Herfindahl-Hirschman index (HHI)	563.35	704.03	1,501.22	674.16	1,611.11	1,707.79	1,854.41	563.35 – 1,854.41
26	K-bank concentration ratio (K=3) – assets (percent)	37.58	35.57	56.14	30.98	57.99	57.06	58.29	30.98–58.29
27	K-bank concentration ratios (K=3) – deposits (percent)	39.55	39.12	55.91	36.51	57.49	58.58	58.05	36.51–58.58
28	K-bank concentration ratios (K=3) – loans (percent)	31.01	35.83	52.26	34.10	56.07	56.93	50.93	31.01–56.93
29	Private credit extended by banks to GDP (percent)	88.16	193.60	143.04	123.61	158.70	98.19	139.33	88.16–193.60
30	Commercial banking assets to GDP (percent)[c]	46.50	149.40	79.80	102.30	121.91	127.37	167.76	46.50–167.76

Appendix 2B. Benchmark Countries: Data Sources and Notes

Sources: By indicator.
1. BIS 2007, various central bank reports, OECD 2007, and World Bank staff calculations.
2. BIS 2007, various central bank reports, OECD 2007, and World Bank staff calculations.
3. World Bank 2006a.
4. World Bank 2006a.
5. BIS 2007, various central bank reports, OECD 2007, and World Bank staff calculations.
6. BIS 2007, various central bank reports, OECD 2007, and World Bank staff calculations.
7. IMF 2007a (New Zealand, BvDEP [Bankscope] 2007 aggregate data).
8. IMF 2007a (New Zealand, BvDEP [Bankscope] 2007 aggregate data).
9. BvDEP (Bankscope) 2007 aggregate data.
10. BvDEP (Bankscope) 2007 aggregate data.
11. BvDEP (Bankscope) 2007 aggregate data.
12. BvDEP (Bankscope) 2007 aggregate data.
13. IMF 2007a (New Zealand, OECD 2007 statistics).
14. BvDEP (Bankscope) 2007 aggregate data.
15. IMF 2007a (New Zealand, OECD 2007 statistics).
16. IMF 2007a (New Zealand. OECD 2007 statistics; Hong Kong, China, BvDEP [Bankscope] 2007 aggregate data).
17. BvDEP (Bankscope) 2007 aggregate data.
18. BvDEP (Bankscope) 2007 aggregate data.
19. World Bank 2007a, BIS 2007, World Federation of Exchanges 2007, and World Bank staff calculations.
20. World Bank 2006b, BIS 2007, and World Bank staff calculations.
21. World Federation of Exchanges 2007.
22. World Bank 2006b, World Federation of Exchanges 2007, and World Bank staff calculations.
23. World Bank 2006b, World Federation of Exchanges 2007, and World Bank staff calculations.
24. World Bank 2006b, World Federation of Exchanges 2007, and World Bank staff calculations.
25. BvDEP (Bankscope) 2007 aggregate data.
26. BvDEP (Bankscope) 2007 aggregate data.
27. BvDEP (Bankscope) 2007 aggregate data.
28. BvDEP (Bankscope) 2007 aggregate data.
29. World Bank 2006b (2006 and New Zealand 2005, IMF 2007b, and World Bank staff calculations).
30. World Bank 2006b.

Note: All benchmark indicators are for selected high-income OECD member and nonmember countries (Australia; Canada; Hong Kong, China; New Zealand; Singapore; the United Kingdom; and the United States).
a. Because of the nonavailability of data for high-income countries, benchmark countries for indicators 3 and 4 include Denmark, Greece, Italy, Malaysia, Singapore, Spain, and Thailand (2001–06).
b. Hong Kong, China and Singapore data are removed as outliers from indicators 5 and 6.
c. Due to nonavailability of data, 2005 ratios are used in 2006 for indicator 30.

Appendix 3. Corporate Governance Matrix: Questionnaire Responses, 2006

1. Ownership Structure and Influence of External Stakeholders

Question	Bangladesh	India	Nepal	Pakistan	Sri Lanka
1.1 Identification of substantial majority holders					
1.1.1 What are the rules that govern disclosure of share ownership? Is the ownership structure transparent?	In AA	✓	x	✓	✓
• Top 10 shareholders and percentage of ownership to be disclosed?	✓	✓	x only to regulator	✓	Top 20
• Threshold of share ownership that needs to be disclosed (e.g., 5% and over)?	10%	1%	0.5%	10%; 3% to SBP	5%
• Is the government's ownership disclosed with its special privileges?	✓ in AA	✓ for public bks nomi.	✓	✓ nomi. For govt. cont. bks	✓ nomi. for state bks
• Does government control the nomination and remuneration process for the board of directors?	✓ nomi.	✓ for public sector bks	x		
• Is there evidence of influence from external stakeholders such as labor unions or banking and securities regulators?	x but regulator can	x	x	x	x
• Are the preemption rights of minority shareholders firmly protected (e.g., are they enshrined in the company law and requiring a supermajority [75%] to disapply them)?	✓		x	✓	✓
1.2 Indirect and beneficial ownership					
1.2.1 Are there rules that govern the disclosure by shareholders of ultimate beneficial ownership?	x (only in indiv. tax returns)	✓	x	✓	x no rules but thresholds
• If so, please specify the threshold for disclosure of ownership.		x		3%	10% for indiv.; 15% for co: 20% agg.
• Are shareholders required to disclose their ownership to an authority?		5% ✓		✓	x
• Where, when, by whom, and to whom are such disclosures to be made?		To bank		Annual a/c and reports to SBP	monitored by CBSL
• Do shareholders have access to this information?		✓		✓	x
• Does the market have access to this information?		✓		✓	✓ on s/holdings thru AR only for listed cos
• Please specify monitoring and enforcement provisions, including penalties for noncompliance.		Fines		Penalties from BCO & PRs[a]	x
• How many cases of noncompliance have been recorded in the past five years, and what actions were taken?		N/A		Action taken case by case	x

(Table continues on next page)

2. Investor Rights

Question	Bangladesh	India	Nepal	Pakistan	Sri Lanka
2.1 Shareholder meetings and voting procedures					
2.1.1 Shareholder meetings					
• Are shareholders informed of shareholder meetings?	✓	✓	✓	✓	✓
• How much notice is given (e.g., four weeks before the meeting)?	3 weeks	21 days	3 weeks	21 days	21 days
• Do banks provide detailed agendas and explanatory circulars along with the notice of meetings?	✓	✓	✓	✓	✓
2.1.2 Voting procedures					
• Can shareholders vote by proxy, by post, or electronically?	Proxy	Proxy, post	Proxy, post	Proxy	Proxy
• Is the counting of votes verified by a third party?	x	✓	✓	✓	x
• Can shareholders vote on a normal range of issues, including major and related-party transactions?	✓	✓	x	✓	x
• Are banks required to disclose special voting rights and caps on voting rights?	✓ 5% cap except for govt.	Not reqd. as it is specified in Banking Reg'n Act	✓	✓	x
2.2 Basic ownership rights					
2.2.1 Are all directors' appointments and dismissals subject to a shareholder vote?	✓	✓ only for pvt bks subject to RBI	x	✓ SBP has power to rule	x
• Can the government control such outcomes due to higher percentage of ownership (where applicable)?	N/A	✓ for public bks	x	By virtue of s/holding	Possible
2.2.2 Is there a clear dividend policy?	✓	✓	x	✓	✓
2.2.3 Are there structural takeover defenses that would prevent a legitimate takeover bid?	x	✓ RBI approval for above threshold limits	x	✓ Purchases more than 5% need SBP approval	✓ Purchases more than 10% need CBS/MOF approval (more than 30%, must make offer to all s/holders)
• Can the government or regulators reserve the right to approve such transactions?	x	✓	x Promoters' share transfers need reg. approval	Bank mgt changes need SBP approval	✓
2.2.4 Can minority shareholders easily nominate independent directors?	x	x not in public blks	x	✓	Depends on internal bank rules

3. Transparency and Disclosure

3.1 Adherence to internationally accepted accounting standards

3.1.1 Do banks prepare their financial statements in accordance with local generally accepted accounting principles and provide reconciliation with international accounting standards?	✓ (ROSC Rpt)[a]	✓ (Local GAAP but some do)	✓	✓	x IASC stds as adopted by country
3.1.2 Are accounting standards in material conformity with international accounting standards?	✓ (ROSC Rpt)[a]	✓ Mostly	✓ (ROSC Rpt)[a]		✓ Except IAS 39 & 40
3.1.3 What is the frequency of reporting of financial statements (e.g., quarterly)?	Annual	Quarterly, semi-annual, & annual	Quarterly		Quarterly, semiannual, & annual
3.1.4 Are bank financials available to the general public? If yes, how? On the Web, in newspapers, upon request?	✓ All	✓ All	✓ All		✓ All
3.1.5 Is disclosure of audit and nonaudit fees paid to the external auditor required?	✓	x	✓		✓
3.1.6 Must the chief executive officer, chief financial officer, or directors sign and certify banks' annual accounts?	CEO + 3 directors	✓ CEO + CFO RBI has directed	CEO + CFO + dirs.		CEO + 3 directors

3.2 Independent internal and external auditors and audit committee

3.2.1 Audit committee

• Has the bank appointed an audit committee?	✓	✓	✓		✓
• If banks appoint such a committee, is there a mandate or charter that clearly delineates its responsibilities?	✓	✓	✓		✓
• How often does the committee meet?	3–4/yr min.	Quarterly	x		Quarterly (min.)
• Does the committee control the selection of auditors?	x	✓ for pvt bks	x		✓
• Does the committee chair attend shareholder meetings, and is the chair available to address questions on the audit?	Not clearly stated but expected as chair is a director	✓ RBI has directed	✓		Not clearly stated but expected as chair is a director

(Table continues on next page)

3. Transparency and Disclosure (continued)

Question	Bangladesh	India	Nepal	Pakistan	Sri Lanka
3.2 Independent internal and external auditors and audit committee (continued)					
3.2.2 External auditors					
• Has the bank appointed a reputed and experienced external auditor?	✓	✓	✓	✓	✓
• Does the bank's auditor rotation policy conform to the requirements set by the regulator?	3 yrs	3 yrs	3 yrs	3 yrs	✓
• Does the auditor perform any nonaudit services for the bank?	✓ (under separate TOR)	x	x	x	x
• Are local auditing rules and practices in line with international standards and practices?	✓ (ROSC Rpt)[a]	✓	✓ (ROSC Rpt)[a]	✓	✓
3.2.3 Internal auditor					
• Has the bank appointed a qualified internal auditor?	✓	✓	✓	✓	
• Is the internal auditor independent? Does he report to the audit committee, board of directors, or other governing authorities?	✓	✓	✓	✓	
• Does the internal auditing program include clearly defined policies, processes, and metrics as performance benchmarks?	✓ (ROSC Rpt)[a]	✓	✓	✓	
• Does the internal auditor provide periodic reports on the risk management, control, and governance processes to the audit committee?	✓	✓	✓	✓	
• If so, what is the frequency of such reports?	Quarterly	Annual	Quarterly	Not specified	Not clear (differs from bk to bk)
4. Board Structure and Effectiveness					
4.1 Role and effectiveness					
4.1.1 Structure					
• What is the average structure of the board (unitary, two-tiered, or hybrid)?	Unitary	Unitary	Hybrid	Unitary	Hybrid
• What is the average size of the board?	13	8–10	5–9	7 min.	5–11
• Are there minimum qualification requirements for appointment of board members by law, regulation, and recommended practice?	✓	x	✓	✓	

Appendix 3. Corporate Governance Matrix: Questionnaire Responses, 2006

4.1.2 Role and responsibility					
• Is the scope of the powers and responsibilities of the board clearly defined?		✓	✓	✓	✓
• Are tasks and objectives individually allocated to board members, including the chair and the board secretary?		✓	x	✓	✓ defined by BOD
• Does the board have a process to identify all the laws and regulations it must comply with?		✓	✓	✓	✓
• Is there a process in place for director induction, training, and continuing education?		✓	x	x	✓ orientation courses (SBP prior approval needed)
4.1.3 For two-tier boards, do key responsibilities include the following? (Please specify whether required by law or regulation or recommended by a code.)	NA	NA	NA	N/A	NA Code of best practice issued by CBSL requires BOD to be responsible for these issues
• Reviewing and guiding corporate strategy and major plan of action.					
• Risk policy.					
• Business plans.					
• Setting performance objectives.					
• Monitoring implementation and corporate performance.					
• Overseeing major capital expenditures, acquisitions, and divestitures.					

(Table continues on next page)

4. Board Structure and Effectiveness *(continued)*

4.2 Compensation

Question	Bangladesh	India	Nepal	Pakistan	Sri Lanka
4.2.1 Determination of board remuneration					
• Is there a law or regulation that sets board remuneration?	✓	✓	✓	✓	x differ from bk to bk
• What role do shareholders play in determining board remuneration?	N/A	In pvt sector bks	Approve it at AGM	Approve it at AGM	
• Who sets remuneration for the CEO?	BOD, with BB approval	Govt. for public bks, s/holders for pvt bks	BOD, approve it at AGM	BOD	
4.2.2 Does the board of directors receive some performance-based in the form of an annual cash bonus, stock, or the like?	x	Exec. directors get perform. bonus for achieving targets from 03/2006 public sector banks pay perform. bonus only from 2006–07 and only to full-time executive directors	✓ As per co. ordinance; approved at AGM	x	N/A
4.2.3 Do banks disclose the board's compensation?		✓	✓	✓	✓
• If so, is disclosure aggregate or detailed?	x	Public, aggregate; private detailed	Detailed	Detailed	Aggregate

Sources: South Asian Central Banks, SECs and Boards, and stock exchanges; Indian Banks' Association 2006a, 2006b, and 2006c; Reserve Bank of India 2006a, 2006b, 2006c, and 2007.
Note: For definitions of acronyms and abbreviations, see the list at the beginning of the report.
N/A = not available; NA = not applicable.
a. The ROSC Report provides information that is contradictory to questionnaire responses (for Bangladesh, see World Bank 2003; for Nepal, see World Bank 2005a).

References

Al-Muharrami, Saeed, Kent Matthews, and Yusuf Khabari. 2006. "Market Structure and Competitive Conditions in the Arab GCC Banking System." *Journal of Banking and Finance* 30: 3487–3501.

Bangladesh Bank. 2007a. *Annual Report, 2006*. Dakha.

———. 2007b. *Financial Sector Review, 2006*. Vol. 2, no. 2. Dakha.

———. 2007c. Central Bank of Bangladesh official Web site. http://www.bangladesh-bank.org/ (accessed in 2007).

BIS (Bank for International Settlements). 2006. Basel Committee on Banking Supervision. "Enhancing Corporate Governance for Banking Organizations." February 2006. Basel.

———. 2007. *BIS 2007 Quarterly Review: 'September 2007*: http://www.BIS 2007.org/ (accessed in 2007).

Barth, Caprio Jr., and Ross Levine. 2001. "The Regulation and Supervision of Banks Around the World—A New Database." Working Paper No. 2588. World Bank, Washington, D.C.

Beck, Demirgüç-Kunt, and Ross Levine. 2000. "A New Database on Financial Development and Structure." *World Bank Economic Review* 14. World Bank, Washington, D.C. (Database Revised September 2005.)

Beck, Thorsten, Asli Demirgüç-Kunt, and Maria Soledad Martinez Peria. 2005. "Reaching Out: Access to and Use of Banking Services across Countries." Policy Research Working Paper No. 3754. World Bank, Washington, D.C.

BvDEP (Bureau van Dijk Electronic Publishing). 2007. Bankscope Database. https://bankscope.bvdep.com/ (accessed in 2006/2007).

Central Bank of Sri Lanka. 2006a. *Annual Report, 2005*. Colombo.

———. 2006b. *Financial System Stability Review, 2006*. Colombo.

———. 2007a *Annual Report, 2006*. Colombo.

———. 2007b. *Financial System Stability Review, 2007*. Colombo.

———. 2007c. Central Bank of Sri Lanka official Web site. http://www.cbsl.gov.lk/ (accessed in 2007).

Colombo Stock Exchange. 2007. Colombo Stock Exchange (CSE). http://www.cse.lk (accessed in 2007).

Djankov, Simeon, Darshini Manraj, Caralee McLiesh, and Rita Ramalto. 2005. "Doing Business Indicators: Why Aggregate and How to Do It." Resource Paper. World Bank and International Finance Corporation, Washington, D.C. http://siteresources.worldbank.org/EXTAFRSUMAFTPS/Resources/db_indicators.pdf.

Enterprise Development Impact Assessment Information Service. 2003. "How to Promote Good Corporate Governance." http://www.enterprise-impact.org.uk/ (accessed in 2006).

Hilbers, Paul. 2001. "The IMF/World Bank Financial Sector Assessment Program." *Economic Perspectives* 6 (1). International Monetary Fund, Washington, D.C.

Hilbers, Paul, Inci Otker-Robe, and Ceyla Pazarbaşıoğlu. 2006. "Going Too Fast?" *Finance and Development* 43 (1). International Monetary Fund, Washington, D.C.

IMF (International Monetary Fund). 2007a. *Global Financial Stability Report.* April. Washington, D.C.

———. 2007b. International Financial Statistics. http://www.imfstatistics.org/imf/ (accessed in 2007).

Indian Banks' Association. 2006a. *Performance Highlights of Foreign Banks 2005–06.* Mumbai.

———. 2006b. *Performance Highlights of Private Sector Banks 2005-06.* Mumbai.

———. 2006c. *Performance Highlights of Public Sector Banks 2005-06.* Mumbai.

Nepal Rastra Bank. 2006. *Annual Bank Supervision Report, 2005.* Bank Supervision Department, Kathmandu.

———. 2007. *Annual Bank Supervision Report, 2006.* Bank Supervision Department, Kathmandu.

———. 2007. Central Bank of Nepal official Web site. http://www.nrb.org.np/ (accessed in 2007).

OECD (Organisation for Economic Co-operation and Development). 2004. *OECD Principles of Corporate Governance.* Paris.

———. 2007. OECD Database on Bank Profitability: Financial Statements of Banks. http://www.oecd.org/ (accessed in 2007).

Okeahalam, Charles. E. 2003. "Concentration in the Banking Sector of the Common Monetary Area of Southern Africa." Policy Research Paper. World Bank, Washington, D.C. http://www.worldbank.org/research/interest/confs/042003/cma_charles.pdf.

Reserve Bank of India. 2006a. *Annual Report, 2005–06.* Mumbai.

———. 2006b. *A Profile of Banks, 2005–06.* Mumbai.

———. 2006c. *Report on Trend and Progress of Banking in India, 2005–06.* Mumbai.

———. 2007. Reserve Bank of India database. http://www.rbi.org.in/scripts/Statistics.aspx (accessed in 2007).

Saving, Thomas. R. 1970. "Concentration Ratios and Degree of Monopoly." *International Economic Review* 2 (1): 139–46.

Securities and Exchange Board of India. 2007. Securities and Exchange Board of India official Web site. http://www.sebi.gov.in/ (accessed in 2007).

Securities and Exchange Commission of Bangladesh. 2007. Securities and Exchange Commission of Bangladesh official Web site. http://www.secbd.org/ (accessed in 2007).

Securities and Exchange Commission of Pakistan. 2007. Securities and Exchange Commission of Pakistan official Web site. http://www.secp.gov.pk/ (accessed in 2007).

Securities and Exchange Commission of Sri Lanka. 2007. Securities and Exchange Commission of Sri Lanka official Web site. http://www.sec.gov.lk/ (accessed in 2007).

Securities Board of Nepal. 2007. Securities Board of Nepal official Web site. http://www.sebonp.com/ (accessed in 2007).

Standard & Poor's. 2004. *Corporate Governance Scores and Evaluations: Criteria, Methodology and Definitions.* New York: Governance Services.

State Bank of Pakistan. 2006a. *Banking System Review.* Bank Surveillance Department, Karachi.

———. 2006b. *Financial Stability Review.* Karachi.

———. 2007. Pakistan Central Bank official Web site. http://www.sbp.org.pk/ (accessed in 2007).

U.S. Department of Justice and the Federal Trade Commission. 1997. "Horizontal Merger Guidelines." Washington, D.C.

World Bank. 2003. *Report on the Observance of Standards and Codes (ROSC), Accounting and Auditing: Bangladesh.* Washington, D.C.

———. 2004. "South Asia Financial Performance and Soundness Indicators Phase I." South Asia Region, Finance and Private Sector Development Unit, Washington, D.C.

———. 2005a. *Report on the Observance of Standards and Codes (ROSC), Corporate Governance Country Assessment: Nepal.* Washington, D.C.

———. 2005b. "South Asia Financial Performance and Soundness Indicators Phase II." South Asia Region, Finance and Private Sector Development Unit, Washington, D.C.

———. 2006a. "Access and Use of Banking Services Across Countries, Data Set 2001–04." Washington, D.C.

———. 2006b. "Financial Development and Structure Database, 2006." Washington, D.C.

———. 2006c. "South Asia Region: PSD Strategy." South Asia Region, Finance and Private Sector Development Unit, Washington, D.C.

———. 2006d. "South Asia Financial Performance and Soundness Indicators Phase III: Getting Finance in South Asia—An Analysis of the Commercial Banking Sector." South Asia Region, Finance and Private Sector Development Unit, Washington, D.C.

———. 2006e. "Microfinance in South Asia: Toward Financial Inclusion for the Poor." Washington, D.C.

———. 2007a. "World Development Indicators Database." Washington, D.C.

———. 2007b. "South Asian Domestic Debt Markets Study—Draft Main Report." Washington, D.C.

World Bank and IMF (International Monetary Fund). 2005. *Financial Sector Assessment: A Handbook.* Washington, D.C.

World Federation of Exchanges. 2007. Statistics, Time-Series 2001–2007. http://www.world-exchanges.org/ (accessed in 2007).

Zaretsky, Adam. M. 2004. "Bank Consolidation: Regulators Always Have the Power to Pull the Plug." *The Regional Economist* (January): 10-11. http://www.stlouisfed.org (accessed in 2007).

Index

The letters *f* and *t* following a page number refer to figures and tables, respectively.

Access to finance
   Bangladesh, 9, 15–16, 46, 46*f*
   development dimension, 4–5
   goals for South Asian countries, 63
   India, 9, 20, 21, 46, 46*f*
   international comparison, 51–52, 55*f*, 58, 59*t*, 60*f*
   measurement, 4, 69–71
   micro indicators, 4, 46. *See also specific indicators*
   microfinance, 10, 11
   Nepal, 9, 26, 46*f*, 63
   Pakistan, 9, 31–33, 46, 46*f*
   ranking of South Asian countries, 9, 44, 46, 46*f*
   Sri Lanka, 9, 37, 38, 46, 46*f*, 63
Accounting and auditing standards
   Bangladesh, 19, 85–86
   India, 24–25
   Nepal, 30
   Pakistan, 36
   Sri Lanka, 42
Afghanistan, microfinance in, 11
ATMs. *See* Demographic ATM penetration; Geographic ATM penetration

Bangladesh
   access to finance in, 9, 15–16, 46, 46*f*
   bank ownership and management structure, 18–19
   Basel II and, 16, 17, 85
   capital market development, 10, 15, 17, 48*f*
   corporate governance, 10, 15, 18–19, 49*f*, 65, 107*t*
   current economic performance, 13–15
   economic growth, 14
   economic sectors, 14
   exports, 14
   financial stability, 9, 15, 16–17, 47, 48*f*, 52, 64
   gross domestic product, 13
   gross national income, 14
   market capitalization, 14, 57*f*
   market concentration and competitiveness, 10, 15, 17–18, 49*f*, 57*f*
   microfinance in, 11, 16
   national debt, 14
   national savings, 14
   performance and efficiency, 9, 15, 16, 46, 47*f*
   population, 13
   prudential regulations and risk management, 17, 18, 85–87
   regional ranking in Getting Finance Indicators, 9, 43, 44, 45*f*
   strategies for financial sector development, 15
   structure of banking system, 14
   tax policy, 19
   See also International comparison; South Asian countries
Basel Committee on Banking Supervision, 7, 105
Basel II framework
   Bangladesh compliance, 16, 17, 85
   goals for South Asian countries, 64
   India and, 22, 88
   Nepal and, 28, 29, 92
   Pakistan and, 34, 96–97
   Sri Lanka and, 39–40, 100–101
Benchmark data, 3–4, 8–9, 13, 51, 65. *See also* International comparison
Bond markets *see* Domestic bonds to equity market capitalization ratio *and* Domestic public bonds outstanding ratio

Capital adequacy ratio
  Bangladesh, 16, 52, 53f, 64, 85
  definition and calculation, 5, 73
  India, 22, 52, 53f, 88–89
  international comparison, 52, 53f, 59t, 61f
  Nepal, 27, 52, 53f, 64, 92, 93
  Pakistan, 33, 52, 53f
  ranking of South Asian countries, 47, 48f, 64
  Sri Lanka, 39, 52, 53f, 100–101
Capital market development
  Bangladesh, 10, 15, 17, 48f
  development dimension, 6
  goals for South Asian countries, 64
  India, 10, 20, 22–23, 48f, 54
  international comparison, 10, 54, 57f, 58, 59t, 61f
  measures of, 6, 75–76
  Nepal, 10, 26, 28, 48f
  Pakistan, 10, 31, 34, 48f
  ranking of South Asian countries, 10, 44, 47, 48f
  Sri Lanka, 10, 37, 40, 48f
Commercial banking assets
  Bangladesh, 14, 14t
  India, 20, 14t
  Nepal, 14t, 26f
  Pakistan, 14t
  Sri Lanka, 14t, 37
Commercial banking assets to GDP ratio
  Bangladesh, 15f, 18, 49f
  definition and calculation, 7, 78
  India, 23, 49f
  Nepal, 29, 49f
  Pakistan, 35, 53, 49f
  ranking of South Asian countries, 49f
  Sri Lanka, 37, 40, 49f
Commercial banking sector
  accounting and auditing standards, 19, 24–25, 30, 36, 42, 85–86
  Bangladesh, 14
  benchmark data, 8–9, 13, 51, 65
  development role, 3, 13, 63
  India, 20
  Nepal's, 26
  ownership and management structure, 18–19, 23, 24, 25, 30–31, 35–37, 40–41, 42, 91
  Pakistan's, 31
  Sri Lanka's, 37
Competitiveness. *See* Market concentration and competitiveness

Corporate governance
  assessment methodology, 4, 7, 78, 79
  Bangladesh, 10, 15, 18–19, 49f, 65, 107t
  Basel Committee on Banking Supervision principles, 7, 105, 106t
  country ranking methodology, 80–83
  data sources, 79
  development dimension, 7, 78
  goals for South Asian countries, 65
  India, 10, 20, 23–25, 49f, 65, 107t
  Nepal, 10, 29–31, 49f, 65, 107t
  opportunities for improvement, 10
  Organisation for Economic Co-Operation and Development best practices, 7, 105, 106t
  Pakistan, 10, 31, 35–37, 49f, 65, 107t
  ranking of South Asian countries, *vii*, 10, 44, 47, 49f
  Sri Lanka, 10, 40–42, 49f, 65, 107t
Demographic ATM penetration
  Bangladesh, 15
  definition and calculation, 4, 70
  India, 21
  international comparison, 58, 59t, 60f
  Nepal, 26
  Pakistan, 31
  ranking of South Asian countries, 46f
  Sri Lanka, 38
Demographic branch penetration
  Bangladesh, 15
  definition and calculation, 4, 69–70
  India, 21
  international comparison, 58, 59t, 60f
  Nepal, 26
  Pakistan, 31
  ranking of South Asian countries, 46f
  Sri Lanka, 38
Deposit accounts per 1,000 people
  Bangladesh, 15
  definition and calculation, 4, 70
  India, 21
  Nepal, 26
  Pakistan, 32
  ranking of South Asian countries, 46f
  Sri Lanka, 38
Domestic bond market to equity market capitalization ratio
  Bangladesh, 17, 48f
  definition and calculation, 6, 75
  India, 22, 48f
  Nepal, 28, 48f
  Pakistan, 34, 48f

ranking of South Asian countries, 48*f*
Sri Lanka, 40, 48*f*
Domestic public bonds outstanding ratio
Bangladesh, 14, 14*f*, 17, 48*f*
definition and calculation, 6, 75
India, 14*t*, 20, 23, 48*f*
international comparison, 58, 59*t*, 61*f*
Nepal, 14*t*, 28, 48*f*
Pakistan, 14*t*, 31, 34, 48*f*
ranking of South Asian countries, 48*f*
Sri Lanka, 14*t*, 40, 48*f*

Equity market capitalization
See also Stock market capitalization ratio

Financial Performance and Soundness Indicators
accomplishments of South Asian countries, 9, 43
country ranking methodology, 80–83
development and application, 3, 7–8
ranking of countries, 9–10, 43–46
selection, 7, 79–80
six dimensions, 4, 43. *See also specific indicator*
Financial sector development
data sources, 13
development dimensions, 4–7
limits of analysis, 10
See also Commercial banking sector
Financial stability
Bangladesh, 9, 15, 16–17, 47, 52, 48*f*
definition, 5
development dimension, 5
goals for South Asian countries, 64
India, 9, 20, 22, 47, 48*f*, 52, 64
international comparison, 52–54, 58, 59*t*
measures of, 5, 73–74
micro indicators, 47
Nepal, 9–10, 26, 27–28, 47, 48*f*, 52, 64
Pakistan, 9, 33–34, 47, 48*f*, 52
ranking of South Asian countries, 9, 44, 47, 48*f*, 83
significance of, in economic development, 5
Sri Lanka, 9, 37, 39–40, 47, 48*f*, 52

Geographic ATM penetration
Bangladesh, 15, 52*f*, 55*f*
definition and calculation, 4, 71
India, 21, 52*f*, 55*f*
international comparison, 52*f*, 55*f*
Nepal, 26, 52*f*, 55*f*

Pakistan, 32, 52*f*, 55*f*
ranking of South Asian countries, 46
Sri Lanka, 38, 52, 52*f*, 55*f*
Geographic branch penetration
Bangladesh, 15, 51, 52*f*
definition and calculation, 4, 70–71
India, 21, 51, 52*f*
international comparison, 51–52
Nepal, 26, 52*f*
Pakistan, 31–32, 52*f*
ranking of South Asian countries, 9, 46*f*
Sri Lanka, 38, 52*f*
Getting Finance Indicators. *See* Financial Performance and Soundness Indicators
Government securities market
Bangladesh, 17
India, 23, 92
Nepal, 26, 28
Pakistan, 34
Sri Lanka, 37, 40
Gross nonperforming loans ratio
Bangladesh, 16, 53*f*, 56*f*, 59*f*, 61*f*
definition and calculation, 5, 74
goals for South Asian countries, 64
India, 22, 53*f*, 56*f*, 59*t*, 61*f*
international comparison, 52, 53, 58, 53*f*, 56*f*, 59*f*, 61*f*
Nepal, 28, 53*f*, 56*f*, 58*t*, 61*f*
Pakistan, 33, 53*f*, 56*f*, 59*t*, 61*f*
ranking of South Asian countries, 47, 48*f*
Sri Lanka, 39, 53*f*, 56*f*, 59*t*, 61*f*

Herfindahl-Hirschman Index
Bangladesh, 17, 55*f*, 57*f*
definition and calculation, 6, 12 n.1, 76
India, 23, 55*f*, 57*f*
international comparison, 54, 55*f*, 57*f*
Nepal, 29, 55*f*, 57*f*
Pakistan, 34, 55*f*, 57*f*
ranking of South Asian countries, 47, 49*f*
Sri Lanka, 10, 40, 54, 55*f*, 57*f*

India
access to finance in, 9, 20, 21, 46, 46*f*
banking system structure, 20
Basel II commitment, 22, 88
capital market development, 10, 20, 48*f*, 64
corporate governance, 10, 20, 23–25, 49*f*, 65, 107*t*
current economic performance, 13, 19–20
economic growth, 19–20

economic sectors, 20
exports, 20
financial stability, 9, 20, 22, 47, 48f, 52, 64
gross national income, 20
market capitalization, 20, 57f
market concentration and
    competitiveness, 10, 23, 47, 49f, 57f
microfinance in, 11, 21
national savings rate, 20
nonperforming loans, 22, 53
outstanding domestic bond, 20
performance and efficiency, 9, 20, 21–22,
    46, 47f
population, 13, 19
prudential regulation and risk
    management, 22, 23, 88–92
regional ranking in Getting Finance
    Indicators, 9, 43, 44, 45f
state-owned banks, 21, 24
strategies for financial sector
    development, 20
See also International comparison; South
    Asian countries
International comparison
  access to finance, 51–52, 55f, 58, 59t, 60f
  benchmark data, 3–4, 8–9, 13, 51
  capital market development, 10, 54, 57f,
    58, 59t, 61f
  financial stability, 52–54, 58, 59t
  market concentration and
    competitiveness, 54, 57f, 58,
    59t, 62f
  performance and efficiency, 52, 56f, 58,
    59t, 60f, 61f
  South Asian countries, 65

K-bank concentration ratios
  Bangladesh, 17, 18, 49f, 55f, 59f, 62f
  definition and calculation, 6, 77
  India, 23 49f, 55f, 59t, 62f
  international comparison, 55f, 59t, 62f
  Nepal, 29, 49f, 55f, 59t, 62f
  Pakistan, 34, 35, 49f, 55f, 59t, 62f
  ranking of South Asian countries, 49f
  Sri Lanka, 37, 40, 47, 49f, 55f, 59t, 62f

Leverage ratio
  Bangladesh, 16
  definition and calculation, 5, 73
  India, 22
  Nepal, 27
  ranking of South Asian countries, 48f
  Sri Lanka, 39

Liquid assets ratio
  Bangladesh, 17
  definition and calculation, 5, 74
  India, 22
  Nepal, 28
  Pakistan, 34
  ranking of South Asian countries, 47, 48f
  Sri Lanka, 39
Liquid assets to liabilities ratio
  Bangladesh, 17
  definition and calculation, 5, 74
  India, 22
  Nepal, 28
  Sri Lanka, 39
  ranking of South Asian countries, 48f
Loan accounts per 1,000 people
  Bangladesh, 15
  definition and calculation, 4, 70
  India, 21
  Nepal, 26
  Pakistan, 32
  ranking of South Asian countries, 46f
  Sri Lanka, 38

Market concentration and
    competitiveness
  Bangladesh, 10, 15, 17–18, 49f, 57f
  goals for South Asian countries, 64–65
  India, 10, 23, 47, 49f, 57f
  international comparison, 54, 55f, 57f,
    58, 59t, 62f
  measures of, 6–7, 76–78
  Nepal, 10, 29, 49f, 57f
  Pakistan, 10, 31, 34–35, 49f, 57f
  ranking of South Asian countries, 10,
    44, 47, 49f
  significance of, in economic
    development, 6
  Sri Lanka, 10, 37, 40, 49f, 54, 57f
Methodology
  access to finance measures, 5, 69–71
  benchmark data, 3–4, 8–9, 13, 51
  capital market development measures,
    6, 75–76
  compilation guide, 4, 69–78
  corporate governance assessment, 4, 7,
    78, 79
  country rankings, 9, 80–83
  financial sector data sources, 13, 79
  financial stability measures, 5, 73–74
  market concentration and
    competitiveness measures, 6–7,
    76–78

performance and efficiency measures, 5, 71–73
scope of data for comparative analysis, 4, 7, 79

Microfinance
access to finance measurement and, 10
Bangladesh, 11, 16
India, 11, 21
limitations, 63
Nepal, 11, 26
Pakistan, 11, 32–33
Sri Lanka, 11, 38

Micro indicators
calculation, 69–78
definition, 4
international comparison for financial performance, 51
ranking of South Asian countries, 46–50
See also specific indicator

Nepal
access to finance in, 9, 26, 46, 46*f*, 63
Basel II and, 28, 29, 92
capital market development, 10, 26, 28, 48*f*
corporate governance, 10, 29–31, 49*f*, 65, 107*t*
current economic performance, 13, 25–26
economic sectors, 25
exports, 25
financial stability, 9–10, 26, 27–28, 47, 48*f*, 52, 64
gross domestic product, 25
gross national income, 25
market capitalization, 25, 29, 57*f*
market concentration and competitiveness, 10, 49*f*, 57*f*
microfinance in, 11, 26
national savings rate, 25
nonperforming loans, 28, 53
outstanding domestic bonds, 25
performance and efficiency, 9, 26–27, 46, 47*f*
population, 25
prudential regulation and risk management, 28, 93–96
regional ranking in Getting Finance Indicators, 9–10, 43–44
state-owned banks, 26
strategies for financial sector development, 26
structure of banking system, 26
tax policy, 28, 94
See also International comparison; South Asian countries

Net interest margin ratio
Bangladesh, 16
definition and calculation, 5, 72
India, 22
Nepal, 27
Pakistan, 32*f*, 33
ranking of South Asian countries, 46, 47*f*
Sri Lanka, 39

Nonbank financial institutions
access to finance, 10
Financial Performance and Soundness Indicators, 3
See also Microfinance

Nonperforming loans
See also Gross nonperforming loans ratio

Operating cost ratio
Bangladesh, 16
definition and calculation, 5, 72
India, 21
Nepal, 27
Pakistan, 33
ranking of South Asian countries, 46, 47*f*
Sri Lanka, 39

Organisation for Economic Co-operation and Development, 3–4, 7–8, 51, 105, 106*t*. *See also* International comparison

Ownership and management structure of banks
Bangladesh, 18–19
best practices, 105
India, 23, 24, 25, 91
Nepal, 30–31
Pakistan, 35–37
Sri Lanka, 40–41, 42

Pakistan
access to finance in, 9, 31–33, 46, 46*f*
Basel II implementation, 34, 96–97
capital market development, 10, 31, 34, 48*f*
corporate governance, 10, 31, 35–37, 47, 49*f*, 107*t*
current economic performance, 13, 31
economic growth, 31
economic sectors, 31
exports, 31
financial stability, 9, 33–34, 47, 48*f*, 52

market capitalization, 31, 34, 57f
market concentration and
  competitiveness, 10, 31, 34–35,
  49f, 57f
microfinance in, 11, 32–33
national savings rate, 31
nonperforming loans, 33–34
performance and efficiency, 9, 31, 33, 46,
  47f
population, 13, 31
prudential regulation and risk
  management, 34, 97–100
regional ranking in Getting Finance
  Indicators, 9, 43, 44, 45f
strategies for financial sector
  development, 31, 33
structure of banking system, 31
tax policy, 33
See also International comparison; South
  Asian countries
Performance and efficiency
  Bangladesh, 9, 15, 16, 46, 47f
  development dimensions, 5
  goals for South Asian countries, 64
  India, 9, 20, 21–22, 46, 47f
  international comparison, 52, 56f, 58,
    59t, 60f, 61f
  measures of, 5, 46, 71–73
  Nepal, 9, 26–27, 47f
  Pakistan, 9, 31, 33, 46, 47f
  ranking of South Asian countries, 9,
    44, 46, 47f
  Sri Lanka, 9, 38–39, 46, 47f
Population, 13
  Bangladesh, 13
  India, 13, 19
  Nepal, 13, 25
  Pakistan, 13, 31
  Sri Lanka, 13, 37
Poverty reduction and economic
  development
  access to finance and, 4
  capital market development and, 6
  corporate governance and, 7
  distribution of development gains, 4
  financial stability and, 5
  market concentration and
    competitiveness and, 6
  performance and efficiency of financial
    institutions and, 5
  risk management and, 8
  role of commercial banking sector, 3
  significance of financial sector reform, 63

Private credit extended by banks
  Bangladesh, 18, 49f
  definition and calculation, 7, 77
  economic significance, 10
  India, 23, 49f
  international comparison, 58, 59f, 62f
  Nepal, 29, 49f
  Pakistan, 35, 49f
  recommendations for South Asian
    countries, 64–65
  ranking of South Asian countries, 49f
  Sri Lanka, 40, 49f
Provisions to nonperforming loans ratio
  Bangladesh, 17, 53f
  definition and calculation, 5, 74
  goals and South Asian countries, 64
  India, 22, 53f
  international comparison, 53, 53f, 54
  Nepal, 28, 53f
  Pakistan, 33, 43f
  ranking of South Asian countriesx, 47,
    48f
  Sri Lanka, 39, 53f

Prudential regulations
  Bangladesh, 17, 18, 85–87
  economic significance, 10
  goals for South Asian countries, 64
  India, 22–23, 88–92
  Nepal, 28, 93–96
  Pakistan, 34, 97–100
  previous Getting Finance Indicators
    studies, 3, 7, 13
  Sri Lanka, 39, 101–103

Recurring earning power ratio
  Bangladesh, 16
  definition and calculation, 5, 72–73
  India, 22
  Nepal, 27
  Pakistan, 32f, 33
  ranking of South Asian countries, 47f
  Sri Lanka, 39
Return on assets
  Bangladesh, 16, 53f
  definition and calculation, 5, 72
  India, 21, 53f
  international comparison, 52, 53f,
    59t, 60f
  Nepal, 27, 53f
  Pakistan, 33, 52, 53f
  ranking of South Asian countries, 47f
  Sri Lanka, 38–39, 53f

Return on equity
  Bangladesh, 16, 52, 53*f*, 56*f*
  definition and calculation, 5, 71
  India, 21, 26, 52, 53*f*, 56*f*
  international comparison, 52, 53*f*, 56*f*, 59*t*, 60*f*
  Nepal, 53*f*, 56*f*
  Pakistan, 33, 52, 53*f*, 56*f*
  ranking of South Asian countries, 47*f*
  Sri Lanka, 38, 52, 53*f*, 56*f*
Risk management
  Bangladesh, 17
  goals for South Asian countries, 64
  importance of, in economic development, 8
  India, 22, 23
  Nepal, 28
  Pakistan, 34
  Sri Lanka, 39–40
  See also Prudential regulation

Self-help groups, 11, 21
Shareholder rights
  Bangladesh, 19
  India, 24
  Nepal, 30
  Pakistan, 36
  Sri Lanka, 41–42
South Asian countries, overall
  access to finance, 9, 44, 46, 63
  accomplishments, 9, 43
  capital market development, 10, 44, 47, 64
  corporate governance in, 10, 44, 47–50, 65
  current economic performance, 13
  economic reform strategies, 9
  economic significance of banking sector, 13
  financial sector data sources, 13, 79
  financial stability, 9, 44, 47, 64
  international comparison of financial performance. *See* International comparison
  market concentration and competitiveness, 10, 44, 47, 64–65
  microfinance movement, 10, 11
  performance and efficiency of financial institutions, 9, 44, 46, 64
  population, 13
  ranking of, in Getting Finance Indicators, 9, 43–50, 80–83
  See also specific country

Sri Lanka
  access to finance in, 9, 37, 38, 46, 46*f*, 63
  Basel II implementation, 39–40, 100–101
  capital market development, 10, 37, 40, 48*f*
  corporate governance, 10, 40–42, 49*f*, 65, 107*t*
  current banking system, 37
  current economic performance, 13, 37
  financial stability, 9, 37, 39–40, 47, 48*f*, 52
  gross domestic product, 37
  market capitalization, 37, 57*f*
  market concentration and competitiveness, 10, 37, 40, 47, 49*f*, 54, 57*f*, 64
  microfinance in, 11, 38
  nonperforming loans, 39
  performance and efficiency, 9, 38–39, 46, 47*f*
  population, 13, 37
  prudential regulations and risk management, 39–40, 101–103
  regional ranking in Getting Finance Indicators, 9, 43, 44, 45*f*
  strategies for financial sector development, 37
  tax policy, 102
  See also International comparison; South Asian countries
Staff cost ratio
  Bangladesh, 16
  definition and calculation, 5, 72
  goals for South Asian countries, 64
  India, 21
  Nepal, 27
  Pakistan, 33
  ranking of South Asian countries, 46, 47*f*
  Sri Lanka, 39
State-owned banks
  Bangladesh, 16–17
  India, 21, 24
  Nepal, 26
Stock market capitalization ratio
  Bangladesh, 14, 17, 57*f*
  definition and calculation, 6, 76
  India, 20, 23, 54, 57*f*
  international comparison, 54, 54*f*, 57*f*, 58, 59*t*, 61*f*
  Nepal, 25, 28, 57*f*
  Pakistan, 31, 34, 57*f*
  ranking of South Asian countries, 48*f*
  Sri Lanka, 37, 40, 57*f*

Stock market turnover ratio
   Bangladesh, 17
   definition and calculation, 6, 76
   India, 23, 54
   international comparison, 54, 54*f*
   Nepal, 28,
   Pakistan, 34
   ranking of South Asian countries, 48*f*
   Sri Lanka, 40
Stock trading value ratio
   Bangladesh, 17
   definition and calculation, 6, 76
   India, 23, 54
   international comparison, 54, 54*f*
   Nepal, 28
   Pakistan, 34
   ranking of South Asian countries, 48*f*
   Sri Lanka, 40
Tax policy
   Bangladesh, 19
   India, 91
   Nepal, 28, 94
   Pakistan, 33
   Sri Lanka, 102
Trading value of the top 10 stocks ratio
   Bangladesh, 17
   definition and calculation, 6, 75
   India, 23
   Nepal, 28
   ranking of South Asian countries, 48*f*

ECO-AUDIT
Environmental Benefits Statement

The World Bank is committed to preserving endangered forests and natural resources. The Office of the Publisher has chosen to print **Getting Finance in South Asia 2009: Indicators and Analysis of the Commercial Banking Sector** on recycled paper with 30 percent postconsumer waste in accordance with the recommended standards for paper usage set by the Green Press Initiative, a nonprofit program supporting publishers in using fiber that is not sourced from endangered forests. For more information, visit www.greenpressinitiative.org.

Saved:
- 6 trees
- 26 million BTUs of total energy
- 492 lbs of net greenhouse gases
- 2,042 gallons of waste water
- 262 lbs of solid waste